Christo

THE ORTHODOX UNDERSTANDING OF SALVATION

"THEOSIS" IN SCRIPTURE AND TRADITION

MOUNT THABOR PUBLISHING
2014

THE ORTHODOX UNDERSTANDING OF SALVATION:
"THEOSIS" IN SCRIPTURE AND TRADITION
Copyright © 2013 by Christopher Veniamin

First edition 2013
Reprint edition (with minor corrections) 2014

Mount Thabor Publishing
106 Hilltop Road
Dalton, PA 18414 USA

www.mountthabor.com

Printed in the United States of America

All rights reserved. No part of this publication may be reproduced, stored in a retrieval system, or transmitted, in any form or by any means, electronic, mechanical, photocopying, recording, or otherwise, without the prior permission of Mount Thabor Publishing.

Library of Congress Cataloging-in-Publication Data

Veniamin, Christopher, 1958-
 The Orthodox understanding of salvation : theosis in Scripture and tradition / Christopher Veniamin.
    pages cm
 Includes bibliographical references/
 ISBN 978-0-9800207-4-8
 1. Salvation--Orthodox Eastern Church. 2. Deification (Christianity) 3. Orthodox Eastern Church--Doctrines. I. Title.
 BT767.8.V465 2013
 234.088'2819--dc23
                                    2013043176

*This work is respectfully dedicated to
Our Fathers in God
Archimandrites Sophrony, 'Kyrill & Zacharias*

Contents

Preface
7

Part I: *Praxis*

The Orthodox Understanding of Salvation: "Theosis" in Saint Silouan the Athonite and Elder Sophrony of Essex
13

The Power of Repentance:
The Ethos of "Metanoia" in the Orthodox Tradition
27

Holy Relics
The Deification of the Human Body
in the Christian Tradition
37

The Sinlessness of the Mother of God
According to St. Nicholas Cabasilas
45

The Orthodox Interpretation of Holy Scripture:
St. Gregory Palamas and the Key
to Understanding the Bible
60

The Significance of Greek Independence Day
for America in the 21st Century
69

Euthanasia: A Theological Approach
75

Part II: *Theoria*

The Light of Tabor
St John Chrysostom and the Language
of Holy Scripture
89

The Resurrection of the Human Body
In the Christology of St Cyril
Pope and Patriarch of Alexandria
104

The Transfiguration of Christ and the Deification of Man in
St Maximus the Confessor
112

The Spiritual Father and Child Relationship
in St Symeon the New Theologian
135

The Interplay Between Mystical and Dogmatic Theology in
St. Gregory the Sinaïte
151

Partakers of Divine Nature
St Gregory Palamas and the Centrality of the Transfiguration
166

BY WAY OF CONCLUSION
On Becoming Theologians
"Hesychia" as a Prerequisite for the Encounter with God
189

PREFACE

THE PURPOSE OF THE WORK IN HAND is to make more readily available certain of my papers and studies, which have appeared in various relatively little-known theological journals and other publications, all of which relate to the question of Salvation in the age-old and unbroken tradition of the Orthodox Christian Faith – the faith of the Patriarchs, Prophets, Apostles, Martyrs and Saints of our Lord, God and Saviour, Jesus Christ. *The Orthodox Understanding of Salvation: "Theosis" in Scripture and Tradition* is thus divided into two parts. Part I, *Praxis*, is comprised of papers delivered chiefly at retreats, clergy symposia and public lectures; while Part II, *Theoria*, is made up of articles, all of which (except for one) were based on my doctoral work on the meaning of the Transfiguration in the Fathers, carried out at Oxford University, under the supervision of His Eminence Kallistos Ware, Metropolitan of Diokleia, to whom I owe a great debt of gratitude. The last chapter of Part II, "On Becoming Theologians", is added simply as "By Way of Conclusion".

"The Orthodox Understanding of Salvation, 'Theosis' in Saint Silouan the Athonite and Elder Sophrony of Essex," is a lecture that was originally presented at the *Twenty-Seventh Annual Adult Education Series* of Saint Tikhon's Seminary, South Canaan PA, under the given title, "The Theology of 'Theosis': The Goal of Two Holy Monks and of Every Christian," which was dedicated to the general theme, *A Modern-Day Saint and His Disciple: Saint Silouan the Athonite and Father Sophrony* (Saint Tikhon's Seminary, September 30, 1997). It has also been published under its original title in *The Tikhonaire* (South Canaan, PA: St Tikhon's Orthodox Theological Seminary, 1998), pp. 53–58.

"The Positive Power of Repentance: The Ethos of 'Metanoia' in the Orthodox Tradition," is a lecture that was originally delivered at the St. Tikhon's *Adult Education Lecture Series*, held in September–October of 1995, and published as "Personal Renewal: A Perspective from the Fathers," in *Alive in Christ*, the Diocesan Magazine of the Diocese of Philadelphia and Eastern Pennsylvania (OCA), Vol. XI, no. 3 (Winter 1995), pp. 43–45; and also in *The Tikhonaire* (South Canaan, PA: St Tikhon's Orthodox Theological Seminary, 1996), pp. 76–79.

"Holy Relics, The Deification of the Human Body in the Christian Tradition," is a paper that originally appeared as, *"God became human that we might be made gods*: The Incarnation of the Word of God and the Deification of Man," in *Alive in Christ,* Vol. XIV, no. 3 (Winter 1998), pp. 20–22. It is reproduced here with minor revisions.

"The Orthodox Interpretation of Holy Scripture: St. Gregory Palamas and the Key to Understanding the Bible," was the keynote address at the *Clergy Continuing Education Symposium*, held at St. Tikhon's Seminary (June 13–15, 2006), entitled, "Saint Gregory Palamas: His Theological Perspective," Delivered on Tuesday, June 13, 2006, and published in *St. Tikhon's Theological Journal,* Vol. 3 (2005, actually published 2007), 1–16. It was also the keynote address for the Sunday of St. Gregory Palamas, at the *Celebration of Books,* March 31, 2013, sponsored by the *Holy Apostles Resource Center* (HARC), held at Holy Apostles Greek Orthodox Church, in Westchester, Illinois.

"The Sinlessness of the Mother of God according to Saint Nicholas Cabasilas," was written in 1983, and first appeared in print in *Alive in Christ,* Vol. XI, no. 2 (Summer 1995), pp. 24–27.

"The Significance of Greek Independence Day for America in the 21st Century," was originally titled, "Thoughts on the Relation

Between the Annunciation of the Most Holy Theotokos and Ever Virgin Mary and Greek Independence Day (25 March 1821)," delivered at the Greek Orthodox Church of the Annunciation in Wilkes-Barre, PA, on 27 March, 2000, by the gracious invitation of the Very Rev. George Demopoulos, of blessed memory (†2012).

"Euthanasia: A Theological Approach," is a lecture that was originally delivered at Holy Cross Greek Orthodox School of Theology in Brookline, Massachusetts, on Tuesday, May 10, 2005, under the title, "*Euthanasia*: Some Thoughts in the Wake of the Terri Schiavo Case." Subsequently, it was also read at the *Clergy Continuing Education Symposium*, St. Tikhon's Seminary (Wednesday, June 14, 2006), and published as "*Euthanasia*: A Theological Approach," in a mildly revised form, in the *St. Tikhon's Theological Journal,* Vol. 3 (2005, actually published 2007), 69–84.

"The Light of Tabor: St John Chrysostom and the Language of Holy Scripture," was originally presented as, "Saint John Chrysostom and the Light of Tabor," as the inaugural paper for the *Patristic and Byzantine Society*, Merton College, Oxford: Hilary Term, 1994. Based on my doctoral work, 'The Transfiguration of Christ in Greek Patristic Literature: From Irenaeus of Lyons to Gregory Palamas' (Oxford D.Phil. thesis, 1991), pp. 95–114, it was first published in *Alive in Christ,* Vol. X, no. 2 (Summer 1994), pp. 29–33.

"The Resurrection of the Human Body in the Christology of St. Cyril, Pope and Patriarch of Alexandria," is a paper that was based on the corresponding section in my, "The Transfiguration of Christ in Greek Patristic Literature," op. cit., pp. 118–136, and published as, "Saint Cyril of Alexandria and the Resurrection of the Body", in *Alive in Christ,* Vol. XI, no. 1 (Spring 1995), pp. 34–36. It is reproduced here with minor revisions.

"The Transfiguration of Christ and the Deification of Man in Saint Maximus the Confessor," was based on the corresponding chapter in my, "The Transfiguration of Christ in Greek Patristic Literature," op. cit., pp. 182–212, and published in Κληρονομία Vol. 27, nos. 1–2 (1995; published 1996), 309–329.

"The Spiritual Father and Child Relationship in St. Symeon

the New Theologian," was also based on a section of my, "The Transfiguration of Christ in Greek Patristic Literature," op. cit., pp. 239–250, and published as, "The Spiritual Father and the Vision of Christ Transfigured in Symeon the New Theologian," in Θεολογία καὶ Κόσμος σὲ Διάλογο [Theology and the World in Dialogue]. *Festschrift* for Professor Georgios I. Mantzarides (Thessalonica, 2004), pp. 157–170; and also in an abridged version in *Alive in Christ,* Vol. XX, no. 3 (Winter 2004), pp. 52–54.

"The Interplay between Mystical and Dogmatic Theology in Saint Gregory the Sinaïte," is a reworking of the corresponding chapter in my, "The Transfiguration of Christ in Greek Patristic Literature," op. cit., pp. 254–270, and was published in the *Festschrift* for Professor John M. Fountoulis, entitled, Γηθόσυνον Σέβασμα· Ἀντίδωρον τιμῆς καὶ μνήμης εἰς τὸν μακαριστὸν καθηγητὴν τῆς Λειτουργικῆς Ἰωάννην Μ. Φουντούλην (†2007) [Joyful Reverence: A Return-Gift in Honour and Memory of Our Blessed Professor of Liturgics, John M. Fountoulis (†2007)], Vol. 1, ed. Panagiotis I. Skaltsis and Archim. Nikodemos A. Skrettas, Thessalonica, 2013: Kyriakides Brothers Puplications, 2013, pp. 273–288; and also in *St. Tikhon's Theological Journal,* Vol. 2 (2005), 25–38.

"*Partakers of Divine Nature*: St Gregory Palamas and the Centrality of the Transfiguration," is a mild revision of a chapter in my "The Transfiguration of Christ in Greek Patristic Literature," op. cit., pp. 270–292, and was first published as, "'*Divinae consortes naturae*': Notes on the Centrality of the Taborian Theophany in Saint Gregory Palamas,' Κληρονομία Vol. 28, nos. 1–2 (Thessalonica, 1996; published 1997), 85–103: *Festal edition in honour of our Father among the saints, Gregory Palamas, Archbishop of Thessalonica, on the seven-hundredth anniversary of his birth* (1296 – 1996).

"On Becoming Theologians: '*Hesychia' as a Prerequisite for the Encounter with God,*" was first delivered as a public lecture at Holy Cross Greek Orthodox School of Theology in Brookline, Massachusetts, on October 18, 2013.

C. V.

ST TIKHON'S SEMINARY
FEAST *of* ST DEMETRIUS THE MYRRHSTREAMER, 2013

Part I: *Praxis*

THE ORTHODOX UNDERSTANDING OF SALVATION: "THEOSIS" IN SAINT SILOUAN THE ATHONITE AND ELDER SOPHRONY OF ESSEX

Coming into contact with Father Sophrony was always an event of a most especial kind. His monastics, first and foremost, but also those who made up his wider spiritual family, "lived", as Father Zacharias put it, "in an abundance of the word of God".

As a young boy, I had the blessing of serving each Sunday in the altar of the Monastery of Saint John the Baptist, Essex, England. One day when I was still a lad of only fifteen or sixteen years of age, following the Divine Liturgy, and whilst standing in the *Prothesis* of All Saints Church, Father Sophrony asked me why I was looking so thoughtful. Embarrassed that I was preoccupied with such mundane matters, I had to confess that school examinations were on the horizon, and that I wanted to do well in them. To my surprise, however, Father Sophrony did not belittle my worldly anxiety, but gently nodded his head, and agreed that it was indeed important to do well in examinations, and that to do so required much toil and sacrifice. But then he also added, as to a friend, that "in this world there is nothing more difficult than to be saved".

The force of the truth of these words struck deep in my heart. We often encounter, in ourselves and in others, the attitude which suggests that Salvation is something that we can leave until later; once, that is, we have taken care of more pressing matters. Father Sophrony's perspective was quite different, however. By pointing to the incomparable difficulty of attaining to Salvation, he was clearly placing it at the very top of our list of urgent priorities. And when one pauses to consider all the great achievements of mankind, past and present, whether they be of a scientific or literary character, in the world of politics or finance or physical endeavour, Father Sophrony's words seem bold and even provocative – "a hard saying" (John 6:60) – but nevertheless fundamentally quite true.

Upon later reflection, I realized that the reason why Father Sophrony's words rang so true that day is because of the wealth of meaning which Salvation has for us in the Orthodox Church. By others, Salvation is often understood simply in terms of "deliverance from sin and its consequences and admission to heaven", in terms of escaping damnation, that is, and reaching a safe place where we can no longer be tormented by the enemy. According to the Fathers of the Church, however, Salvation is not so prosaic a matter, for it involves the "theosis" (the deification or divinization) of the entire human person in Christ; it involves, that is, becoming like unto Christ to the point of identity with Him; it involves acquiring the mind of Christ (as Saint Paul affirms in the second chapter of the *First Epistle to the Corinthians,* verse sixteen), and indeed it signifies the sharing in His very Life.

In our brief and humble examination of the content and meaning of theosis or deification in Saint Silouan and Staretz Sophrony, I should like to focus on three main areas: 1. Christ as the measure of our deification, 2. Love for enemies as the measure of our likeness to Christ, and 3. Holy Relics as a witness to the love of Christ in us.

1. Christ as the Measure of Our Deification

CHRIST IS THE MEASURE of all things, both divine and human. Since the divine Ascension, our human nature has been raised up to the right hand of God the Father. As Father Sophrony points out, in His divine Person, the Son and Word of God was of course always seated on the right hand of the Father, being consubstantial with Him. The divine purpose for the human race, however, is seen in the union of our human nature to the divine Person of Christ, the Second Person of the Holy Trinity, in its being raised to the right hand of the Father.

St Paul, the great Apostle of the Word of God made flesh, identifies the divine purpose of the Incarnation with our adoption as sons of God: "But when the fulness of the time was come, God sent forth his Son, made of a woman, made under the law, To redeem them that were under the law, *that we might receive the adoption of sons*. And because ye are sons, God hath sent forth the Spirit of his Son into your hearts, crying, Abba, Father. Wherefore thou art no more a servant, but a son; and if a son, then an heir of God through Christ" (Gal. 4:4-7).

In Christ Jesus, therefore, we encounter both true and perfect God and true and perfect man. In other words, we see in Him not only the great God and Saviour (Tit. 2:13), but also what or who we have been called to become – sons and heirs of God the Father. In fact, the Lord Himself, quoting the Psalmist in response to the Jews' objection that He was making Himself equal to God, says, "Is it not written in your law, I said, Ye are gods?" (John 10 34, cf. Psalm 82:6). And St Paul, pointing to the great mystery of the communion of all the members of the Body of Christ with one another, explains that when "one member is glorified [εἴτε δοξάζεται ἐν μέλος], all the members rejoice with it" (συγχαίρει πάντα τὰ μέλη, 1 Cor. 12:26).

St Irenaeus of Lyons, in refuting the heresy of the Gnostics of the second century, described the divine purpose thus: "If the Word is made man, it is that men might become gods".[1] And the champion of Nicene Orthodoxy, Athanasius the Great, who in his *Paschal Letter* of 367 (*39th Festal Letter*) gives us the New Testament canon, reaffirms the Biblical and Irenaean position: "God became man," he says, "that we might be made gods" (αὐτὸς γὰρ ἐνηνθρώπησεν, ἵνα ἡμεῖς θεοποιηθῶμεν).[2]

---

1. *Adversus Hereses* V, pref.
2. *De Incarnatione* LIV.

"God became man that we might be made gods." What a daring statement! But what exactly does it mean for us to become gods? Can we created mortals become uncreated and immortal? Is this not an impossibility? An impiety? Or even a blasphemy? In what, then, does our becoming gods, our deification or divinization – our theosis – consist?

As Archimandrite Sophrony explains in his spiritual autobiography, *We Shall See Him As He Is:*

Christ manifested the perfection of the Divine image in man and the possibility for our nature of assimilating the fulness of divinization to the very extent that, after His ascension, He placed our nature "on the right hand of the Father".[3]

Note here that the expression "on the right hand of the Father" (ἐκ δεξιῶν τοῦ Πατρός) denotes nothing less than equality with the Father. Thus, since the time of the divine Ascension of Christ, our human nature has been deified in Him, and raised up to the right hand of God the Father.

Significantly, however, Fr. Sophrony also adds the following:

But even in Him our nature did not become one with the Essence of the Uncreated God. In Christ, incarnate Son of the Father, we contemplate God's pre-eternal idea of man.[4]

So, in Christ Jesus we find man's rightful place, "on the right hand of the Father", sharing in the divine Life; but, as with the two natures in Christ, man has been called to be united with God without mixture or confusion of any kind, that is to say, we never cease to be His creatures, since He alone is Uncreated. This fundamental distinction is of inestimable significance in Patristic theology.

Nevertheless, in the union of our human nature to the Second Person of the Holy Trinity, we also see what in theological terminology is called the *communicatio idiomatum*, that is, the exchange of natural properties belonging to each of Christ's two natures. This may also

---

3. *We Shall See Him As He Is,* translated by Rosemary Edmonds (Tolleshunt Knights, Essex: Patriarchal and Stavropegic Monastery of St. John the Baptist, 1988), p. 193.
4. Ibid.

be described in terms of the interpenetration of the natural energy of each of the two natures in Christ in the other.

As a simple illustration of this we have the Gospel narrative of the Transfiguration in Luke 9:28, where we first see Christ praying, performing, that is, an act which is proper to His human but not to His divine nature; while moments later, we find His humanity sharing in, indeed resplendent with, His divine glory, which is proper only to the divine nature. Saint Cyril of Alexandria describes the scene in this way:

The blessed disciples slept for a short while, as Christ gave Himself to prayer. For He voluntarily fulfilled His human obligations (τὰ ἀνθρώπινα). Later, on waking they became beholders (θεωροί) of His most holy and wondrous change.[5]

Staretz Sophrony points out that the union of the human nature in Christ is of course hypostatic or prosopic, that is to say, that Christ is a divine Person, the Person of the Son and Word of God; but, it is equally important to note that the union of the two natures in Christ is also energetic.[6] The significance of this energetic interpenetration

---

5. *Homiliae diversae IX in transfigurationem* (*Patrologia Graeca* 77:1013B); cf. *Ad Nestorium 12, anathema 4* (*Acta Conciliorum Oecumenicorum* I,1,1:41), where the concept of the *communicatio idiomatum* is formulated in a succinct manner. The reality of the hypostatic union and the *communicatio idiomatum* in Christ can be discerned in the fact that Christ conversed with the people sometimes οἰκονομικῶς, as man, and sometimes with divine authority (μετ' ἐξουσίας τῆς θεοπρεποῦς), as God, *Ad Successum episcopum Diocaesareae* 171.6 (*ACO* I,1,6:153). As a result of the *communicatio idiomatum*, it is also permissible to say that the Son of God was born, cf. *Contra Nestorium 2* (*ACO* I,1,6:18–21), and *Ad Nestorium* 6.3 (1:35), and died, cf. ibid., 4.5 (27–28) and 12, *anathema* 12 (42); *Contra Nestorium* 5; 7 (6:101–3;105–6). See also *De adoratione in spiritu et veritate* 10 (*PG* 68:656C) and cf. *Thesaurus de Trinitate* 32 (*PG* 75:560C), where Cyril maintains that the human nature of Christ possessed essential ἰδιώματα of God, while at the same time remaining distinct from His divinity, cf. also *De recta fide ad Arcadiam et Marinam* 177 (*ACO* I,1,5:107–8). For further details see my "The Transfiguration of Christ in Greek Patristic Literature: From Irenaeus of Lyons to Gregory Palamas" (Oxford D.Phil. thesis, 1991), pp. 134–135.

6. *Asceticism and Contemplation* [in Greek], translated by Hieromonk

of the divine and human natures in each other is of paramount importance for us human beings in that it forms the basis of our own union with God, which is also energetic and not essential or hypostatic. In other words, it proves to us that the example of Christ is also realizable, also attainable, by us human persons, and that theosis to the point of divine perfection, far from being optional, is in fact an obligation. It is in this sense that Staretz Sophrony understands the exhortation: "Be ye therefore perfect, even as your Father which is in heaven is perfect" (Matt. 5:48).

Father Sophrony also highlights another mystery concerning the Life of Christ on earth as a model and pattern for our own Life in Christ. This is revealed in the fact that even with the human nature of Christ we may observe a certain growth or dynamism, or, as Holy Scripture puts it, a certain "increase": "And Jesus increased in wisdom and stature, and in favour with God and man" (Luke 2:52). Thus, before all things had been fulfilled, even after the hypostatic union of human nature to the divine Person of the Word – even after His assumption of our humanity into His divine Person – even Christ, in His human aspect, appears as increasing in perfection. Hence, He also undergoes temptations (Luke 4:1–13, Hebr. 2:18); and even reached the point of agony (Luke 22:44). This, as Father Sophrony remarks, is due principally to a certain division which may be observed in Christ before His glorious Ascension, owing to the asymmetry of His natures. Following His Ascension, and the sitting of Christ the Son of Man on the right hand of God the Father, we have the new vision of the Christ-Man as equal to God, not of course according to His nature, but according to His energy.

Father Sophrony cautiously notes, however, that this does not refer to Christ's hypostatic "aspect", for the pre-eternal and uncreated Word remained such even after His Incarnation. Nevertheless, in the human "aspect" of His union and existence, we find once again the model and pattern for our own Life in Christ, for, as Staretz Sophrony puts it:

Zacharias (Tolleshunt Knights, Essex: Patriarchal and Stavropegic Monastery of St. John the Baptist, 1996), p. 152.

Christ is the unshakable foundation and the ultimate criterion for the anthropological teaching of the Church. Whatever we confess concerning the humanity of Christ is also an indication of the eternal divine plan for man in general. The fact that in the Christ-Man His hypostasis is God, in no way diminishes the possibility for us humans to follow His example (cf. John 13:15),[7] after which "in all things it behoved him to be made like unto his brethren" (Hebr. 2:17).

If it is true that Christ is the "Son of Man", consubstantial with us, then it follows that everything that He accomplished in His earthly life must likewise be possible for the rest of the "sons of men".

And for this reason, Father Sophrony adds that "if we confess His full and perfect theosis, it behoves us also to hope for the same degree of theosis for the saints in the age to come".[8]

The fundamental theological concern behind all that we have said so far is soteriological, that is to say, it concerns our salvation in a most fundamental way. Why? Because of the simple fact that we cannot live with Christ if we are not like Him in all respects. As the great hierophant John the Theologian and Evangelist proclaims:

> We know that, when he shall appear, we shall be like him; for we shall see him as he is. And every man that hath this hope in him purifieth himself, even as he is pure (1 John 3:2–3).

"We shall be like him; for we shall see him as he is." So, if we wish to be eternally with Christ, we must become like Him; and this process of becoming Christlike, this purification, invariably involves repentance – a fundamental change in our whole way of life, in our very "mode of being".

Saint Symeon the New Theologian, in his *Hymn* no. 44 reiterates this point in the following way:

> The Master is in no way envious of mortal men that they should appear equal to Him by divine grace, neither does He deem His servants unworthy to be like unto Him, but rather does He delight and rejoice

---

7. 'For I have given you an example, that ye should do as I have done to you.'
8. For all of the above, see: *Asceticism and Contemplation*, pp. 138–139.

to see us who were made men such as to become by grace what He is by nature. And He is so beneficent that He wills us to become even as He is. For if we be not as He is, exactly like unto Him in every way, how could we be united to Him? How could we dwell in Him, as He said, without being like unto Him, and how could He dwell in us, if we be not as He is?[9]

And again concerning the awesomeness of our inheritance, the great Paul, in *Romans*, writes the following:

The Spirit itself beareth witness with our spirit, that we are the children of God: *And if children, then heirs; heirs of God, and joint-heirs with Christ; if so be that we suffer with him, that we may be also glorified together.* For I reckon that the sufferings of this present time are not worthy to be compared with the glory which shall be revealed in us (Rom. 8:16–18).

Father Sophrony also makes another very interesting and important observation concerning the example given by Christ and our own theosis or deification. He points to the fact that even though the deification of Christ's human nature was, as Saint John Damascene says, effected from the very moment in which He assumed our nature, nevertheless Christ as Man shied away from anything which might give the impression of *autotheosis,* that is to say, self-deification or self-divinization. That is why we see the action of the Holy Spirit underlined at His Holy Birth: "The Holy Ghost shall come upon thee... therefore also that holy thing which shall be born of thee shall be called the Son of God" (Luke 1:35); also, the Holy Spirit descends upon Christ at His Baptism in the Jordan (Matt. 3:15); and concerning the Resurrection, the Scriptures speak thus: "God, that raised him up from the dead, and gave him glory" (1 Pet. 1:21); and finally, Christ Himself, teaching us the way of humility and how always to ascribe glory to Our Heavenly Father, says: "If I bear witness of myself, my witness is not true. There is another that beareth witness of me; and I know that the witness which he witnesseth of me is true" (John 5:31–32).

The same movement may be observed in the Divine Liturgy. The Words of Institution – "take eat, this is my body", "drink of this all of you, this is my blood" – *by themselves* are not regarded

---
9. See ibid., pp. 151–152.

as sufficient to effect the consecration of the Holy Gifts; they must be accompanied by the *Epiklesis,* the invocation of the Holy Spirit, precisely in order to avoid any notion of self-deification, to avoid, that is, giving the impression that simply by speaking the words which Christ spoke, *we are able* to transform the Holy Gifts into the precious Body and Blood of Christ. (Of course, at the heart of this movement lies the truth that the action of Father, Son and Holy Spirit is always *one and the same:* the Three Divine Hypostases always act together, always act in unison, which is an expression of Their consubstantiality.) Thus, it behooves us to beseech God the Father to send down the Holy Spirit, by Whose power the change of the bread and wine into the Body and Blood of Christ is effected.[10]

2. Love for Enemies as the Measure of Our Likeness to Christ

NOW ALTHOUGH SAINT SILOUAN HIMSELF, as far as I am aware, does not actually use the term theosis, the deification of the human person in Christ is certainly a golden thread which may be traced throughout his writings. For Saint Silouan, the fundamental criterion by which a person may measure his or her likeness to Christ is love for one's enemies (cf. Matt. 5:43–45). As he says:

Christ prayed for them that were crucifying him: "Father, forgive them; for they know not what they do" (Luke 23:34). Stephen the Martyr prayed for those who stoned him, that the Lord "lay not this sin to their charge" (Acts 7:60). And we, if we wish to preserve grace, must pray for our enemies.

Herein lies the mystery of the divine "mode of being", God's very way of life: humility. Humility on the ascetic plane, explains Father Sophrony, is manifested as regarding one's self as the worst of all sinners, while on the theological plane, humility is revealed as love, which is given freely and completely.[11] Saint

---

10. Ibid., p. 153.
11. Ibid., p. 156.

Silouan, who was himself possessed of this divine love, humbly warns us to be watchful:

> If you do not feel pity for the sinner destined to suffer the pains of hell-fire, it means that the grace of the Holy Spirit is not in you, but an evil spirit. While you are still alive, therefore, strive by repentance to free yourself from this spirit.[12]

The struggle for Christlike love for one's enemies and humility, and against pride, is a very great one indeed; and that is why the saints, the true imitators of Christ and sharers in His love, are great indeed. Saint Silouan writes:

> I am a sorry wretch, as the Lord knows, but my pleasure is to humble my soul and love my neighbour, though he may have given me offence. At all times I beseech the Lord Who is merciful to grant *that I may love my enemies;* and by the grace of God I have experienced what the love of God is, and what it is to love my neighbour; and day and night I pray the Lord for love, and the Lord gives me tears to weep for the whole world. But if I find fault with any man, or look on him with an unkind eye, my tears will dry up, and my soul sink into despondency. Yet do I begin again to entreat forgiveness of the Lord, and the Lord in His mercy forgives me, a sinner.

"Brethren," Saint Silouan continues:

> before the face of my God I write: Humble your hearts, and while yet on this earth you will see the mercy of the Lord, and know your Heavenly Creator, and your souls will never have their fill of love.[13]

So, we see that the love of Christ fills the very being of His saints.

3. Holy Relics as a Witness to the Love of Christ in Us

BUT WITHER DOES THIS ALL-EMBRACING Christlike love lead? The answer for Saint Silouan is a simple one:

---

12. *Saint Silouan the Athonite,* translated by Rosemary Edmonds (Tolleshunt Knights, Essex: Patriarchal and Stavropegic Monastery of St. John the Baptist, 1991), p. 352.
13. Ibid., pp. 362–363.

Love of God takes various forms. The man who wrestles with wrong thoughts loves God according to his measure. He who struggles against sin, and asks God to give him strength not to sin, but yet falls into sin again because of his infirmity, and sorrows and repents – he possesses grace in the depths of his soul and mind, but his passions are not yet overcome. But the man who has conquered his passions now *knows no conflict:* all his concern is to watch himself in all things lest he fall into sin. Grace, great and perceptible, is his. But he who feels grace in both soul and body is a perfect man, and if he preserves this grace, his body is sanctified and his bones will make holy relics.[14]

There are, described in this passage, four stages of love, the fourth and highest of which is that which is attested to by the penetration of Divine Grace into the body, into the very marrow of a persons being. And this is identified by Saint Silouan as the highest state of perfection, the highest state of holiness. "He who feels grace in both soul *and body* is a perfect man, and if he preserves this grace, *his body is sanctified* and *his bones will make holy relics.*"

As with Christ's voluntary death, in which it was not possible for the Body of the Logos of Life to see corruption, and which was thus raised together with His human soul on the third day,[15] so too will it be with the bodies of those saints which have known great grace in this life, and who have been able to preserve it.[16] They too, even after death, are not separated from the grace and love of God, neither in soul nor in body, and hence their bodies are revealed as holy relics.

Here we are confronted with an overwhelming mystery: that man is not truly man, not truly a human person or hypostasis, without his body. For this reason, even great saints patiently await

---

14. Ibid., pp. 438–439.
15. Cf. the troparion: "In the tomb according to the flesh, As God in hell with the soul, In paradise with the thief, And on the throne with the Father and the Spirit wast thou, O Christ, omnipresent, incircumscript." Translation taken from *The Orthodox Liturgy* of the Patriarchal and Stavropegic Monastery of St. John the Baptist, Essex (Oxford University Press, 1982), p. 63.
16. Cf. Saint Gregory Palamas' Homily XVI, *On Holy Saturday,* §17.

the Second and Glorious Coming of Christ, when by Grace they will become united once more with their bodies. There will not be a Judgment for them; for they have already been judged – by holy self-condemnation. The Second Coming of Christ, then, will be for them the moment of their full realization as persons, and thus the inauguration of their full and perfect participation in the Life in Christ, which is at one and the same time the Life of the Most Holy Trinity.

The sole exception to this, of course, is the Mother of God, the Theotokos (whose Feast of the Holy Protection we celebrate tomorrow, October 1), who, as the Mother of Life, even after death, could not be held by the grave, but, like her Son, "passed over into life". She, therefore, even now, as a fully realized human hypostasis, enjoys the blessed Life to which we have all been called.

In our first section, we noted an important passage in Saint Paul, from his *Epistle to the Romans,* concerning sonship, suffering and the final glory. Allow me to repeat it once more:

> The Spirit itself beareth witness with our spirit, that we are the children of God: And if children, then heirs; heirs of God, and joint-heirs with Christ; if so be that we suffer with him, that we may be also glorified together. For I reckon that the sufferings of this present time are not worthy to be compared with the glory which shall be revealed in us (Rom. 8:16–18).

"The sufferings of this present time are not worthy to be compared with the glory which shall be revealed in us," that is to say, in our adoption as sons, in our Salvation, in our theosis in Christ. That is why Saint Gregory Palamas affirms, "Except for sin nothing in this life, even death itself, is really evil, even if it causes suffering".[17] Speaking of the torments that the martyrs were willing to endure, Saint Gregory explains, "The martyrs made the violent death which others inflicted on them into something magnificent, a source of life, glory and the eternal heavenly kingdom, because they exploited it in a good way that pleased God."[18]

---

17. Ibid., §33.
18. Ibid. Quotations taken from *Saint Gregory Palamas: The Homilies,*

Christ's word is charged or loaded with His divine energy, life and power; so too are His divine actions and His Life on earth as Man. When we fill ourselves with His words, and strive earnestly to live according to His command and example, to love even our enemies as He did – as He does – so too do we, by the grace of the Holy Spirit, enter into the sphere of Life which is contained in them. There is, as Father Zacharias puts it, "an exchange of lives" which takes place. We thus become, in our souls and in our bodies, "partakers of the divine nature" (2 Pet. 1:4) through union with His flesh, His humanity – sharers, that is, in the very divine Life of Christ Himself, which is at the same time the Life of the Most Holy Trinity.

We are saved not as individuals but as persons-hypostases, as members of the Body of Christ, of which Christ is the Head. We are united with Him – and through Him, with the other members of His Body.

Notice the following words from Father Sophrony's *We Shall See Him As He Is*:

Through His incarnation the everlasting Logos of the Father gives us to partake of His Blood and His Flesh in order thereby to pour into our veins His eternal Life, that we may become His children, flesh of His Flesh, bone of His Bone (cf. John 6:53–57).[19]

In Holy Relics, therefore, we do not see dead bones – far from it! In Holy Relics we see the result of communion with the Lord, the result of sharing the very Life of the Most High God (cf. Rom. 9:5) – communion with Him Who is Self-Life, Life Itself (αὐτοζωή). United with Christ, then, though we pass through "the valley of the shadow of death" (Ps. 23:4), we pass from death unto Eternal Life (cf. John 5:24). This is the point at which the created meets the uncreated, the point at which earth meets "heaven face to face", and the point at which we created, mortal human beings are transfigured by Him into Divine Life.

---

edited and translated from the original Greek with an introduction and notes by Christopher Veniamin (Dalton, PA: Mount Thabor Publishing, 2nd ed., 2013), p. 130.

19. Op. cit., pp. 192–193.

Thus are the perfect. Thus are the saints. Thus are they whose very bones have preserved grace to the end. Holy Relics are the earthly remains of those who have been taught by none other than Christ Himself to love their enemies even unto death, the death of the Cross, which is His glory, and which by grace becomes their glory, too. Love for enemies is not a moral injunction, it is the fundamental criterion for the Christian way of life. This is Salvation. Yea, this is *theosis*.

Truly, then, "In this world there is nothing more difficult than to be saved". But as we begin to perceive Salvation as theosis, so too do the dry bones seen by the Prophet Ezekiel begin to receive Life:

The hand of the Lord was upon me, and carried me out in the spirit of the Lord, and set me down in the midst of the valley which was full of bones, And caused me to pass by them round about: and, behold, there were very many in the open valley; and, lo, they were very dry. And he said unto me, Son of man, can these bones live? And I answered, O Lord God, thou knowest. Again he said unto me, Prophesy upon these bones, and say unto them, O ye dry bones, hear the word of the Lord. Thus saith the Lord God unto these bones; Behold, I will cause breath to enter into you, and ye shall live: And I will lay sinews upon you, and will bring up flesh upon you, and cover you with skin, and put breath in you, and ye shall live... And ye shall know that I am the Lord, when I have opened your graves, O my people, and brought you up out of your graves, And shall put my spirit in you, and ye shall live, and I shall place you in your own land: then shall ye know that I the Lord have spoken it, and performed it, saith the Lord (Ezek. 37:1–14).

"[I] shall put my spirit in you, and ye shall live." "Even so, come, Lord Jesus" (Rev. 22:20).

THE POWER OF REPENTANCE
THE ETHOS OF "METANOIA"
IN THE ORTHODOX TRADITION

THAT WE ARE ALL IN NEED OF REPENTANCE is beyond dispute, as this is clearly indicated at the beginning of the Gospel, in the very first words preached by both St. John the Baptist and Christ Himself: "Repent: for the Kingdom of heaven is at hand" (Matt. 3:2 and 4:7); but also at the end of the Gospel (in Luke 24:47), where the Lord commissions His disciples: "that repentance and remission of sins should be preached in his name among all nations, beginning at Jerusalem."

So the question that I should like to pose at the outset of our reflection on this fundamentally crucial theme is: What is repentance and how does it bring about our "personal renewal"?

"Repentance," says St. John of the Ladder (c. 570 – c. 649, whose memory we celebrate on the Fourth Sunday of Great Lent), "is the renewal of baptism".[1] We know from Holy Scripture and our life in the Church that baptism means dying to the old man and being raised together with Christ in newness of life. As the great Paul says:

"Know ye not, that so many of us as were baptized into Jesus Christ were baptized into his death? Therefore we are buried with him by baptism into death: that like as Christ was raised up from the dead by the glory of the Father, even so we also should walk in newness of life... Knowing this, that our old man is crucified with him" (Rom. 6:3–4, 6).

So if, as St. John of the Ladder teaches us, repentance is the renewal of baptism, then it too must signify the renewal of the very same death and resurrection in Christ that we receive at baptism. But what exactly is this kind of death, and what is this kind of resurrection? The short answer to this question, as the holy Apostle Paul himself goes on to say in Romans 6:7, must be, *that* death which sets us free from sin, "For he that is dead is freed from sin".

So, in practical terms, how do we die to sin? Christ Himself tells us plainly that "If any man will come after me, let him deny himself, and take up his cross daily, and follow me" (Luke 9:23; and cf. also Matt. 16:24 and Mark 8:34). But what do these words really mean? Is this just an exalted metaphor that is intended to encourage us to be good and honest citizens? Most certainly not. For if Jesus Christ is truly "the way" (John 14:6), then surely, if we would be His disciples, we must also follow Him, follow His way; and, as Archimandrite Sophrony (of blessed memory) says, His way is that of the Cross: "where I am, there shall also my servant be" (John 12:26) – and "Where is Christ?" asks Fr. Sophrony. "On the Cross," he answers.[2]

In His Sermon on the Mount (Matt. 5:1 – 7:29), Our Lord God and Saviour Jesus Christ gives us a vivid description of the divine way of life, that is to say, He teaches us how to live as He does. This is especially evident when we bring to mind such verses as:

"Ye have heard that it was said of them of old time... Thou shalt love thy neighbour, and hate thine enemy... But I say unto you, Love your enemies, bless them that curse you, do good to them that hate you, and pray for them which despitefully use you, and persecute you; That ye may be the children of your Father which is in heaven: for he maketh his sun to rise on the evil and on the good, and sendeth rain on the just and on the unjust" (Matt. 5:43–45).

If we look closely at these and other such pronouncements, what we shall find is nothing less than Christ's self-revelation. In other words, Christ is telling us how He lives, and how, therefore, we too should strive to live, if we would be perfect; if, that is, we would be *as He is*.

The beloved disciple John the Theologian and Evangelist, whose memory we celebrated today (September 26), makes this clear when he says,

> "we know that, when he shall appear, we shall be like him; for we shall see him as he is. And every man that hath this hope in him purifieth himself, even as he is pure" (1 John 3:2–3).

Thus, if we wish to be eternally with Christ, we must become like Him; and this process of becoming Christlike, this purification, invariably involves repentance – a fundamental change in our whole way of life, in our "mode of being".

Our reactions, then, in any and every circumstance should be Christlike. Each time we find ourselves in difficult circumstances; each time that we are tempted to think or act according to the way of the world, and every time that we resist this impulse for the love of Christ, and ask for His help and mercy, we are indeed taking up our cross, we are indeed striving to change our way of life in accordance with Christ's commandments and example, we are indeed beginning to repent.

Let us listen briefly to how St. Silouan the Athonite (1866 – 1938), a saint of our own age, speaks of repentance:

> "Glory be to the Lord that He gave us repentance. Through repentance we shall all, every one of us, be saved. Only those who refuse to repent will not find salvation, and therein I see their despair, and shed abundant tears of pity for them. They have not known through the Holy Spirit how great is God's mercy. But if every soul knew the Lord, knew how deeply He loves us, no one would despair, or murmur against his lot.

> "Every soul that has lost peace should repent and the Lord will forgive her her sins, and there will be joy and peace in the soul. We have no need of other witnesses, for the Spirit Himself testifies that our sins are forgiven. Here is a token of forgiveness: if you now detest sin, it means the Lord has forgiven you your sins.

> "And what more could we expect? That some voice from heaven sing us a heavenly song? But in heaven everything has life through the Holy

Spirit, and the Lord has given us on earth the same Holy Spirit; in desert, mountain and cave, in every place, Christ's warriors who fight the good fight live by the Holy Spirit. If we preserve the Holy Spirit we shall be free of all darkness, and life eternal will be in our souls.

"If all men would repent and keep God's commandments, there would be paradise on earth, for 'the Kingdom of Heaven is within us.' The Kingdom of Heaven is the Holy Spirit, and the Holy Spirit is the same in heaven and on earth."[3]

But even though we know these things intellectually, even though we hear them at every Church service, yet we resist the challenge of Christ's first call to repentance, because we fear that we shall in some way loose our freedom; when, in fact, "true freedom" comes to him, says St. John of the Ladder, who "voluntarily delivers himself into servitude" – servitude, that is, to God.[4]

Based on the tradition of the Fathers, we can say that there are two basic ways by which one may arrive at the realization that a fundamental change of life must take place.

Firstly, there is what we might be allowed to call the "way of light", and secondly, there is what we may be allowed to term the "way of darkness". By the "way of light", then, we refer to such exceptionally rare occasions as when Christ Himself appears to His creature in His uncreated divine glory, and recognizing thereby how far we stand from what we have been called to become, we cannot but react by beseeching Him to save us, and help us to change.

By the "way of darkness" we refer to the more common way by which the chasm that divides us from Christ is revealed to us. God, in His mercy, allows us to see ourselves as we really are; He allows us to come to the realization, as St. Silouan the Athonite says, that without Him we cannot do or even think any good thing.[5] And the soul, seeing this, begins to cry out for help, asking Christ to enlighten, to illumine our darkened soul.

Now it should be emphasized here that both of these "ways" are a gift from God, and as such are the result of His saving uncreated grace operating in our lives. In other words, we are speaking here neither of an emotional nor of a psychological state or condition;

for there is no similarity between the uncreated grace of God and any other created thing.[6]

Repentance, then, is not an emotion. But how can we be sure that we are repenting, and that we are not simply indulging in emotion and sentimentality? Indeed, how can we be sure that we are living and acting in accordance with the will of God?[7]

Let us turn now to examine more closely the culture of repentance as expressed in the daily life of the Orthodox Church, and let us look in particular at the monastic life, at the life as it were of our "specialists" in the ascetic life.[8] For as St. John of the Ladder puts it, "Angels are a light for monks, and the monastic life is a light for all men. Therefore let monks strive to become a good example in everything..."[9]

We laymen, then, must also be prudent enough to learn from the light of the monastic life and polity, recognizing that it is the generator and measure of our own lives in the world. And let us not forget that asceticism – *ascesis* in Greek or in Russian *podvig* – understood as "spiritual labour", refers to monks and layman alike, since this is nothing more or less than living according to the commandments of Christ.

When speaking of repentance, the way of the cross, or following the commandments of Christ – for, as we have seen these terms are synonymous with one another[10] – the Fathers place a special emphasis on the importance of obedience, by which they refer not so much to an outward discipline as to the laying aside – or sacrifice – of one's own will in order to learn the will of God.

This, as we all know, is by no means an easy task, especially in our self-confident modern times. Archimandrite Sophrony explains why:

The educated man of the present day, with his developed critical approach, is incomparably less fitted for the ascetic exercise of obedience than the man of a simple turn of mind who is not seduced by intellectual curiosity. The cultured man, enamoured of his own critical intelligence, which he is accustomed to consider his principal dignity and the one solid foundation of his "personal" life, has to renounce this wealth of his before becoming a novice, or it will be difficult for him to enter the Kingdom.[11]

The age-old tradition of the Church teaches us that none of us is capable of discerning the will of God by ourselves, however, and therefore we all require the advice and guidance of an experienced fellow-Christian, of one who is at least a little further along the path of salvation than we are – a spiritual father. Indeed, asks St. Theodore the Studite (759 – 826), "What is more to be desired than a true father – a father-in-God?"[12] Such a man, says Symeon the New Theologian (949 – 1022), is found by persistently beseeching God to guide us to one capable of shepherding us well. And once found, he should be obeyed, just as though he were God Himself, even when his advice seems harmful to us and appears to go against our better judgment.[13]

"I know of monks," says St. Antony the Great, "who fell after much toil and lapsed into madness, because they trusted in their own work and neglected the commandment that says: 'Ask your father, and he will tell you'" (Deut. 32:7).[14] And St. Symeon also warns us of this danger when he insists that it is 'better to be called a disciple of a disciple and not to live according to the fashion of one's own style of life, gathering up the unprofitable fruits of one's own will'.[15]

It is certainly true that Abba Dorotheus of Gaza (6th century) teaches that if one truly wishes to learn the will of God, God will reveal His will to such a person even when there is no guide to be found, even, for instance, from the lips of a child. But the same holy father, quoting Proverbs, also states that "those who have no guidance fall like leaves but there is safety in much counsel" (Prov. 11:14). "We need assistance," he urges, "we need guidance in addition to God's grace;"[16] and he adds, "I know of no fall that happens to a monk that does not come from trusting his own judgment. Some say, 'A man falls because of this, or because of that,' but I say, and I repeat, I do not know of any fall happening to anyone [*please note here the words*, "to anyone"] except from this cause". "Do you know someone who has fallen?" asks Dorotheus, "Be sure that he directed himself."[17]

So, then, we ought to be humble and realistic enough to seek advice and guidance from a spiritual father. It should be noted, however, that the personal relationship between spiritual father and child is an extremely subtle one, requiring much caution and attention. In the *Admonition of the Father to his Son,* a text from Kievan Russia (?eleventh century), we read the following words of advice:

> I show you, my son, true refuges – monasteries, the houses of the saints: have recourse to them and they will comfort you; shed your sorrows before them and you will be gladdened: for they are sons of sorrowlessness and know how to comfort you, sorrowing one… In the city where you are living or in other neighbouring towns seek a God-fearing man – and serve him with all your strength. Having found such a man, you need grieve no more; you have found the key to the Kingdom of Heaven; adhere to him with soul and body; observe his life, his walking, sitting, looking, eating, and examine all his habits; first of all, my son, keep his words, do not let one of them fall to the ground; they are more precious than pearls – the words of the saints.[18]

By sacrificing his own will, by not yielding to vainglory (*kenodoxia*), sluggishness (*okneria*) or apathy (*rathymia*), and by eagerly doing those things which he is advised, the disciple may be saved.[19]

Now let us conclude these brief and humble observations with a quotation taken again from Silouan the Athonite:

> "Do not murmur, O children of God, because you find life difficult. Only wrestle with sin and entreat help from the Lord, and He will hearken, for He is full of compassion and loves us.

> "O, all ye peoples, I weep as I pen these lines. My soul's desire is that you should know the Lord and contemplate His mercy and glory. I am an old man of seventy-two years and must shortly die, and I write to you of the Lord's mercy that He gave me to know by the Holy Spirit; and the Holy Spirit taught me to love the people. Would that I could set you on a high mountain, that from the height thereof you might behold the gentle and compassionate countenance of the Lord, that your hearts would rejoice. Verily I tell you: I find no good in me, only many sins, but the grace of the Holy Spirit has effaced the multitude of my sins, and I know that to the man who wrestles against sin the Lord grants, not only forgiveness

but likewise the grace of the Holy Spirit, Who brings joy to the soul and a profound, sweet peace."[20]

At the ancient close of the Liturgy, the priest says 'Let us depart in peace'. Now as Archimandrite Kyrill (Abbot of the Monastery of St. John the Baptist in Essex, England), explains,[21] it is clear from the New Testament that the word "peace" can refer only to the person of Christ, Who is Himself the only true peace. And so when we bare this in mind we begin to understand that the priest is in fact exhorting the faithful to "depart in Christ". That is to say, that it is our responsibility as Christians, once we have received Christ at the Divine Liturgy, through the Holy Eucharist, not to forget the things of God at the Church doors as we leave, but to take Christ with us out into the world, thereby witnessing by our very way of life that we are His disciples. And how do we ensure that we take Christ with us? By taking the cup of salvation and continually calling upon His holy Name: "Lord Jesus Christ have mercy upon me."

ENDNOTES

1. "Step 5 On Painstaking and True Repentance which Constitutes the Life of the Holy Convicts; and about the Prison," in St. John Climacus, *Ladder of Divine Ascent*, tr. by Archimandrite Lazarus Moore with an introduction by Muriel Heppell (Willits, CA: Eastern Orthodox Books, 1959), p. 98.

2. From Hieromonk Zacharias' homily "On Repentance," delivered in the "Atelier," Stavropegic Monastery of St. John the Baptist, Essex, England, January 29, 1983.

3. Archimandrite Sophrony, *Saint Silouan the Athonite* (1991), pp. 347–348.

4. Patrologia Graeca (*PG*) lxxxviii, 680C; found in Sophrony, "Principles of Orthodox Asceticism," tr. from the Russian by Rosmary Edmonds and reprinted from *The Orthodox Ethos: Studies in Orthodoxy*, vol. 1, edited by A. J. Philippou (Oxford: Holywell Press, 1964), p. 273.

5. *Saint Silouan the Athonite, passim.*

6. Fr. Zacharias, loc. cit.

7. St. Silouan points to a useful criterion: "If you think evil of people, it means you have an evil spirit in you whispering evil thoughts about others. And if a man dies without repenting, without having forgiven his brother, his soul will go to the place where lives the evil spirit which possessed his soul. This is the law we have: if you forgive others, it is a sign that the Lord has forgiven you; but if you refuse to forgive, then your own sin remains with you." *Saint Silouan the Athonite*, p. 351.

8. Cf. Sophrony, "Principles of Orthodox Asceticism," p. 259.

9. "Step 26 On Discernment of Thoughts, Passions and Virtues," *Ladder of Divine Ascent*, pp. 206–207.

10. Based on a homily "On the Passions of the Lord" given by Hieromonk Zacharias, in the Chapel of St. Silouan, Stavropegic Monastery of St. John the Baptist, Great Lent, 1984.

11. Sophrony, "Principles of Orthodox Asceticism," p. 273.

12. Found in Bishop Kallistos T. Ware's article, "The Spiritual Father in St. John Climacus and St. Symeon the New Theologian," *Studia Patristica* xviii, 2 (1989), 299. Also reprinted as the "Foreword" in the study made by Irénée Hausherr, entitled *Spiritual Direction in the Early Christian East*, Cistercian Studies Series: no. 116, tr. Anthony P. Gythiel (Kalamazoo, Michigan: Cistercian Publications, 1990), p. vii.

13. From my own "The Transfiguration of Christ in Greek Patristic Literature: From Irenaeus of Lyons to Gregory Palamas" (Oxford D. Phil. thesis, 1991), p. 241 (hereafter cited as Veniamin, "Transfiguration"); and cf. §104 of Step 4 "On Blessed and Ever-memorable Obedience", in St. John Climacus, *Ladder of Divine Ascent*, p. 91, where he says: "Let us trust with firm confidence those who have taken upon themselves the care of us in the Lord, even though they order something apparently contrary and opposed to our salvation. For it is then that our faith in them is tested as in a furnace of humiliation. For it is a sign of truest faith if we obey our superiors without any hesitation, even when we see the opposite of what we had hoped for happening".

As an illustration of this, St. John then tells of a certain Acacius, placed under obedience to an elder "who was extremely careless and undisciplined", and who "tormented [Acacius] daily not only with insults and indignities, but even with blows". However, Acacius' obedience, as St. John quite cautiously points out, "was not mere senseless endurance"; and this is borne out by the fact that, five days after his repose, even from the grave Acacius replies to his disbelieving elder's question ("Are you dead, Brother Acacius?") with the following words: "How is it possible, Father, for a man who is a doer of obedience to die?"

14. *Apophthegmata*, Alphabetical collection, Antony 37 and 38 (*PG* 65: 88B); Ware, "The Spiritual Father in St. John Climacus and St. Symeon the New Theologian," op. cit., 300, n. 11.

15. Veniamin, "Transfiguration", loc. cit.

16. "On the need for Consultation: That a man ought not to rely on his own judgment," *Dorotheos of Gaza: Discourses and Sayings,* Cistercian Studies Series, no. 33, tr. Eric P. Wheeler (Kalamazoo, Michigan: Cistercian Publications, 1977), p. 122.

17. Ibid., p. 126.

18. Ware, "The Spiritual Father in St. John Climacus and St. Symeon the New Theologian," op. cit., 301.

19. Veniamin, "Transfiguration", loc. cit.

20. *Saint Silouan the Athonite*, p. 345.

21. Archimandrite Kyrill, "Homily on Bringing up Our Children in the Church," Chapel of St. Silouan the Athonite, December 13, 1992.

Holy Relics: THE DEIFICATION OF THE HUMAN BODY IN THE CHRISTIAN TRADITION

*DELIVERED DURING THE CHRISTMAS FAST

IN OCTOBER OF 1978 A SMALL COMPANY left San Lorenzo de Campo in the north of Italy for Thessalonica in Northern Greece. The members of this party included the Metropolitan of Thessalonica, Panteleimon, his Chancellor, and the Roman Catholic Bishop of the Italian province from which they were leaving. This was a very low-key event. Perhaps the local newspaper had written a couple of lines in reference to it, but in any case very few people even noticed, or much cared about, what was taking place.

The retinue quietly made its way to the harbour, whence, virtually unnoticed, they embarked upon their voyage for Thessalonica.

The journey itself, though uneventful, was pleasant enough. But as their ship approached the Thessalonian harbour, a faint sound was heard emanating from it. At first it was hardly discernible from the sound of the sea, but as it grew louder it revealed a sense of excitement, until, as the ship drew even closer to shore, it developed into the sound of ten-thousand voices singing in unison.

The Roman Catholic Bishop could hardly disguise his surprise. With raised eyebrows he asked, "Was this throng waiting to greet *them*?"

"They have come to welcome the Saint," said one of the company. The others nodded in agreement.

"But how many must there be?" asked the Bishop in disbelief. "It looks as though the whole city has come down to the harbour!"

"It seems so," said the Chancellor.

"All these people for the sake of some old bones . . . hum, I mean, for the relics of St. Demetrius?"

"Yes," the Metropolitan replied, "the people have come to greet the Holy Relics of our beloved St. Demetrius. It is for this that the whole city rejoices."

The celebration of the return of the Saint's Holy Relics took the form of church services, all-night vigils, sermons and long speeches delivered by various dignitaries, and so forth.

But why, we may well ask – together with the Roman Catholic Bishop – why so much excitement and rejoicing over a few "old bones"? Why do the Orthodox Christians (not only of Thessalonica, but all over the world) still venerate Holy Relics with such reverence and piety? What is it about them that the Orthodox peoples know, which others – even fellow Christians – appear to have forgotten?

It will come as no surprise to you, if I answer this question by saying that Holy Relics witness to the great sanctity of a Christian, to his or her faithfully following the commandments of Christ, to receiving His Grace, and to truly becoming like Him.

But what exactly does "great sanctity" mean? Or, in other words, what kind of sanctity is it that produces Holy Relics? To what kind of person do Holy Relics bear witness? And finally, what do Holy Relics have to do with Christmas, the great mystery of the Incarnation?

In attempting to answer this question, I should like first to quote a few lines from a great saint of our own age, St. Silouan the

Athonite (1866 – 1938), because the saints have a wonderful way of cutting straight to the heart of the matter. Drawing therefore a direct connection between Holy Relics and the Love of God, St. Silouan writes:

> Love of God takes various forms. The man who wrestles with wrong thoughts loves God according to his measure. He who struggles against sin, and asks God to give him strength not to sin, but yet falls into sin again because of his infirmity, and sorrows and repents – he possesses grace in the depths of his soul and mind, but his passions are not yet overcome. But the man who has conquered his passions now *knows no conflict:* all his concern is to watch himself in all things lest he fall into sin. Grace, great and perceptible, is his. But he who feels grace in both soul and body is a perfect man, and if he preserves this grace, his body is sanctified and his bones will make holy relics (*Saint Silouan the Athonite,* translated by Rosemary Edmonds, Tolleshunt Knights, Essex: Patriarchal and Stavropegic Monastery of St. John the Baptist, 1991, pp. 438–439).

There are, described in this passage, four stages of love, the fourth and highest of which is that which is attested to by the penetration of Divine Grace into the body, into the very marrow of a persons being. And this is identified by St. Silouan as the highest state of perfection, the highest state of holiness: "He who feels grace in both soul *and body* is a perfect man, and if he preserves this grace, *his body is sanctified* and *his bones will make holy relics.*"

And we could justifiably add to St. Silouan's remarks here that this is in fact the whole point of the Incarnation – to save the whole human person – soul *and body;* to raise, that is, our fallen human nature to its intended place – at the right hand of God the Father.

Let us now bring to mind St. Athanasius the Great's famous saying, which refers to the purpose of Christ's coming in the flesh: "God became man that we might be made gods" (*On the Incarnation* 54. It was St Athanasius, *c.* 296 – 373, Pope and Patriarch of Alexandria, who championed the defence of the true Faith against the Arians, and also gave us the present New Testament canon, in his *Paschal Epistle* of 367).

"God became man that we might be made gods." In the Epistle Reading for the Divine Liturgy on Christmas Day, where the Apostle Paul identifies the Incarnation as "the fullness of time," he also makes the following very important point:

> But when the fullness of the time was come, God sent forth his Son, made of a woman, made under the law, To redeem them that were under the law, *that we might receive the adoption of sons*. And because ye are sons, God hath sent forth the Spirit of his Son into your hearts, crying, Abba, Father. Wherefore thou art no more a servant, but a son; and if a son, then an heir of God through Christ (Gal. 4:4–7).

Thus the purpose of Christ's redemption of mankind is "that we might receive the adoption of sons" *through union with Him,* for thereby we receive the Spirit, Who cries in our hearts, "Abba, Father;" and thereby we truly become "heir[s] of God through Christ."

It is in Christ Jesus, therefore, that we not only encounter true and perfect God, but also true and perfect man. In other words, we see in Him not only the great God and Saviour, but also what *we* have been called to become.

As Archimandrite Sophrony (1896 – 1993) says in his spiritual autobiography:

> Christ manifested the perfection of the Divine image in man and the possibility for our nature of assimilating the fullness of divinization to the very extent that, after His ascension, He placed our nature "on the right hand of the Father."

To this, however, he also adds:

> But even in Him our nature did not become one with the essence of the Uncreated God. In Christ, incarnate Son of the Father, we contemplate God's pre-eternal idea of man (*We Shall See Him As He Is,* translated by Rosemary Edmonds, Tolleshunt Knights, Essex: Patriarchal and Stavropegic Monastery of St. John the Baptist, 1988, p. 193).

In Christ Jesus we find man's true place, "on the right hand of the Father," sharing in the divine life; but, as with the two natures in Christ, united without confusion; in other words, we never cease to be His creatures, for He alone is Uncreated and Pre-eternal.

Throughout the History of Salvation – in the Old Testament as well as in the New – it was this same Son and Word of God, Who was in the beginning with the Father, Who of old revealed Himself to our spiritual forefathers. In other words, it was the Pre-Incarnate Word, He Who by His Incarnation became the Christ, it was He Who visited Abraham under the Oak at Mamre, it was He Who wrestled with Jacob, it was He Who spoke with Moses and the Prophets. This is He of Whom the Prophet-King David tells, "The LORD said unto my Lord, Sit thou at my right hand, until I make thine enemies thy footstool" (Ps. 110:1).

And of His coming as a man, the Prophet Isaiah speaks the well-known lines:

Unto us a child is born, unto us a son is given: and the government shall be upon his shoulder: and his name shall be called Angel of Great Counsel, Wonderful Counselor, Mighty God, Potentate, Prince of Peace, Father of the Age to Come (Isa. 9:6 in the Septuagint (LXX), the version used by the Church).

These are the names which we use today in Great Compline during Great Lent, when we sing "For God is with us" (*hoti meth' hemôn ho Theos*); and they are the names of none other than Jesus Christ.

Just as Christ became the New Adam in order to save the whole Adam, that is to say, to save all mankind, so too do we, by becoming Christlike – through the purification of the passions and the cultivation of the virtues, by living according to the commandments of Christ – *so too do we* embrace, as does Christ, *the whole Adam* in our person.

Now what we are referring to here is not a moral or ethical state, but an ontological or rather an *experiential* one; and this produces in us the ability to repent in the same way as did Adam our forefather. This Adam-like repentance, moreover, gives birth to hypostatic-personal prayer for the world.

The reason why we insist that this repentance and the prayer that springs from it are not to be understood as operating on a moral level, but rather on a hypostatic or personal one, is because our archetype is none other than the divine Person of

Christ Himself, Who contains within Himself both heaven and earth – full and perfect divinity and full and perfect humanity.

Of the experience of hypostatic, personal prayer, St. Silouan the Athonite writes:

> He who has the Holy Spirit in Him, *to however slight a degree,* sorrows day and night for all mankind. His heart is filled with pity for all God's creatures, more especially for those who do not know God, or who resist Him and therefore are bound for the fire of torment. For them, more than for himself he prays day and night, that all may repent (*Saint Silouan the Athonite,* p. 352).

The great and wonderful mystery here is that when a person reaches out and embraces the whole Adam, he finds himself, by the grace of the Holy Spirit, *actually living the spiritual state or condition of the whole human race* – even that of the most sinful man – and in this way such a person truly prays for his neighbour as for himself.

Hypostatic prayer – this prayer for all creation as for one's self – is at the very heart of the Divine Eucharist – the Liturgy – and can be seen very clearly both in Holy Scripture and Sacred Tradition:

In the Old Testament, for instance, we find Moses imploring God to forgive the people of Israel, after falling into the grave sin of idolatry:

> Yet now, if thou wilt forgive their sin —; and if not, blot me, I pray thee, out of thy book which thou hast written (Exod. 32:32).

And in the New Testament too, St. Paul says of his fellow Jews:

> I say the truth in Christ, I lie not, my conscience also bearing me witness in the Holy Ghost, That I have great heaviness and continual sorrow in my heart. For I could wish that myself were accursed from Christ for my brethren, my kinsmen according to the flesh (Rom. 9:1–3).

In Holy Tradition too, in the lives of the saints, we find exactly the same thing. As St. Silouan says:

> Christ prayed for them that were crucifying him: "Father, forgive them; for they know not what they do" (Luke 23:34). Stephen the Martyr prayed for those who stoned him, that the Lord "lay not this sin to their

charge" (Acts 7:60). And we, if we wish to preserve grace, must pray for our enemies (*Saint Silouan the Athonite*, p. 352).

Holy Relics, therefore, are the earthly remains of those who have been taught by none other than Jesus Christ Himself to love their enemies – just as He did . . . just as He does. Love for enemies is not, then, simply a moral injunction – it is the fundamental criterion for the Christian way of life. That is why St. Silouan, himself possessed of this divine love, humbly warns us to be watchful:

> If you do not feel pity for the sinner destined to suffer the pains of hellfire, it means that the grace of the Holy Spirit is not in you, but an evil spirit. While you are still alive, therefore, strive by repentance to free yourself from this spirit (*Saint Silouan the Athonite*, p. 352).

It is no coincidence that the altars of the earliest churches were built over the tombs of the martyrs, that is, over their holy relics; and that the celebration of the Divine Eucharist took place over them. (And to this day, in accordance with tradition, particles of holy relics are typically embedded in our holy altars and sewn in to our *antimensia*.) For, as mentioned earlier, the hypostatic or personal prayer of the saints *is* liturgical and eucharistic prayer, and this is so *precisely* because both kinds of prayer embrace the whole Adam, the whole of humankind, in the love of Jesus Christ.

We are saved, not as individuals, but as persons, that is to say, as members of the Body of Christ, of which Christ is the Head. We are united with Him – and in and through Him, with the other members of the Body.

Notice how the following words by Elder Sophrony underline the fact that the sanctification of the human body is intimately bound up with the Incarnation of Christ and the Divine Eucharist:

> Through His incarnation the everlasting Logos of the Father gives us to partake of His Blood and His Flesh in order thereby to pour into our veins His eternal Life, that we may become His children, flesh of His Flesh, bone of His Bone [cf. John 6:53–57] (*We Shall See Him As He Is*, pp. 192–193).

In Holy Relics, therefore, we do not see dead bones – far from it. What we see in Holy Relics is the result of communion with the Lord, the result of sharing the very Life of the Most High God (cf. Rom. 9:5) – communion with Him Who is Self-Life (*autozoë*), Who is Life itself. United with Christ, then, though we pass through "the valley of the shadow of death" (Ps. 23:4), we pass from death unto Eternal Life (cf. John 5:24). This is the point where the created meets the uncreated, where earth meets heaven face to face, the point at which our life is transformed by Him into divine Life (cf. Ezek. 37:1–14).

"God became man that we might be made gods." The deification of man is thus the express purpose of the first Parousia of Christ. It is for the sake of us human beings, for the purpose of our deification, that the Son and Word of God – He "who is above all being" – was born of the Virgin. There was no need for God to do this: deification is a pure gift freely given by God Himself. For this reason, Salvation bears witness to God's great mercy and ineffable love for mankind.

The question naturally arises: "What shall I render unto the Lord for all his benefits toward me?" (Ps. 116:12) And the Psalmist, inspired by the Holy Spirit, teaches us what the correct response to the divine offering ought to be: "I will take the cup of salvation, and call upon the name of the Lord" (Ps. 116:13). What else is there left for us to do, in other words, but to accept what God is offering us in humility, confess the great things which God has done for us in both word and deed, and give all glory, honour and worship to Him alone?

That is what the Church, by every means at Her disposal, teaches us to do. And so we sing:

Today Christ is born of the Virgin in Bethlehem. Today He who knows no beginning now begins to be, and the Word is made flesh. The powers of heaven greatly rejoice, and the earth with mankind makes glad. The Magi offer gifts, the shepherds proclaim the marvel, and we cry aloud without ceasing: Glory to God in the highest, and on earth peace, good will among men (*Hymn* by John the Monk, sung at "Both Now…" for the *Lauds* of the Feast of the Nativity According to the Flesh of our Lord, God and Saviour, Jesus Christ).

THE SINLESSNESS OF THE MOTHER OF GOD
ACCORDING TO ST NICHOLAS CABASILAS

Historical Background

ST. NICHOLAS CABASILAS was born *circa* 1322 of noble parentage in the ancient city of Thessalonica, the second city of the Christian Roman Empire.[1] His lifetime spanned

1. Second in importance only after Constantinople. On the life and times of Cabasilas, see *passim* in the following works: P. Nellas, ed., Ἡ Θεομήτωρ· Τρεῖς Θεομητορικὲς Ὁμιλίες τοῦ Νικολάου Καβάσιλα (Athens, 1974), p. 14; Myrrha Lot-Borodine, *Un Maître de la spiritualité byzantine au XIVe siècle, Nicolas Cabasilas* (Paris, 1958); A.A. Angelopoulos, Νικόλαος Καβάσιλας Χαμαετός· ἡ ζωὴ καὶ τὸ ἔργον αὐτοῦ (Thessalonica: Patriarchal Institute for Patristic Studies, Vlatadon, 1970); W. Völker, *Die Sakramentsmystik des Nikolaos Kabasilas* (Wiesbaden, 1977); H.-G. Beck, *Kirche und theologische Literatur im byzantinischen Reich* (München: C.H. Beck'schebuchhandlung, 1977), pp. 780–783; P. Chrestou, Ἐκκλησιαστικὴ Γραμματολογία· Πατέρες καὶ Θεολόγοι τοῦ Χριστιανισμοῦ, Vol. 1 (Thessalonica: Brothers Kyriakides Press, 1981), pp. 54–56; J. Gouillard in *Dictionnaire d'Histoire et de Géographie Ecclésiastique* xi (1949), cols. 14–21, and S. Salaville, A.A., in *Dictionnaire de Spiritualité* ii (1953), cols. 1–9, H.D. Hunter, in *New Catholic Encyclopedia* (*NCE*) ii (1981), p. 1036, and A.-M. Talbot, in *Oxford Dictionary of Byzantium* (*ODB*) ii (1991), p. 1088, all s.v., with bibl.;

a period which saw the gradual decline of Byzantine hegemony in the East. Civil wars, religious conflict, and continual threats of invasion all conspired to produce a state of turmoil from which the Empire was never to recover, draining it, almost inevitably, "of its last vestige of strength".[2]

At the same time, however, amidst the endless power struggles for imperial rule and the fierce politico-religious disputes of the Zealots, this also proved to be an age of remarkable and profound creativity; and nowhere is this more apparent than in the arena of theological disputation with the so-called Palamite or Hesychast Controversy of the fourteenth century.[3]

Viewed against the backdrop of such strife, the figure of Nicholas Cabasilas acquires even greater stature. Put simply, Nicholas was what we would term a "Renaissance man". Himself a Hesychast,[4] Cabasilas first studied in his native Thessalonica under his celebrated uncle, Neilus[5] (Metropolitan of Thessalonica

---

O. Tafrali, *Thessalonique au XIVe siècle* (Paris, 1913), and G. Ostrogorsky, *History of the Byzantine State*, trans. by Joan Hussey (Oxford: Basil Blackwell, 1984), pp. 499–519, and esp. 516.

2. Ostrogorsky, op. cit., p. 511.
3. Ibid., pp. 511–522.
4. Ibid., p. 522. But cf. B. Tatakis, *La philosophie byzantine* (Paris, 1949), pp. 277–281, who while he "recognizes Nicholas Cabasilas as 'a fervent palamite and the pre-eminent mystical theologian of his time', also affirms 'that there are few evidences of Palamism in his mysticism", from B. Bobrinskoy's "Introduction" to deCatanzaro's, *The Life in Christ* (Crestwood, NY: SVS Press, 1974), p. 18, which is a reprint of the second part of Bobrinskoy's study on Cabasilas (see *Sobornost*, series 5: No. 7 [Autumn, 1968], pp. 483–505); and Beck, op. cit., pp. 780–781, who maintains that not only did Cabasilas have little to do with the Hesychast Controversy *per se*, but that his particular brand of Christocentric mysticism appears to be almost totally untouched by that of the Hesychasts.
5. For reasons of prestige, Nicholas preferred "Cabasilas", his mother's family name, to his paternal surname, "Chamaetos". That Neilus has sometimes been confused with his nephew may be due to the fact that Neilus as a layman was also called Nicholas, Talbot, op. cit., p. 1087, s.v. "Kabasilas, Neilos".

Note also that it was Neilus who, together with Philotheus Kokkinos

from 1361 to 1363),[6] and alongside Demetrius Cydones, who later translated some of the works of Aquinas into Greek.[7]

From 1335 to 1340 Nicholas continued his studies in Constantinople. Here, in addition to philology, philosophy and theology, his wide range of interests also encompassed such diverse disciplines as rhetoric, law, astronomy and mathematics.[8]

Owing to his privileged background and noble upbringing, Cabasilas moved in the most sophisticated and influential circles of his time. It appears, for instance, that up until 1335 he was closely associated with Isidore I Boucheras (one of the leading Hesychasts of his time and, from 1347, Patriarch of Constantinople), whom he appears to have had as his spiritual father. Isidore, himself a highly influential figure in the city of St. Demetrius, had sat at the feet of St. Gregory the Sinaïte (c. 1265 – 1346) and was later tonsured by St. Gregory Palamas (c. 1296 – 1359).[9]

Later, from around 1350, Nicholas was to distinguish himself as a government official, diplomat and courtier, serving in the entourage of John VI Cantacuzenus (1347–54) with, among others, his old fellow-student, Demetrius Cydones.[10] Interestingly, Cabasilas is also found in an official capacity accompanying

---

(Patriarch from 1354 to 1355, and again from 1364 to 1376), composed the famous *Synodical Tome* of 1351, Hunter, op. cit., p. 1036, s.v. "Cabasilas, Nilus".

6. It appears that Neilus never actually took up residence in his See, Talbot, op. cit., p. 1087, s.v. "Kabasilas, Neilos".

7. Though also a pupil of Neilus, Demetrius Cydones (b. c. 1324) was very much an anti-Hesychast, opposing the theology of St. Gregory Palamas, and an exponent of Thomist theology. Encouraged by Neilus, he translated into Greek Aquinas' *Summa Contra Gentiles,* and parts of the *Summa Theologiae* (as did also his younger brother, Prochorus the Hieromonk, 1333/4 – 1369/70). Later, c. 1357, Demetrius Cydones converted to the Latin Church and "supported John V's [Palaeologus] profession of faith made in Rome before Pope Urban V in 1369", see F. Kazhdan, in *ODB* ii (1991), p. 1161, s.v. "Kydones, Demetrios".

8. A.-M. Talbot, ibid., s.v., p. 1088, "Kabasilas, Nicholas".

9. Idem, ibid., p. 1015, s.v., "Isidore I Boucheras".

10. Chrestou, op. cit., p. 54; and cf. Kazhdan, ibid., p. 1161, s.v. "Kydones, Demetrios".

Palamas, the newly elected Metropolitan of Thessalonica, to the outer gates of the city, and then later, upon being refused entry by the Zealots, to the Holy Mountain. In 1353 or 54 we find him appearing as a candidate for Patriarch.[11] How exactly Cabasilas spent the latter part of his life still remains uncertain, although the opinion that he eventually became Metropolitan of Thessalonica is now widely rejected.[12]

Beyond dispute, however, is the fact that as scholar, diplomat and theologian, Cabasilas stands out as a man of rare and remarkable talent. He is best known to us through two works in particular: his *Concerning the Life in Christ*[13] and his *Interpretation of the Divine Liturgy*;[14] both of which, deservedly, have come to be regarded as classics of Christian mystical theology. Their strong Christocentric and sacramental character – written in a flowing

---

11. Beck, op. cit., pp. 780–781.

12. See H.D. Hunter, loc. cit.: "the view that he succeeded his uncle in the see of Thessalonica is false"; based on R. Loenertz, "Pour la chronologie des oeuvres de Joseph Bryennios," *Revue des Études byzantines* 7 (1949), 16f, and Beck, op. cit., p. 780. Among those who in the past have supported the view that Nicholas also served as Metropolitan of Thessalonica are A.K. Demetracopoulou, Ὀρθόδοξος Ἑλλάς (Leipzig, 1872), p. 83; and I. Karmiris, Θωμᾶ τοῦ Ἀκινάτου· Σούμε Θεολογική, Vol. 1 (Athens, 1935), p. 46.

Among those who disagree with this view are Nellas, op. cit., p. 14, and see his Προλεγόμενα εἰς τὴν μελέτην τοῦ Νικολάου Καβασίλα (Athens, 1968), pp. 10–11 (reprint from the Θρησκευτικὴ καὶ Ἠθικὴ Ἐγκυκλοπαιδεία, Vol. xii, s.v. "Nikolaos Kavasilas"). Nellas, following Beck (loc. cit.), who is cautious enough to use the word, "höchstwahrscheinlich", that is, "most probably" or "likely", maintains that Cabasilas remained a layman throughout his life. Note, however, that Angelopoulos (op. cit., pp. 67–74) supports the view that Cabasilas was tonsured a monk towards the end of his life; and that Chrestou (op. cit., p. 54), goes so far as to suggest that Nicholas lived as much as the second half of his life as a monk, "devoting himself entirely to writing and the Liturgy".

13. W. Gass, *Die Mystik des Nikolaus Cabasilas vom Leben in Christo* (Greifswald, 1849, second edition, 1899); reprinted in *Patrologia Graeca* (*PG*) 150, 493–725. Eng. trans. by deCatanzaro, op. cit.

14. *PG* 150, 368–492. Eng. trans. by J. M. Hussey and P. McNulty, *A Commentary on the Divine Liturgy* (London: SPCK, 1960).

style, imposing and unsurpassed in elegance – have earned Cabasilas the reputation of being one of the foremost authorities on the mysteries of Baptism, Chrismation and especially the Divine Eucharist.

Cabasilas' Homilies on the Mother of God

NOT SO WELL KNOWN, however, is the fact that Cabasilas wrote considerably more than the two works mentioned above.[15] Among his lesser known works are to be found three homilies on the *Nativity, Annunciation,* and *Dormition of the Mother of God,*[16] which display the same genius evident in both the *Life in Christ* and the *Interpretation of the Divine Liturgy*; and which form the basis of our present study.

The chief reason for this study is to investigate the claim originally made by Martin Jugie, to whom we owe a debt of thanks for the publication of the text of the three homilies, that Cabasilas' teaching on the sinlessness and purity of the Mother of God is in keeping with the Latin dogma of the *Immaculata Conceptio*, proclaimed by Pope Pius IX in 1854, which affirms that

---

15. Cabasilas wrote works on "socio-political ethics", as is instanced by his treatise *On Usury* (*PG* 150, 727–750, and R. Guilland, ed., in *Eis mnemen Spyridonos Lamprou* [Athens 1935] 269–77, found in Beck, op. cit., p. 782), and his *Discourse Concerning Illegal Acts of Officials against Things Sacred* (Talbot, op. cit., s.v. "Cabasilas, Nicholas Chamaetos"). And in addition to his three homilies on the Theotokos (see note following), he wrote against the skepticism (particularly) of Sextus Empiricus, sermons on the Ascension and the Saving Passion of Christ, as well as encomiums to SS. Demetrius, Theodora, Nicholas, Andrew the Younger of Jerusalem, and the Three Hierarchs. For a list of all Cabasilas' works, see Bobrinskoy, loc. cit.; Nellas, op. cit., pp. 30–36; Chrestou, Νικόλαος Καβάσιλας· εἰς τὴν Θείαν Λειτουργίαν καὶ περὶ τῆς ἐν Χριστῷ ζωῆς, Vol. 22 in the series Φιλοκαλία τῶν Νηπτικῶν καὶ Ἀσκητικῶν, which is itself part of the collection, Ἕλληνες Πατέρες τῆς Ἐκκλησίας (Thessalonica: Patristic Editions "Gregory Palamas", 1979), pp. 11–17; and also Beck, op. cit., pp. 781–782.
16. M. Jugie, ed., *Patrologia Orientalis* (*PO*) 19, 465–510 (with Latin translation and French introduction). See also Nellas, op. cit., pp. 40–221 (with Modern Greek translation and *scholia*).

the Blessed Virgin Mary was delivered from original sin *from the very moment she was conceived* by her mother, St. Anna.[17]

Now, the doctrine of the immaculate conception first appeared in the West during the eighth century as a "theological opinion". During the Middle Ages, and more specifically about the thirteenth century, this teaching was vigorously supported by the Franciscans; though, it should be noted, it was also categorically rejected by such notable figures as Bernard of Clairvaux (1090 – 1153), Albert the Great (*c.* 1200 – 1280), Bonaventure (*c.* 1217 – 1274) and the Dominicans – including Thomas Aquinas himself (*c.* 1225 – 1274). Indeed, according to the Scholastic tradition of this period, it was held that the Mother of God was in fact conceived in "original sin",[18] from which she had been freed while still in her mother's womb.[19]

---

17. Prologue to Cabasilas' homilies in *PO* 19, pp. 458–459.
18. Strictly speaking, there is in Orthodox Patristic tradition no "original sin" in the sense that the Latins and Protestants have come to understand the term. Orthodox often prefer to use the expression "ancestral sin", as it points away from the notion that human nature has inherited the very guilt of Adam. According to the Fathers, Adam's fall resulted in death (which is not created by God) and corruption, which in turn causes man to sin. Hence, our inclination towards evil. Note too that the Orthodox doctrine avoids the concept of necessity and preserves thereby the free choice or "self-governance" (τὸ αὐτεξεούσιον) of the human person-hypostasis. For a fuller investigation into the Patristic understanding of the Fall *vis-à-vis* Western Latin and Protestant doctrines, see the groundbreaking work by J.S. Romanides, *Τὸ Προπατορικὸν Ἁμάρτημα* (Athens, 1957; reprint of second edition by Domos Publications, 1992; Eng. trans. as *The Ancestral Sin*, by Zephyr Publishing, 2002); and for a more recent account of Romanides' views, see Hierotheos Vlachos' *Empirical Dogmatics: According to the Spoken Teaching of Father John Romanides*, Vol. 2 (Levadia: Birth of the Theotokos Monastery, 2013), pp. 168–190. Also, see B. Englezakis, "Rom. 5,12–15 and the Pauline Teaching on the Lord's Death: Some Observations," *Biblica* 58,2 (1977), 231–236, who points to the ABBA schema of Paul's theology of the Fall, that is to say, that of Sin–Death–Death–Sin.
19. Thomas Aquinas wrote of two "sanctifications" of the Ever-Virgin Mary: *Sanctificatio prima*, during the period between just after her conception in her mother's womb and her birth; and *sanctificatio secunda*,

It should be noted, however, that in the East too, in the second half of the fourteenth century, we have the example of Isidore Glabas (1341/2 – 1396), Metropolitan of Thessalonica (1380 – 1384 and 1386 – 1396), who appears to have preached that the Mother of God was delivered from the ancestral sin at the moment of her conception. In his homily *On the Entry of the Ever-Virgin Mary into the Holy of Holies*, Isidore suggests that the words, "Behold, I was shapen in iniquity; and in sin did my mother conceive me" (Ps. 50 [51]:5), do not apply to the Mother of God, and that her exemption is attributable to "the great things" that "he that is mighty hath done" (Luke 1:49).[20]

This paper, therefore, attempts to demonstrate that whilst at times appearing to incline towards such sentiments, a closer reading of Nicholas Cabasilas' teaching on the Theotokos will show quite clearly that he follows a rather different line of thought; indeed, a line of thought that suggests a set of presuppositions fundamentally different to those of all the distinguished figures of the Western theological tradition mentioned above.

Firstly, then, Cabasilas speaks of Joachim and Anna not merely as instruments (ὄργανα) of God but as co-workers (συνεργοί) with Him, as actively sharing in the divine economy, in God's work of salvation. Of all the righteous of the Old Dispensation – Moses, Noah, Abraham and the others – through whom great benefices had come to the human race, none, argues Cabasilas, could compare with the righteousness of the Ever-Virgin's parents, who must have been the most perfect keepers of the Law and so also the most beloved of God (καὶ τὸν νόμον φύλακες καὶ μάλιστα πάντων θεοφιλεῖς). Cabasilas, therefore, praises Joachim and

---

during her conception of Christ. With the first sanctification, her soul was freed from the flaring up of the passions, from the action of original sin; while at the second sanctification, her body was also freed, or completely cleansed of, the very essence or existence of the passions, and from the potential operation of original sin, that is from the corruption of the body itself (*infectio carnis*), which can also corrupt others with original sin. For further discussion, see I. Kaloyerou, Μαρία ἡ ἀειπάρθενος Θεοτόκος κατὰ τὴν Ὀρθόδοξον πίστιν (Thessalonica, 1957), p. 86.

20. *PG* 139, 52C–53A; found in Kaloyerou, ibid., p. 52.

Anna for their great virtue (ἀρετή), which was made manifest through their *synergy* or cooperation (συνέργεια or συνεργία) with God. Addressing them directly, he says that Mary's was indeed a natural birth, though not a simple birth of nature (μηδὲ φύσεως ὑμῖν ἁπλῶς ἐγένετο τόκος), for the birth of the Θεοτόκος was also the work of their prayer and righteousness (τῆς ὑμετέρας εὐχῆς καὶ δικαιωσύνης ἔργον ὑπῆρξεν). Nature, represented by the old age of the holy Progenitors, was barren (στεῖρα), but not barren in virtue; for it was by the virtue of SS. Joachim and Anna, which gave force to their prayer (ἡ δὲ τῆς εὐχῆς δύναμις παρὰ τῆς ἀρετῆς τοὐνδόσιμον ἔλαβεν), that God allowed such a wonder to take place (Θεῷ δὲ τὸ πᾶν ἐπετράπη).[21] Joachim and Anna's great favour before God is justified by the fruit which they bore (cf. Matt. 7:16), namely, the Mother of God, the magnitude of which also reveals the magnitude of their virtue. And Cabasilas adds that this indeed must be so, since "it is impossible for God to be a respecter of persons" (προσωπολήπτην τὸν Θεὸν ἀμήχανον εἶναι, cf. Acts 10:34).

Hence, though certainly describable as "supranatural" and even as "divine",[22] yet the Holy Virgin's birth is not described here as "virginal" or "maidenly". And this certainly seems to be in keeping with the earlier Patristic consensus, summed up in the words of St. John Damascene's rhetorical exclamation: "O loins of Joachim most blessed, out of which came blameless seed" (Ὦ ὀσφὺς τοῦ Ἰωακεὶμ παμμακάριστε, ἐξ ἧς κατεβλήθη σπέρμα πανάμωμον),[23] and "Thou (*sc*. the Mother of God) from us (*sc*. Adam and Eve) hast inherited a corruptible body" (σὺ φθαρτόν ἐξ ἡμῶν σῶμα κληρονομήσασα).[24] "Mary is our sister," says Athanasius the

---

21. *On the Nativity of the Mother of God PO* 19, 467.
22. Cf. the *troparion* of the 8th Ode, Second Canon by Basil the Monk, *Feast of the Entry of the Most Holy Theotokos into the Temple* (21 November): "They that divinely bore thee, O Undefiled and Pure..." (πανάχραντε Ἀγνή, οἱ θείως τεκόντες σε), see *The Festal Menaion,* trans. Mother Mary and Archimandrite [now Metropolitan] Kallistos Ware (Faber and Faber: London, 1969; reprinted by St. Tikhon's Seminary Press: South Canaan, PA, 1990), p. 189.
23. *On the Nativity of the Theotokos PG* 96, 664B.
24. *On the Dormition of the Theotokos*, ibid., 733C.

Great (c. 296 – 373), "for we are all of Adam" (ἀδελφὴ γὰρ ἡμῶν ἡ Μαρία, ἐπεὶ καὶ πάντες ἐκ τοῦ Ἀδάμ ἐσμεν).²⁵ Thus, the Mother of God, like the rest of mankind, inherited original sin, because she was born of the seed of Joachim. And in such lines as "from men did she spring" (ἐξ ἀνθρώπων ἀνέφυ), and "she was partaker of every common characteristic of the human race" (τῶν αὐτῶν μετέσχε πάντων τῷ γένει), we can see that Cabasilas is merely re-affirming this fundamental doctrine.

At the same time, however, with such lines as, "She did not inherit the same frame of mind nor was she tempted by the great evils of this life, but triumphed over sin (φρονήματος δὲ οὐκ ἐκληρονόμησεν ἴσου οὐδὲ παρεσύρη τῇ τοσῇδε τῶν κακῶν συνηθείᾳ, ἀλλ' ἔστη μὲν κατὰ τῆς ἁμαρτίας),"²⁶ Cabasilas also underlines the absence of personal sins, which are the result of the wilful operation of original sin: he maintains that the Holy Virgin alone of all mankind did not convert the potential to sin into actual operation (μόνη τῶν ἐξ αἰῶνος ἀνθρώπων ἐξ ἀρχῆς εἰς τέλος κατὰ πάσης ἔστη κακίας, καὶ τῷ Θεῷ τὸ παρ' αὐτοῦ δοθὲν ἡμῖν ἀκήρατον ἀπέδωκε κάλλος καὶ τῇ δυνάμει πάσῃ καὶ τοῖς ἀποτεθεῖαιν ὅπλοις ἐχρήσατο).²⁷ And this he attributes to the steadfastness of the Holy Virgin's will (καὶ γνώμης εὐθύτητι).²⁸

---

25. *Letter to Epictetus* 7 PG 26, 1061B. Kaloyerou believes that Augustine (354 – 430) clearly teaches that the Ever-Virgin was also an inheritor of original sin, op. cit., p. 84.
26. *Homily on the Dormition of the Mother of God* PO 19, 503.
27. *On the Nativity of the Mother of God*, ibid., 471. Fr. Sergei Nikolaevich Bulgakov maintains that the Theotokos had inherited original sin, but that her ability to sin was diminished even from her birth, reduced to a simple *potentia*. He accepts that she had never converted this potential into operation, and that from the moment of the Annunciation, Mary was completely freed from the hereditary inclination (*robê*), see *Kupina neopalimaja: opyt dogmaticheskago istolkovanija nekotorykh chert v pravoslavnom pochitanii Bogoroditsy* (Paris: YMCA Press, 1927), pp. 68ff; found in Kaloyerou, op. cit., p. 89.
28. *On the Nativity of the Mother of God*, loc. cit., and *Homily on the Dormition of the Mother of God*, loc. cit. Cf. Vladimir Lossky: "Like other human beings, such as St. John the Baptist... the Holy Virgin was born

The Mother of God was prefigured in the Holy of Holies (τὰ ἅγια τῶν ἁγίων), the "place" of the "presence of God": "The Holy of Holies," insists Cabasilas, "certainly pointed to the Most Holy Ever-Virgin";[29] and that she was allowed to enter that holy place – a place where the high-priest alone entered but once a year (cf. Heb. 9:7) – must surely be a sign that she was completely free from all evil.[30] Parallels once again can be found in St. John Damascene (*c.* 675 – *c.* 749), who teaches that the fruition of Mary's virtue and sanctity begins with her entry into the Temple, and that while there "she became a resting-place of every virtue" (πάσης ἀρετῆς καταγώγιον γέγονε).[31]

On this point, it is fair to say, Cabasilas does appear to hold a more extreme position. He maintains that it was in the person of the Mother of God that we first see the manifestation of the strength to oppose evil, implanted in man by God. Furthermore, Cabasilas argues that not only could the Mosaic Law be kept – as is witnessed by the righteous of the Old Covenant – but that it was the Theotokos who was the first person to actually keep it in its entirety. She alone lived as God intended man to live; she alone revealed human nature as the Creator originally intended it to be.[32]

Elsewhere, Cabasilas makes what at first sight appears to be a remarkably daring affirmation, namely, that "she herself [the Mother of God] destroyed the enmity which existed in human nature against God and opened heaven and attracted grace and received the strength to strive against sin".[33] But even here, as Nellas points out, one should not be under the impression that Cabasilas is claiming that the Ever-Virgin's struggle against

---

under the law of original sin... But sin never could become active in her person; the sinful heritage of the Fall had no mastery over her right will," *In the Image and Likeness of God* (London and Oxford: Mowbrays, 1974), p. 204.

29. *On the Nativity of the Mother of God PO* 19, 479.
30. Ibid.
31. *Exposition on the Orthodox Faith* iv, 19 *PG* 94, 1160A.
32. Op. cit. (480–481).
33. Ibid. (473–474).

sin did not require the help of God – this, as the words "and received the strength to strive against sin" indicate, would be a misinterpretation – but rather that she did not receive any extra special help from God.³⁴ "Consequently, the help with which He helped His Mother is in no way greater than that which he gave to all men." The greatness of the Mother of God, therefore, resides precisely in the fact that she is no different than we.

God, explains Cabasilas, was awaiting the appearance of man's true nature so that he could be united to it; and it was the Holy Virgin that offered it to Him pure and spotless. For this reason Cabasilas also ascribes to the Theotokos the phrase, "becoming [God's] most fitting fellow-worker" (συνεργοῦ τυχὼν ἐπικαιροτάτου).³⁵ For this reason, she, alone throughout all history, was counted worthy to hear the salutation, "Rejoice!"

Now, it is at this point that Cabasilas makes his most daring statement. On the Annunciation, he insists that "nowhere in the joyful tidings of the Angel was word mentioned concerning deliverance from guilt and forgiveness of sins."³⁶ This, however, seems to be in contradiction with Patristic tradition. Both St. Cyril of Jerusalem (c. 315 – 386)³⁷ and St. Gregory of Nazianzus (329 – 389,

---

34. Ibid. (475).
35. Ibid. (482): ἐπικαιρότατος, lit. "most opportune" or "most seasonable". And cf. also in the same passage the line, καὶ βοηθὸς ὑπῆρξε τῷ πλάστῃ, καὶ τὸ ἄγαλμα συνειργάσατο τῷ τεχνίτῃ.
36. Ibid. (480). Lossky warns of a possible exaggeration on this point: "We cannot say that the humanity assumed by Christ in the womb of the Holy Virgin was a complement of the humanity of his Mother. It is, in fact, the humanity of a divine person, that of the 'man of heaven' (1 Cor. 15:47–48). The human nature of the Mother of God belongs to a created person, who is the offspring of the 'man of earth'. It is not the Mother of God, but her Son, who is the head of the new humanity, 'the head over all things for the Church, which is his body' (Eph. 1:22–23). Thus the Church is the complement of his humanity. Therefore it is through her Son, and in His Church, that the Mother of God could attain the perfection reserved for those who bear the image of the 'man of heaven'", see "Panagia", op. cit., pp. 204–205.
37. *Catechism* 17,7 *PG* 33, 976.

also called the Theologian),[38] for example, teach that the Holy Spirit *cleansed* the Mother of God during the Annunciation. And St. John Damascene writes thus: "After therefore the consent of the Holy Virgin, the Holy Spirit came upon her according to the word of the Lord, which the Angel did say, *purifying* her and giving her the strength both to receive and to give birth to the Word of God."[39]

Cabasilas, however, fully aware of what the Fathers have said on this point, interprets their references to the Holy Virgin's "cleansing" as implying an "addition of grace" (ἀλλὰ τὴν κάθαρσιν προσθήκην χαρίτων αὐτοῖς βούλεσθαι χρὴ νομίζειν).[40] Moreover, when Mary asks, "How shall this be?" (Luke 1:34), she is not asking because she is in need of further cleansing, but because the things of which the archangel spoke are contrary to the laws of nature.[41] Thus, we can see that Cabasilas' concept of the Holy Virgin's perfection inclines towards the absolute perfection and purity of the Theotokos *even before* the Annunciation.

This, however, is not the case with St. Basil the Great (*c.* 330 – 379), who gives an example of the Holy Virgin's *imperfection*. Basil

38. *Dogmatic Epp.*, 9, v, 68 and 10, v, 5 *PG* 37, 462A and 469; and *Oration on Holy Easter PG* 36, 633.

39. *Exposition on the Orthodox Faith PG* 94, 985B. The italicization is my own. Metrophanes Critopoulos (1589 – 1639) accepts that following the Annunciation the Holy Virgin was delivered from original sin, although he adds that she too was in need of cleansing and salvation, and quotes Luke 1:46-47: "My soul doth magnify the Lord, And my spirit hath rejoiced in God my Saviour", see I. Karmiris, Τὰ Δογματικὰ καὶ Συμβολικὰ Μνημεῖα τῆς Ὀρθοδόξου Καθολικῆς Ἐκκλησίας, Vol. ii (Athens, 1953), pp. 550–551. Florovsky writes that "Mary herself was participating in the mystery of the redeeming re-creation of the world. Surely, she is to be counted among the redeemed. She was most obviously in need of salvation. Her Son is her Redeemer and Saviour, just as he is the Redeemer of the world." But he adds also that "she is the only human being for whom the Redeemer of the world is also a son, her own child whom she truly bore. Jesus indeed... is 'the fruit of the womb' of Mary," in *Creation and Redemption*, Vol. iii in the *Collected Works of Georges Florovsky* (Belmont: Nordland, Mass., 1976), p. 177.

40. *On the Nativity of the Mother of God PO* 19, 477.

41. *On the Annunciation of the Mother of God PO* 19, 490.

correlates the "sword" which the Righteous Simeon prophesied would pierce through the Holy Virgin's soul (cf. Luke 2:35), with the doubts and fears that she felt at the beginning of her Son's mission as well as during His Crucifixion.[42]

In St. John Chrysostom's interpretation of Matt. 12:46–50, he analyses the shortcomings and human weaknesses of the Holy Virgin and Christ's "brethren". Indeed, when he examines the reason why Christ's Mother and brethren desired to see Him at that particular moment "While he yet talked to the people" – Chrysostom (c. 347 – 407) attributes this to a sort of vainglory on their part. Chrysostom continues his homily by emphasizing that even the Holy Virgin's divine motherhood would be worthless without her being virtuous.[43] By contrast, Cabasilas' interpretation of this same incident differs substantially from that of Chrysostom. He maintains that Christ is referring here to the supremacy of His Mother, and that "these which hear the word of God, and do it" (Luke 8:21) is referring exclusively to the Ever-Virgin, who is the measure of every virtue.[44] Consequently, according to Cabasilas, the main purpose behind Christ's words was in fact to glorify His Mother.[45]

Finally, Cabasilas, in referring to the very close relationship between the Holy Virgin and Christ, makes what seems to be

---

42. *Epistle to Bishop Optinus* PG 32, 965–968. Dositheus of Jerusalem (1641 – 1707) writes that the imperfections and weaknesses of the saints (including St. John the Baptist and the Mother of God) belong to the "fruits" of original sin, which all men feel in this life, Karmiris, op. cit., p. 750.
43. *Homily on Matthew* 44 PG 57, 465–466.
44. *On the Nativity of the Mother of God*, op. cit., 359.
45. Interestingly, Lossky notes that it is not insignificant that Luke 8:19–21 comes just after the Parable of the Sower: "It is precisely this faculty of keeping the words heard concerning Christ in an honest and good heart – the faculty which elsewhere Christ exalts above the fact of corporeal maternity (Luke 11:28) – which the Gospel attributes to no individual except the Mother of the Lord. St. Luke insists upon it, as he mentions it twice in his Infancy narrative: 'But Mary kept all these things pondering them in her heart' (Luke 2:19, 51)," op. cit., pp. 199–200.

another bold and daring statement: "She has become equally honoured (*homotimos*), sharing the same throne (*homothronos*) and being one with God (*homotheos*)."[46] Her blood, says Cabasilas, became His blood – the blood of God incarnate. Most significant, however, is the fact that the Mother of God stands as the first created person to realize fully the potential holiness to which we have all been called. As Lossky puts it: "Alongside the incarnate divine hypostasis there is a deified human hypostasis."[47]

"Mariology," as has rightly been said, "is simply an extension of Christology".[48] The essential issue in the whole question of the sinlessness of the Mother of God must be the preservation of the uniqueness of Christ's sinlessness. Christ's salvific work would be debased or even nullified if we were to accept that someone else also fulfils the conditions of His sinlessness; if we were to accept, that is, that the Ever-Virgin was born free from original sin. That would automatically isolate her from the rest of humanity and place her in another category – in that of the divine – a category to which Christ uniquely as the God-man belongs, by virtue of his conception through the Holy Spirit and the Virgin Mary.[49] The Orthodox understanding of this question is admirably expressed by Vladimir Lossky: "The Orthodox Church does not admit the idea that the Holy Virgin was thus exempted from the lot of the rest of fallen humanity – the idea of a "privilege" which makes her into a being ransomed before the redemptive work, by virtue of the future merits of her Son. It is not by virtue of a privilege... that we venerate the Mother of God more than any other created being... She was not, at the moment of the Annunciation, in a state analogous to that of Eve before the Fall... The Second Eve – she who was chosen to become the Mother of God – heard and under-

---

46. *On the Dormition of the Mother of God* PO 19, 503.
47. Op. cit., p. 208.
48. Timothy Ware (Bishop Kallistos of Diokleia), *The Orthodox Church* (London: Penguin, 1993), p. 258.
49. Kaloyerou, op. cit., pp. 91–92; and see also *Saint Gregory Palamas: The Homilies*, Hom. XIV *On the Annunciation of Our Exceedingly Pure Lady, Mother of God, and Ever-Virgin Mary*, ed. and trans. by C. Veniamin (Dalton PA: Mount Thabor Publishing, 2013), pp. 100–107.

stood the angelic word in a state of fallen humanity. That is why this unique election does not separate her from the rest of humanity... whether saints or sinners, whose best part she represents."[50]

The secondary issue here is the determination of the exact moment at which divine grace began to act upon the Holy Virgin so as to cleanse and strengthen her, and it is largely on this point that Cabasilas presents a somewhat peculiar line of thought. And while some of his phrases and certain shifts of emphasis could be construed as resembling the opinions of the thirteenth century Scholastics, and even, at times, as diverging from Cabasilas' immediate predecessors, such a view would not take into account sufficiently the fact that his theological presuppositions belong to a fundamentally different world. Indeed, the diversity of opinion in the Patristic tradition is not necessarily mutually exclusive on the question of the Holy Virgin's sinlessness and purity, as the work of Cabasilas' contemporary, St. Gregory Palamas, clearly shows, with whom Cabasilas has much in common.[51] Both Palamas and Cabasilas chose to focus chiefly on the preparation by God of His Most Holy Mother from her very conception by Joachim and Anna, and on the unique state of virtue to which she had attained, through her extraordinary collaboration with the will and grace of God, since earliest childhood, pointing to the fact that her election as the Mother of the Saviour of the world was by no means a coincidence.

It has been suggested that Cabasilas "overemphasizes" and "over-extols" the Mother of God, so as to result in a general exaltation of her person and the role she played in our salvation.[52] But surely, this is nothing more than the effusion of Cabasilas' profound veneration of the Most Holy Mother of God. What is certainly beyond dispute, however, is the fact that nowhere in the theology of St. Nicholas Cabasilas is the immaculate conception accepted, mentioned or inferred.[53]

---

50. Lossky, op. cit., pp. 203–204.
51. See esp. Homs. LII and LIII, *On the Entry into the Holy of Holies of Our Exceedingly Pure Lady, Mother of God, and Ever-Virgin Mary*, in Veniamin, ibid., pp. 407–444.
52. Kaloyerou, op. cit., pp. 92–93.
53. Cf. Jugie, loc. cit.

THE ORTHODOX INTERPRETATION OF HOLY SCRIPTURE
ST GREGORY PALAMAS AND THE KEY TO UNDERSTANDING THE BIBLE*

Introduction

*Luminary of the Orthodox faith,
support of the Church and teacher,
splendour of monastics,
invincible champion of theologians,
O wonderworker Gregory,
boast of Thessalonica,
preacher of grace,
pray without ceasing
that our souls be saved.*

So we sing in the Troparion for the Saint on the Second Sunday of Great Lent, situated between the Sunday of Orthodoxy and the Sunday of the Precious and Life-giving Cross. But why is Saint Gregory Palamas given such a prominent place in the liturgical calendar of the Orthodox Church?

It was in 1334, while on Mount Athos, in his third year at the hermitage of Saint Sabas, which belongs to the Great Lavra, that Palamas experienced a vision in which he was encouraged to share the wisdom bestowed upon him from on high. It seemed that he was carrying a vessel overflowing with milk, which subsequently turned into the finest of wines. The wine emitted such a strong fragrance that it brought great joy to his soul. A youth appeared and rebuked him for not sharing the wine with others and for allowing it to go to waste, for this wine, as he explained, was inexhaustible. The angel then warned Gregory, reminding him of the parable of the talents (*cf.* Matt. 25:14–30). As he later related to his friend and disciple Dorotheus, Palamas understood this vision to mean that the time would come when he would be called upon to transfer his teaching from the simple plane of the ethical (the milk) to the higher plane of the dogmatic word (the wine), which leads heavenward. Thus at the age of about thirty-eight Gregory began to write his Encomium for Saint Peter the Athonite, and, at about the same time, he also began to compose what is without doubt the most famous of all his works, Homily 53, "On the Entry of the Mother of God into the Holy of Holies", in which the *Theotokos* is presented as the archetype of the hesychastic way of life, the way of "stillness" (Gk. *hesychia, cf.* Ps. 46:10).

The teaching of Saint Gregory and his fellow Hesychasts of the fourteenth century was based on the understanding that man, the greatest of all God's creatures, had been called to enter into direct and unmediated communion with God even from this present life. The chief manner by which this is achieved is through the grace of God and *noetic* prayer, that is, through the Prayer of the Heart, also known as the Jesus Prayer: *Lord Jesus Christ, Son of God, have mercy upon me.* For the Hesychasts, therefore, true theology, true knowledge of God, is given not to those whose minds have been exercised in lofty concepts *about* God, but to those who, through prayer and ascetic striving in accordance with the commandments of Christ, have been made worthy to behold the vision of Christ in glory, to those who have seen God face to face and who share in His very Life.

St. Gregory Palamas is, above all, the theologian of the

Transfiguration: that great New Testament theophany, which gives us, in a graphic and concrete manner, the vision of God's purpose in creating man. In Christ's resplendent form, as it appeared before the three chosen disciples on Mount Tabor not long before His crucifixion, we see *our* future hope: Human nature filled with divine glory; human nature *suffused* with the grace of God, the very Life of the Most Holy Trinity.

Christ as the Image of the Father

But in the vision of Christ Transfigured, Peter, James and John, first and foremost, behold Christ as God, consubstantial and equal *in every respect* with God the Father, Whose exact image He is (cf. Hebr. 1:3).

"No man hath seen God at any time; the only begotten Son, which is in the bosom of the Father, he hath declared him" (John 1:18).

Our Lord, God and Saviour Jesus Christ teaches us that He is the image of the Father: "He that hath seen me hath seen the Father" (John 14:9), and that "No man cometh unto the Father, but by me" (John 14:6). This has tremendous consequences for our understanding of the divine economy, and for our reading of Holy Scripture.

For example, we note the profound significance of the Apostolic greeting in *Second Corinthians*, which in earliest times marked the beginning of the Liturgy: "The grace of the Lord Jesus Christ, and the love of God [the Liturgy specifies, "God the Father"], and the communion of the Holy Ghost, be with you all" (2 Cor. 13:14). The fact that Christ is mentioned first, *before* the Father, testifies to the Son's equality with the Father in His divine status. Christ is thus *homoousios* or consubstantial with the Father, and in no way inferior to Him in His divinity.

But that is not all that this Apostolic greeting tells us. For in addition to witnessing to the divine equality of the Son and Word of God with His divine Father, it also gives us the *shape* of the divine economy. That is to say, it bears witness to the fact that in God's revelation, in His self-disclosure, to the world, Christ is the chief protagonist, the central figure. So, every manifestation of God, every revelation of God, comes *in and through Christ*, the Son and Word of God the Father. Hence, Christ is at the heart of all the great revelations of God, in the Old as well as in the New Testament. As examples of this we have:

The three men or angels that appeared to Abraham at Mamre: Christ is the central angel (Gen. 18:1–33).[2] The man with whom Jacob wrestled at Peniel, which means "the Face of God", after which he exclaims, "for I have seen God face to face, and my life is preserved [lit. 'my soul is saved']" (Gen. 32:30). And the greatest Old Testament theophany of all: Moses' vision of the burning bush on Sinai, with the disclosure of the Name of God, "I AM" (Exod. 3:2–4:17). It is Christ that is referred to as the Angel of the LORD, Who spoke with Moses from the Burning Bush; and it is Christ Who is "I AM" – as is also witnessed to most clearly on almost every icon depicting Him.

All of these revelations, and many more besides, are revelations of Christ. (For further confirmation of this basic hermeneutical key, all one has to do is read the services of the Church for the Great Feasts of the year.) In all of these great events in the history of our salvation, Saint Gregory Palamas teaches us that it was none other than Christ Himself that was revealed first and foremost; precisely because it was He, and not the Father or the Holy Spirit, Who was to become flesh. In other words, because it was the will of God the Holy Trinity to save us by the coming of the Messiah, that is, by the Incarnation of the Son and Word of God.

But if it is indeed true that "he that hath seen the Son hath seen the Father" (cf. John 14:9), and that "no man can say that Jesus is the Lord, but by the Holy Ghost" (1 Cor. 12:3), then the revelation of Christ must at the same time be a revelation of the Holy Trinity. St. Gregory teaches us that the Christocentric character of God's dispensation towards man should not blind us to the great mystery of the unity and common action of the Holy Trinity. Ultimately, in other words, Christology and Trinitarian theology are one and the same doctrine. What the three persons do, they do together, in unison. As St Gregory of Nyssa, in his *Letter to Ablabius: That There Are Not Three Gods,* teaches: "We do not learn that the Father does something on his own, in which the Son does not co-operate. Or again, that the Son acts on his own without the Spirit. Rather does every energy which extends from God to creation... have its origin from the Father, proceed through the Son, and reach its completion in the Holy Spirit."3 Here we have the classic *schema* of the divine economy: *from* the Father, *through* the Son, *in* the Holy Spirit – the divine operation of the Most Holy Trinity is always *from* the Father, *through* the Son, *in* the Holy Spirit.

But the fact remains that the distinction of persons, the diversity in God the Holy Trinity, is also necessary to maintain, since, as we have said, only *one* of the Three Divine Persons became man; only *one* of the Holy Trinity was born and crucified, though this is accomplished with the consent of the Father and the Holy Spirit. It is true, of course, that the Father gives His only-begotten Son (cf. John 3:16), and the Holy Spirit testifies of Him as Lord and God. But the distinction of persons remains. We see this most concretely in the mystery of the Divine Eucharist, where the Spirit is present in Holy Communion as well as the Son, but it is a different kind of presence: the Spirit did not become incarnate, therefore the Spirit has no body and blood. We receive the body and blood of Christ, the Second Person of the Holy Trinity, not the body and blood of the Holy Spirit.

Christ as the Image of Man

But as Saint Gregory Palamas also points out, Christ is not only the Sole Revealer of God, He is also the Sole Revealer of God's purpose in His creation of man. In simple terms, what is true of Christ's humanity can also be true for us – *by grace*. Christ is unique in that the union of human nature with His divine Person is hypostatic or personal. But the consequence of this hypostatic union, namely, the exchange of the natural properties of each of His two natures (the *communicatio idiomatum*), serves as a model for our own salvation and deification (*theosis*). What is true of

Christ's humanity can also be true for us – *by grace*, that is to say, *as gift*.

This is how salvation is understood in the tradition of the Orthodox Church; not in merely moral or ethical terms, but as the attainment of Christlike perfection. This is the purpose of our human existence – to become *by divine grace* what Christ is *by nature*.

This is a high calling indeed, and one which only God Himself can accomplish in us. But it *is* attainable, and the Church sets before us the example of Saint Gregory Palamas on the Second Sunday of Lent precisely in order to emphasize the importance of personal experience in the life of the Church.

On the first Sunday of Lent we celebrated the Triumph of Orthodoxy. We celebrated the fact that, by keeping the Faith which those who have gone before us – the faith confessed by all those who through the ages have become Christlike – we too may come to know the Truth which *is* Christ. So, we receive the Orthodox Faith through those men and women who have successfully followed the "Way" which Christ revealed to us. The teachings or doctrines of the Church are like a map that points us in the direction of salvation, of eternal union with God. We learn, therefore, from those who have been tried and tested, and who, by means of Christlike humility, have emerged from the good fight as victors. That is why, in his first sermon on the Transfiguration, Saint Gregory Palamas writes: "We believe what we have been taught by those enlightened by Christ, things which they alone can know with certainty".[4]

And the Church, on the Second Sunday of Lent, as I say, puts none other than Saint Gregory Palamas forward as a prime example of what man can become, when he voluntarily unites his will and his life to God; but also, as a clear statement that it is such persons as Saint Gregory, a true master of, and trustworthy guide in, the Life in Christ, that we Orthodox Christians must follow. The history of the Church is in fact replete with examples of such saints, both men and women, who stand as proof to us that this salvation – perfection in Christ – is possible. As the great Paul himself proclaims in the epistle reading for Orthodoxy Sunday, we have a "cloud of witnesses" (Hebr. 12:1), who testify to this truth; who testify to *the* Truth. And, by the grace of God, we are also blessed to have such people as examples and guides even today, in the twenty-first century.

The Cross as the Way of Christ

But as Saint Gregory Palamas also teaches, along with all the great Fathers of the Church, the vision of Christ in glory – our salvation – is synonymous with the mystery of the precious and life-giving Cross. And this is true precisely because the Cross reveals to us the Way of Christ, and as such is the *only* way to salvation: to the cleansing of the passions and the cultivation of the virtues, to the illumination of the mind, heart and soul, and the sanctification of the body, and to the vision of God, that is to say, to perfect union with God. For the vision of Christ in glory is given only when we arrive at the foot of the Cross, in imitation of Christ's own self-emptying (His *kenosis*), in His descent from on high down to the nethermost parts of the earth. This inevitably involves repentance, a profound and *continuous* change on the part of the human person, without which it is impossible to become Christlike, since His perfection has no end.

What this means, in practical terms, is each time we find ourselves in difficult circumstances, each time that we are tempted to think or act according to the way of the world, and *every* time that we resist this impulse for the love of Christ, and ask for His help and mercy, we are indeed taking up our cross, we are indeed striving to change our way of life in accordance with Christ's commandments and example, we are indeed beginning to repent.

The fact is that if we wish to be *with* Christ, then we must become *like* Him (cf. 1 John 3:2-3). This is the mystery of the adoption of sons, of which the great Paul speaks (Rom. 8:17), which is offered to each and every one of us. We can never be God. Only God is divine by nature, but as St. Maximus the Confessor says, "the person who has been deified by grace will be in every respect as God is, except for His very essence".5 This means that we have been created to contain the very Life of the Holy Trinity. That is what is meant by being created in the image of God: to have the God-given capacity of containing and living the divine Life.

As Saint John, the most theological of the evangelists, instructs us, "God is love" (1 John 4:8, 16). And so the criterion of whether we are truly following the Way of Christ is love; but not just any love – divine Love. In the Sermon on the Mount (Matt. 5–7), Christ Himself exhorts us to love even our enemies (Matt. 5:44), which is humanly speaking impossible. But by this exhortation, He reveals to us the all-embracing character of His love – of *how* He is; and *how* we must exist, if we would be like Him and with Him.

The Fathers teach us that the root of all evil is pride, otherwise referred to as "self-love" (*philautia*).6 Self-love is a sinful anthropocentrism; it is the refusal to relate to those who are different to us, and to embrace them. Love of one's self places man at the centre of the universe, and hence seeks to usurp that which belongs to God alone. This was the sin of Adam, and before him, of Lucifer. But love of enemies, the opposite of self-love, is divine, for it is, as we have said, the way that God exists: unconditional love – unconditional and infinite personal love and care for each and every one of us, no matter how different to Him we may be, no matter how sinful we may be. God's love, by which death itself was destroyed, is able to forgive all, accept and embrace all.

This is the great discovery that St. Gregory Palamas tells us the Mother of God made, when she entered into the Holy of Holies at the tender age of three. In her diligent practice there of "holy stillness" (in Gk. *hesychia*), she arrived at the *knowledge* of the vision of God, where simultaneously she discovered her kinship with the whole of creation, and so began to intercede for the whole world. For, as St. Gregory explains, "She found that the purest thing in us [the human mind or *nous*] is precisely intended by nature for this holy and divine love"; and the result of this communion of divine love is prayer for the entire world,7 which is the prayer and longing of all the saints, of all of those who have truly become like Christ, of all those who can say, "His Life is mine"; and this is the unceasing prayer and inner life of the One Holy Catholic and Apostolic Church – the Orthodox Church: the Church which has as its head, not a book, nor a pontiff, but Christ Himself.

ENDNOTES

* Delivered at the Clergy Continuing Education Symposium, which took place at St. Tikhon's Seminary, South Canaan PA, on June 13.

2. The reference is actually to "three men" (Gen. 18:2); whereas later it says, "And there came two angels to Sodom at even" (Gen. 19:1).

3. PG 45:116–136.

4. Hom. XXXIV, 17, trans. taken from *Saint Gregory Palamas: The Homilies*, ed. and trans. by C. Veniamin (Dalton PA: Mount Thabor Publishing, 2013), p. 542, n. 88.

5. *Letters to Thalassius* XXII (PG 90:320); quoted by St. Gregory Palamas, Hom. VIII, 13, *On Faith,* op. cit., pp. 90–91, delivered on the Sunday of Orthodoxy.

6. See e.g., his *Centuries on Love* II, 8 and III, 8 (PG 90:985C and 1020BC).

7. See esp. Hom. LIII, 49 and 53, *On the Entry into the Holy of Holies of Our Exceedingly Pure Lady, Mother of God and Ever-Virgin Mary, and Her Divine Manner of Life There.* English trans. in *Saint Gregory Palamas: The Homilies,* op. cit., pp. 436 and 438.

THE SIGNIFICANCE OF GREEK INDEPENDENCE DAY FOR AMERICA IN THE 21st CENTURY

"Today is the crown of our salvation and the manifestation of the mystery that is from all eternity. The Son of God becomes Son of the Virgin, and Gabriel announces the good tidings of grace. Therefore let us also join him and cry aloud to the Theotokos: Hail, thou who art full of grace: the Lord is with thee" (*Hymn of the Feast*).

Σήμερον τῆς σωτηρίας ἡμῶν τὸ κεφάλαιον, καὶ τοῦ ἀπ' αἰῶνος Μυστηρίου ἡ φανέρωσις· ὁ Υἱὸς τοῦ Θεοῦ, Υἱὸς τῆς Παρθένου γίνεται, καὶ Γαβριὴλ τὴν χάριν εὐαγγελίζεται. Διὸ καὶ ἡμεῖς σὺν αὐτῷ τῇ Θεοτόκῳ βοήσωμεν· Χαῖρε Κεχαριτωμένη, ὁ Κύριος μετὰ σου (*Ἀπολυτίκιον τῆς ἑορτῆς*).

IT IS NO COINCIDENCE that the independence of the modern state of Greece took place on 25 March, on the celebration of the Annunciation of the Theotokos and Ever-Virgin Mary. Because the Annunciation marks the beginning of the Salvation of the world! 25 March of 1821 was indeed a great event in modern history, because it has far-reaching consequences not only for the Greek people, and not just for all the Orthodox peoples of the world, but in fact for the whole world.

The first thing that we should bear in mind is that wherever the Orthodox Church is, there also is the Cross of Christ: "Where I am", as the Lord Himself says, "there shall also my servant be" [ὅπου εἰμὶ ἐγὼ ἐκεῖ καὶ ὁ διάκονος ὁ ἐμὸς ἔσται] (John 12:26). And where is Christ? On the Cross. And what is true for the life of each Christian soul is also true for Orthodox peoples as a whole. Indeed, we have many, many instances in recent history, as well as in times of old, which show us clearly "that judgment", as Saint Peter says, "must begin at the house of God" [ὅτι [ὁ] καιρὸς τοῦ ἄρξασθαι τὸ κρίμα ἀπὸ τοῦ οἴκου τοῦ θεοῦ] (1 Pet. 4:17)

Now it is precisely "the preaching of the cross" [Ὁ λόγος γὰρ ὁ τοῦ σταυροῦ] (1 Cor. 1:18), which was "to the Greeks foolishness" [Ἕλλησι δὲ μωρίαν] (1 Cor. 1:23); "but unto us which are being saved", says Saint Paul to the Corinthians, "it is the power of God" [τοῖς δὲ σῳζομένοις ἡμῖν δύναμις θεοῦ ἐστιν] (1 Cor. 1:18). But how can this be? Is this not simply a sophisticated way of preparing us for a life of misery and suffering? What is it, therefore, that lies behind the preaching of the Cross? What is it that led our forefathers to embrace the Cross with all their hearts and with all their might, and to cling to it in the face of every kind of adversity, preferring to die with Christ, as Christians, rather than to live in comfort without Him?

Those to whom we refer as the *New Martyrs* did exactly that. Once upon a time, virtually the whole of the eastern Mediterranean and the Middle East was Christian, and indeed Orthodox. Through the invasions which culminated in the capture and conquest of Constantinople in 1453, these Christians came under increasing pressure to renounce Christ, because socially, economically and politically, this would have meant a far easier way of life for them. It was far easier to reject Christ, and save themselves from continual and systematic pressures (and often persecution), than to continue as Christians, with all the restrictions of freedom and obstacles to personal and social progress that that entailed. And, it must be said, many, many of them capitulated (many of the *New Martyrs*, for example, were among those who had become Mohammedans, and later repented, returning to Christianity once more, for which they were put to death, which was the penalty for renouncing Islam). It is no coincidence, therefore, that there are very few Christians left in Asia Minor and the Middle East – although, as I said, these areas used to be *predominantly* Christian.

But we are descendants of those who did not give in to any of the abovementioned pressures, we are descendants of those who loved Christ and His Cross more than life itself: and they are the true heroes of the revolution, because it is they who preserved and passed on to us our language, our customs, and our faith.

When, by the grace of God, through the prayers of the Most Holy Theotokos, our Panagia, "the victorious leader of triumphant hosts" (Τῇ ὑπερμάχῳ στρατηγῷ τὰ νικητήρια), significant areas of present-day Greece gained their independence – for let us not forget that Northern Greece, from the area of Volos northwards, did not gain their independence until 1912; and certain parts of the Greek-speaking world even today are once again not free – this was truly a great occasion for rejoicing, especially for the people of Greece, but also for Orthodox Christians everywhere. And this because we were able to really be Greek, *Romioi*, once again; we were free once more to openly worship the true God, Christ, without fear of persecution.

But how are the events of 25 March 1821 connected with the Salvation of the world? Is this not a national holiday, pertaining exclusively to a specific group of people, in this instance solely to the Greeks? In order to answer this question, we need to look first at Salvation, as it is understood in the Orthodox tradition. As one Athonite elder of our own day once told me: "In this world there is nothing more difficult than to be saved." We often encounter the attitude that Salvation is something that we can leave until later; once, that is, we have taken care of more pressing matters. By saying this, however, this holy man was clearly placing Salvation at the very top of our list of urgent priorities. And when we pause to consider all the great achievements of mankind, past and present, whether they be of a scientific or literary character, in the world of politics or finance or physical endeavour, this utterance, this "word", seems "a hard saying" indeed [Σκληρός ἐστιν ὁ λόγος οὗτος] (John 6:60) – but it is nevertheless fundamentally true.

Now the reason why these words are so true is because of the wealth of meaning which Salvation has for us in the Orthodox Church. By others, Salvation is often understood simply in terms of "deliverance from sin and its consequences and admission to heaven", that is, in terms of escaping damnation, and reaching a safe place where we can no longer be tormented by the devil. According to the Fathers of the Church, however, Salvation involves the "theosis" (the deification or divinization) of the entire human person in Christ; it involves, that is, becoming like Christ to the point of identity with Him; it involves acquiring the mind of Christ (as Saint Paul says in the second chapter of his *First Epistle to the Corinthians*, 2 Cor. 2:16), and indeed it signifies the sharing in His very Life – the life of God.

Now this brings us back to the Cross, with which we began, because Salvation begins with "repentance". This is clearly indicated by the very first words preached by both St. John the Baptist and Christ Himself: "Repent: for the Kingdom of heaven is at hand" [Μετανοεῖτε· ἤγγικεν γὰρ ἡ βασιλεία τῶν οὐρανῶν] (Matt. 3:2 and 4:17).

But what does repentance mean, and *how* do we repent? Repentance in Christian terms means changing, becoming like Christ; and we repent by reacting in any and every circumstance as Christ Himself would. (Now this, of course, can only be achieved with God's help.) But, each time we find ourselves in a difficult situation; each time that we are tempted to think or act according to the way of the world, and every time that we resist this impulse for the love of Christ, and ask for His help and mercy, we are taking up our cross, we are striving to change our way of life in accordance with Christ's commandments and example, and we are indeed beginning to repent.

Now you may say, "That's all very well, but what does all this have to do with our national holiday?" The answer is: Very much indeed. Firstly, because we must be very careful, that is, we bear a great responsibility, not to throw away what our ancestors fought so courageously to preserve and pass on to us. And we need to continue and grow in and also contribute to our tradition.

The second point relates more specifically to the Greeks of the Diaspora, and in particular to the Greek Americans here in this country, and their children: What is the significance of 25 March 1821 for their future? Does it have any real relevance for them? I believe that it does, in the sense that it places a great challenge before us. *Because of 25 March 1821, we stand here as Greek Orthodox Christians*, and we are here in this great land to bear witness to the Orthodox faith. By the will of God, and we must believe this, we have been entrusted with the awesome responsibility of implanting Orthodoxy here in America, so that it will become an organic and integral part of American and Western civilization, and no longer something foreign and exotic. God's will is for all men to be saved and to come to the knowledge of the Truth (1 Tim. 2:4), which is the Orthodox vision of Christ and His Church. This is the challenge before us now, which for us Greek Orthodox Christians was made possible by the events of 1821 and after: to transform Western society from within in an Orthodox way into a truly Christian society. No one is in a better position to do this than the Orthodox of this country. What a responsibility! What an honour!

Look at how many great gifts have been bestowed upon us. In addition to the legacy of "the glory that was once ancient Greece", of Alexander the Great, and so on, we are heirs of the Christian Roman Empire of Constantine the Great, Justinian, and the Palaeologi; among the greatest literary contributions to the world are: the oldest surviving version of the Old Testament, the Greek Septuagint (translated *c.* 300 BC), the New Testament which, of course, was originally written in Greek; Greek was also the original language of the worship and theology of the Church, in the West as well as in the East; and the vast majority of the great Fathers of the Church (Saint Athanasius the Great, Saint Basil the Great, Saint Gregory the Theologian, Saint John Chrysostom, Saint Cyril of Alexandria, Saint Maximus the Confessor, Saint John Damascene, Saint Symeon the New Theologian, Saint Gregory Palamas, to name but a few) wrote in Greek; the *New Martyrs* which we mentioned previously, Saint Kosmas the Aetolian, Saint Nicodemos of the Holy Mountain, and many, many more, were all *Romioi*, and wrote in Greek. And this tradition continues to this very day. So we have the longest literary tradition and legacy *with Christ at its very epicentre* than any other nation in the world! Yes, we have a lot to be thankful for, to cherish and to preserve; and a lot, therefore, also to bear witness to and share with the world.

Now the heroes of 1821, like you and I, all came out of this tradition. And it was precisely in reference to this tradition that Father Georges Florovsky, the great Russian Orthodox theologian of the twentieth century, used to say: "We must all become Greeks." That is to say, we must all become part of this very tradition, which at its heart has Christ the Saviour.

Today, Greece has once again become a "superpower" – not in political or economic terms, but in spiritual terms. No other country in Europe at present has greater dynamism in its religious life; and very few countries in the world can be compared to Greece in terms of religious tradition; and this is certainly even more the case when one thinks exclusively in terms of Christianity. (We need only mention the renewed vigour and influence of Mount Athos, a truly unique bastion of our civilization and inheritance.)

We have a responsibility, then, to be devout and sincere Greek Orthodox Christians. Because with our history and customs, with our language and culture, to be anything else would be an insult, not only to the heroes of 1821, but to all of our ancestors and Fathers, and to our inheritance, which is none other than Jesus Christ our Lord, the only true God and Eternal King: "O Lord, by the prayers of Thy Most Holy Mother, Save thy people and bless thine inheritance" (Κύριε, δι' εὐχῶν τῆς Ὑπεραγίας Θεοτόκου, σῶσον τὸν λαόν Σου καὶ εὐλόγησον τὴν κληρονομίαν Σου). Amen.

Euthanasia
A THEOLOGICAL APPROACH

Point of Departure

ONE OF THE WAYS BY WHICH the level of a society's culture may be measured is how it treats its members both at the beginning and at the end of life. Much of what our senses and imagination are exposed to in our times could be described in terms of a distortion or perversion of the point at which life begins, that is to say, in terms of sex outside marriage, and the point at which biological life ends, that is to say, in terms of extreme acts of violence.

Now, one of the consequences of the Teresa Schiavo case is that it has forced us once again to revisit and to seek to understand, in the context of 21st century American social, legal and medical values and progress, the *Christian* perspective on questions pertaining to the end of our biological human existence.

The Schiavo case, I maintain, has brought into sharp relief just how important Orthodox theology is to our modern age; just how much of a contribution it could make to the seemingly insurmountable moral dilemmas of our times.[1]

---

[1] From 1990 to 2005, the Teresa ("Terri") Shiavo case centered on the question of whether to remove life-support from a person who had been diagnosed as existing in a vegetative state following a cardiac arrest.

Many Christians, of all denominations, pleaded in favour of the preservation of Terri Schiavo's life; but many Christians, it must be conceded, were persuaded by the arguments of the various court rulings, allowing doctors to remove from her the means of sustaining her life.

The disappointing thing about all this was the fact that those in favour of preserving Mrs. Schiavo's life lacked a certain depth when it came to explaining *why* her life should be preserved in what was described as a physically and mentally "vegetative state". Of course, there were many statements made in favour of the sanctity of life, of the need always to err on the side of life, that only God could decide if and when a life should be terminated, and so on. But, for the most part, such statements were unaccompanied by theological explanation as to why even a "vegetative" human life is worth preserving. And so, despite the apparent self-evident nature of these statements, with which it would be hard for Orthodox to disagree, many professing to be Christians did exactly that. How so?

Now it is my position in this paper that the fundamental problem in the Terri Schiavo case in particular, and on the question of Euthanasia and other ethical issues in general, is the divorce between doctrine and ethics, between faith and the life in Christ, which in turn stems from the fact that when applied to practical, every-day, ethical or moral situations, western theology is sadly found wanting. Hence, what we witnessed, on the one hand, was that for those in favour of preserving Mrs. Schiavo's life, theology *as such* played a very limited rôle, and we were once again relegated to protestations on a simple moralistic level, which when scrutinized – *if* scrutinized – left us with a sad silence, the uncomfortable silence of having very little in fact to say about the intrinsic value of a human life which is both physically and mentally incapacitated. On the other hand, for those against maintaining Mrs. Schiavo's life, the argument was based on "quality of life", or rather the lack thereof, precisely because she was physically and mentally incapacitated. In other words, this was a case in which "theology", apparently, did not help.

The reason for this, I believe, is that the respective theologies of both sides are fundamentally the same. They are the same, that is, *vis-à-vis* their vision of the nature and purpose of human life. Therefore, they share the same theological and so also anthropological presuppositions. After all, αὐτογνωσία is the product of Θεογνωσία: "knowledge of one's self" comes from "knowledge of God", and not vice versa.

The Theological Background

For Christians, Christ is the measure of all things, both divine and human, and His Word is saving, and provides us with the solution to every human situation or problem in every age and generation;[2] and therefore, when considering this question, we must look to none other than the God-man, to the Θεάνθρωπος, for a deeper and more perfect understanding of human existence. In that aspect of the union of the divine and human in the Person of Christ, which is referred to as the "exchange of natural properties" (the ἀντίδοσις ἰδιωμάτων or *communicatio idiomatum*), we find the model and pattern for our own union with God. And so, except for the "hypostatic union" itself, everything in the humanity of Christ also applies to us. Christ is our Life, and Christ is our Way.

As Christians, moreover, we are called to imitate Christ, not only in His life, but also in His death. There is, perhaps, nothing greater in this life than being able to choose the manner in which one is to die.[3] Indeed, this is precisely what we learn to pray for in the Divine Liturgy: "For a Christian ending to our life, painless, without shame and peaceful." Surely, this must be our definition of *euthanasia* (εὐ-θανασία) – "a good death". For Christians, it is not death but sin, or, as Saint John Chrysostom puts it, "death in

---

2. Archimandrite Zacharias (Zacharou), *The Enlargement of the Heart: "Be ye also enlarged" (2 Corinthians 6:13) in the Theology of Saint Silouan the Athonite and Elder Sophrony of Essex*, ed. C. Veniamin (South Canaan PA: Mount Thabor Publishing, 2005; 2nd. ed., 2013), p. 62.

3. Ibid., p. 9.

sin", which is evil.4 Saint Gregory Palamas, urging his people to resist sin "even unto death" if need be, makes what seems to be a bold statement indeed, when he says:

Except for sin nothing in this life, even death itself, is really evil, even if it causes suffering. The company of the saints brought bodily sufferings upon themselves. The martyrs made the violent death which others inflicted on them into something magnificent, a source of life, glory and the eternal heavenly kingdom, because they exploited it in a good way that pleased God.5

As the saints, following the example of Christ Himself, show, it is the way we approach death that is of the utmost importance. What matters in all things is our spiritual disposition. Thus, by accepting whatever may befall us as from the hand of God, the followers of Christ transform a painful and just death into a glorious and unjust death, and this they do by voluntarily following the Way of Christ, in obedience to His ordinances and example. In other words, by doing so, the saints place themselves in the stream of the Life of Christ, and thus beget Him as their companion, as did, for example, the Three Young Men in the fiery furnace (Daniel 3:1–23; Song of the Three Children 1–66).6 And this is the mystery of the Cross.

At the same time, however, the Christian view of human life is based on the indelible and unrepeatable reality of each and every human person. And this is indubitably bound up with the question of the value of human life, and therefore the even more fundamental question of the definition of human life: What is human life?

As already noted, this question, considered within the context of Orthodox Christian ethics, can only be treated fully and properly on the basis of the hypostasis, of the person, and

---

4. *On Statues* (Εἰς ἀνδριάντας) V, 2 (PG 49:71–72); found in G. Mantzarides, *Christian Ethics*, p. 653 [in Greek].

5. Hom. XVI, 33: *On the Dispensation of our Lord in the Flesh;* trans. taken from *Saint Gregory Palamas: The Homilies,* edited and translated from the original Greek with introduction and notes by Christopher Veniamin (Dalton PA: Mount Thabor Publishing, 2013), p. 130.

6. Archimandrite Zacharias, op. cit., p. 72.

then only within the context of the human person's vocation of union and communion with God, and in and through God, with one's neighbour, which is nothing less than our *reason d'être*.

The Nature of the Problem

Now, I realize that this is far too complex a subject to be treated in all of its aspects in the context of a short presentation. So, what I would like to do here is draw your attention to one aspect of the problematic around Euthanasia in particular, which is all too easily overlooked, but which is in fact of fundamental determinative significance: the theological presuppositions *vis-à-vis* the human person and the purpose of our existence.

In considering this question, let us turn first to the modern psychological contextual framework, which, as I maintain, begins with Saint Augustine's "I believe that I may understand" (*Credo ut intelligam*) and is expressed most succinctly in modern times by Descartes', "I think therefore I am" (*Cogito ergo sum* or *Je pense donc je suis*). In both cases, significantly, we find an exaltation of the activity of the mind (however understood)[7] as a definition of existence.

The fundamental problem here is how the fact of communion – κοινωνία – is understood. Therefore, the root of the problem of Euthanasia, as I see it, is to be found in the doctrine of the *filioque,* precisely because it is by means of the *filioque* that Saint Augustine developed his notion of the person; a notion that has influenced every aspect of our modern intellectual and spiritual tradition.

In brief, then, Saint Augustine's understanding of the triune God of Christianity, and the image of God in man, is based on the concepts of "mind" and "relation". This we see most clearly

---

7. As different as they may be in terms of their understanding of the nature and purpose of the mind, both Saint Augustine of Hippo (354–430) and René Descartes (1596–1650) are firmly focused on the activity of the mind as man's highest mode of existence, which is significantly different to the Orthodox patristic tradition, according to which union and communion with God surpass even the mind, that is, the *nous*.

in his analogy of the Trinity of Love (*Lover, Beloved,* and *Love*), and in his two uni-personal analogies of Mind: first, the Mind, its Knowledge of itself, and its Love of itself; and second, Memory, Understanding, and Will. The key notions in all this are inter-relation and inter-action.

The person is thus defined as, and consequently reduced to, a series of inter-relations and interactions, which brings us back to the Terri Schiavo case.

These inter-relations and interactions are understood primarily in the physical and rational sense. Hence, if one is physically incapacitated this is regarded as a serious handicap to one's personal existence *in via,* in this earthly life; as a handicap, in other words, in terms of doing and acting, and therefore to being a person. (And this seems to be the perspective despite the fact that on the level of eternity – *in patria* – there is no discernibly organic rôle for the body.)

The emphasis as regards eternal human existence is clearly and most significantly on the rational. Thus, if one is incapacitated in terms of rational activity and one's reasonable interaction with fellow human beings, then one is also handicapped in terms of one's spiritual communion with God, Who is perceived principally as Mind (*mens*).

The emphasis on the mind in man's communion with God is evident in many ways that touch upon the every-day life of the Christian, for example, even in the rôle of Church pews. Significantly, Church pews imply in a concrete way the restriction of physical movement, while the mind, by contrast, is left free and encouraged to sore up to the summit of the finger-like Gothic church spires, and beyond, to the realm of divine concepts.

So, the person is seen as a series of inter-actions and inter-relations. In the case of God the Holy Trinity, this is based on origin, and on how each of the divine Hypostases stands in relation to the other Two. Hence, the Father is from No One, the Son is from One, the Holy Spirit must be from Two (*filioque*). Otherwise, since generation and procession are seen as the same – that is to say, no real distinction is made between the two – there would be no difference between the Spirit and the Son, inasmuch as they would both be from One. The *filioque* thus becomes a *sine qua non*.

The human person, consequently, is seen and defined as the sum of its relationships and inter-actions, which is why, in respect to our earthly existence, such emphasis is placed on "doing", and why, on the eternal plane, we are seen primarily as spirits or minds, either beholding God's substance *intellectually* from a distance (as in the Roman Catholic tradition), or simply enjoying "fellowship" with God (as in the various Protestant traditions). But again, both of these views are understood *rationally* in terms principally of the mind.

As one can see from what has been said above, there has been, between Saint Augustine and Descartes, a radical shift from "mind" (*mens* or *intellectus*) to "reason" (*ratio*). But be that as it may, what concerns us most at this point is the emphasis on "thought" of some kind, of conceptualizing, and the absence of communion with God on the level of the Uncreated, which surpasses both reason and mind, and which, in Orthodox theology, refers to the level of deification, the level of *glorificatio* or *theosis*.

In summing up, the startling fact is that once Terri Schiavo had become incapacitated in her faculty of reason she ceased to be regarded as a person possessing the capacity for communion, and was subsequently never treated as one still capable of enjoying a personal relationship with other human beings in this life; and even more startling, as one still capable of enjoying a full and perfect communion with God.

The Orthodox Perspective

How does this differ from the person as understood in the Orthodox tradition? And wherein lies the intrinsic and eternal value of the human hypostasis or person according to the Orthodox patristic tradition?

As we have already noted, the key question here is that of communion: communion with God, in the first instance, and simultaneous to this, communion with one's neighbour, with other people.

Speaking of the unity of the divine Hypostases, of God the Father, the Son, and the Holy Spirit, Saint Basil the Great affirms, "It is in the communion of the Godhead (κοινωνία τῆς θεότητος) that the unity consists".[8]

Christians agree, I think it's safe to say, that the human person is a unity of soul and body; not in the sense in which this was understood among the "areopagites" of antiquity – not, that is, as a coming together of two distinct elements merely for the duration of earthly life – but as a unity *from the beginning of human existence*, intended to continue into eternity, and beyond. This, of course, is the Biblical or Scriptural view of the person, and is expressed most emphatically and brilliantly in the ascetico-theological vision of Saint Maximus the Confessor. In 1 Thess. 5:23, Saint Paul adds the "spiritual" dimension, which underlines the fact that the human person is not a person in the fullest and truest sense unless he or she is in communion with God: "And the very God of peace sanctify you wholly; and I pray God your whole *spirit* and *soul* and *body* be preserved blameless unto the coming of our Lord Jesus Christ."

But let us pause for a moment to take a more detailed look at this holistic view of the person in the Orthodox tradition, most sublimely elaborated by none other than Saint Gregory Palamas, who in his Sixth Homily refers to man as the crowning point of God's Creation.

At the Creation first one thing was brought into existence, then another, then another and so on in turn. Last of all came man (Gen. 1:26), who was worthy of God's greater honour and consideration both before and after his creation. All the visible world was made before him for his sake. Immediately after the foundation of the world, before he existed, the kingdom of heaven was made ready for him. A divine Counsel concerning him preceded him, and he was created by God's hand and in His image. He did not take his whole being from matter or the visible world, like the other living creatures did, but only his body. His soul he took from the heavenly realms, from God Himself when He breathed life into him in a

---

8. *On the Holy Spirit* 18 (PG 32:194C, and cf. 153A and 156A), or in the other numbering, 45.

way that defies description (Gen. 2:7). Man was a great wonder surpassing all else, towering above everything, superior to all. Man was capable of knowing God, as well as receiving Him and declaring Him, and was most certainly the highest achievement of the Creator's sublime majesty.[9]

Remarkable as this may seem, Palamas also claims that man possesses the image of God more fully even than the angelic powers, for just as God is Trinity: Mind (νοῦς), Word (λόγος), and Spirit (πνεῦμα) – a *schema* borrowed from another great Gregory, Saint Gregory the Theologian (329–389) – so it is, argues Palamas, that man's soul alone possesses mind, reason, and a "life-giving spirit" (πνεῦμα ζωοποιόν).[10] Even though angels and archangels, as *noetic* and reasonable beings, also possess mind and reason, they do not possess *a body that is quickened by a life-generating spirit*. And although God's image is found *principally* in man's soul, the fact that the human body is conjoined with and quickened by the human spirit makes man superior to the angels.[11] Indeed, as he states even more emphatically in Homily LX, 4: "he alone [that is, the human person] is in the image of the Trinity".[12]

Now the important thing to bear in mind here is that we are saved as persons, that is to say, as members of the Body of Christ, the Church, and not as individuals in the common sense of the term. (I make this qualification simply because the term "individual" (ἄτομον) in Patristic theology means precisely "person" or "hypostasis", as seen for example in Saint John Damascene's *Dialectica*.) So we are saved as members of the Body of Christ, as we find in Saint Paul's First Letter to the Corinthians 12: 25–27, where he explains that "if one member suffers, all the members suffer with it; or if one member be honoured [the Greek, in fact, reads δοξάζεται, "is glorified"], all the members

---

9. Hom. VI, 10: *To Encourage Fasting;* trans. op. cit., p. 45.
10. See his *Natural and Theological Chapters* 37; and cf. Saint Gregory the Theologian *Oration* XII, 1.
11. *Natural and Theological Chapters* 38.
12. Hom. LX, 4: *On the Holy Feast of Theophany,* op. cit., p. 495.

rejoice with it.¹³ Now ye are the body of Christ, and members in particular." Our life in the Church and our life in Christ, therefore, is based on *communion*: communion with Christ, in the first instance, but simultaneously, through Christ, communion with one another. And this is nothing less than a reflection of the communion seen in Father, Son, and Holy Spirit, which constitutes Their very unity, Their very Oneness of being.

Thus, the human person, created in the image of God, is only fully and properly such as a member of Christ's Body, and our communion with God involves the body (σῶμα), the soul (ψυχή) and the spirit (πνεῦμα). The emphasis, therefore, is on the human person's communion with God on every level of existence: the physical, that of the soul, and also that of the spirit. Human existence is embraced in its entirety; it is healed, sanctified and transfigured in God, and at the same time, the union of the created with the Uncreated signifies a transcendence, that is to say, the raising of the human person to the right hand of God the Father (cf. the Ascension), which means above and beyond necessity and all the limitations of created existence.

Now, in the Orthodox understanding of the person-hypostasis, we have as the distinguishing unique and indelible characteristic of each what is referred to as the "mode of existence" (τρόπος ὑπάρξεως, as used in the Cappadocians).¹⁴ In the communion of the flesh of Christ we come face to face with none other than God Himself. This, after all, is the very achievement of the Incarnation: the Divine Eucharist which is the Church.

As mentioned earlier, in the Orthodox tradition we have three levels of existence, three aspects which come together in man *qua* man, that is to say, when the person is what he or she

---

13. Gk. καὶ εἴτε πάσχει ἓν μέλος, συμπάσχει πάντα τὰ μέλη· εἴτε δοξάζεται ἓν μέλος, συγχαίρει πάντα τὰ μέλη.

14. We should note here, however, that there is a second way in which this phrase is applied, when it is utilized to refer to the way of life revealed in and through the hypostasis or person of Christ. But here again, this is simply because of the fact that it is only through the flesh of Christ that we have a personal relationship with God.

has been created to be, namely, in communion with God on the physical plane, on that of the rational soul, and also on that of the spiritual or pneumatological level of existence (1 Cor. 12:25–26).

Thus, there is the level of reason, the level of the *nous,* and the level of perfect union and communion in Christ, which both includes and goes beyond the other two. The amazing thing about this *schema* is that the body is included on all levels of personal existence.

Now I realize that there is much more that could be said on this question, as also on other related questions that I have not even touched upon. But since my intention is merely to point to certain oftentimes neglected considerations, allow me to conclude these brief remarks on the question of Euthanasia, by stressing that *communion* with God and one's fellow human beings cannot be measured either by how physically active we are or by what an Electroencephalogram (EEG) is able to detect, however sophisticated. For this reason, it is of vital importance for us as a society to be mindful of the fact that *communion* with God and our neighbour is a state that *at one and the same time* includes and goes far beyond every aspect of our created nature: beyond, therefore, the physical aspects of our existence, beyond the rational or reasonable aspects of our existence, and even beyond the *noetic* or intellectual aspects of the God-like human mind itself.

Part II: *Theoria*

The Light of Tabor
ST JOHN CHRYSOSTOM
AND THE LANGUAGE OF HOLY SCRIPTURE

CHURCHMAN *par excellence*, St John, Patriarch of Constantinople (398–404), is often regarded more as a moralist than a theologian. Such a view, however, which surely stems from the fact that Chrysostom's greatest literary legacy is his homilies,[1] apart from betraying a false distinction, also fails to take into account, and ascribe proper weight to, the profound theological influence of homiletic tradition upon the formulation of Christian doctrine. Homilies, of course, imply church services – *Liturgy* in the wider, Western sense of the word;[2]

---

1. A careful reading of Chrysostom's homilies would show, despite their non-expository character, that they are in fact replete with doctrinal significance. That Chrysostom was more than capable of writing a theological treatise may be inferred from his *De incomprehensibili Dei Natura*, also known as *Contra Anomoeos*, which stands in its own right among the most notable products of Patristic literature, comparable in style and theological content to the finest works of the great Cappadocian Fathers.
2. Note too here that Chrysostom's influence on hymnography is also very much in evidence, as even a cursory reading of the services for the Feast of the Transfiguration will show, see: *The Festal Menaion*, translated by Mother Mary and Archimandrite [now Metropolitan] Kallistos Ware (London and Boston, 1984), pp. 468–503, and the chapter on the Transfiguration in

hence, we should not ignore the reciprocal relationship between faith and worship. Indeed, approximately three thousand homilies on Holy Scripture have been ascribed to Chrysostom, a truly remarkable legacy by any standards; and his sermons are widely acknowledged as the foundation upon which subsequent homiletic tradition in the Greek-speaking East is based.

Now it seems to me that this assertion is no less true in the case of the Transfiguration of Christ, the main source of which is St John's *Homilia LVI in Matthaeum*, which is the first homily *per se* on the Transfiguration in the history of the Church, and indeed constitutes the first extensive treatment of the subject since Origen's *Commentarius in Matthaeum*.[3] Equally significant are the references to the Transfiguration in Chrysostom's *In Eutropium Eunuchum*,[4] his *Adhortationes ad Theodorum Lapsum*,[5] his *De futurae vitae deliciis*,[6] and his *Ad Viduam Iuniorum*,[7] which also shed light on Chrysostom's understanding of the nature and significance of the revelation on Tabor.

There can be little doubt that Origen's *Commentarius in Matthaeum*[8] influenced Chrysostom's homily on the Transfiguration;

Elizabeth Briere's thesis on "Scripture in Hymnography" (Oxford D. Phil. thesis, 1983), *passim*.

3. *Clavis Patrum Graecorum* 2:4424; BHG 1984, 1984b, BHG^n 1984bd; PG 58:549–558. So far as I am aware, none of the homilies believed to be wrongly ascribed to Chrysostom precede this one. For further details, see: M. Sachot, "Edition de l'Homélie Pseudo-Chrysostomienne BHG 1998 (*CPG* 5017) sur la Transfiguration," *Recherches de science religieuse* 58 (1984), 91–104; his *L'homélie pseudo-chrysostomienne sur la Transfiguration, Contextes liturgiques; restitution à Léonce, prêtre de Constantinople; édition critique et commentée; traduction et études connexes*, (Frankfurt–Bern, 1981), see esp. pp. 22–37; and also his *Les Homélies Grecques sur la Transfiguration: Tradition Manuscrite* (Paris, 1987), pp. 107–27.

4. *CPG* 2:4528; PG 52:395–414.
5. *CPG* 2:4305; SC 117:51–6.
6. *CPG* 2:4388; PG 51:347–54.
7. *CPG* 2:4314; SC 138:211–15.
8. *CPG* 1:1450.1; 31–43 *GCS* 40:136–70.

but as in other notable writers, such as Maximus the Confessor,[9] this influence is found more in terms of structure and (more significantly) in the kinds of question posed. Origen's rôle is thus primarily one of catalyst. Hence, we find in Chrysostom's treatment many subtle but significant shifts of emphasis on a number of themes away from Origen's own position.[10] Now in my opinion the most important example of this resides in the fact that while Origen places very little or no emphasis on the Transfiguration Light,[11] Chrysostom focuses on it in such a way as to signify considerably more than mere metaphor.

For the purposes of this seminar,[12] then, I have chosen to focus exclusively on the question of the nature and significance of the Light of Tabor in St John, even though his treatment of the Transfiguration, it should be noted, is an extremely rich and varied one, and touches on a much wider variety of themes than we are able to cover here.[13] My choice of subject, moreover, is governed principally by the fact that not only is it one which, over the centuries subsequent to Chrysostom's own period, gains in prominence and indeed becomes central to the theological debates of the fourteenth century, but also that the Patristic

---

9. See my doctoral dissertation, "The Transfiguration of Christ in Greek Patristic Literature: From Irenaeus of Lyons to Gregory Palamas" (Oxford D. Phil. thesis, 1991), pp. 182–212, and esp. 196–97 (hereafter cited as Veniamin, "Transfiguration"), and the relevant chapter in this work.
10. For further details on Origen's contribution, see: M. Eichinger, "Die Verklärung Christi bei Origenes: die Bedeutung des 'Menschen Jesus' in seiner Christologie," *Wiener Beiträge zur Theologie* 24 (1969); and Veniamin, "Transfiguration", pp. 50–72.
11. Ibid. Origen circumvents the question of the Transfiguration light, because he, like the Neoplatonists and later St Augustine himself (*Contra Adimantum* 28.2 PL 42:171–2), regarded the Light of the Transfiguration as a lesser, visible, and therefore more material manifestation of God; and consequently somewhat removed from the simple intellectual nature (*intellectualis natura simplex*) of the One.
12. Paper presented at the inaugural seminar of the *Oxford University Patristic and Byzantine Society*, which met at Merton College on January 19, 1994.
13. See Veniamin, "Transfiguration", pp. 99–119.

understanding of the Taborian Light is a subject which remains a controversial one to this day.

What, then, does Chrysostom have to say specifically about the Light of Tabor? In addressing this question I first propose to examine Chrysostom's references to the Light as supranatural, and then secondly, I shall attempt to place what he says about the divine Light in St John's own gnosiological context, which will enable us to evaluate its nature and significance more accurately.

The Supernatural Light of Tabor

In a way which is highly reminiscent of St Irenaeus, Bishop of Lyons (d. *c*. 202), St John Chrysostom's appreciation of the Taborian revelation is fundamentally eschatological.[14] So as to prepare His disciples for the trials that they were about to endure in this life (cf. John 16:33), Christ chose to give them a foretaste, concrete proof, of the heavenly blessings of which he had hitherto only spoken:

These things [*sc.* trials and tribulations] were in the present life and at hand, while the good things were still in hope and expectation; as in for example, they save their life who lose it; His coming in the glory of His Father, to render His rewards. But willing to assure their very sight, and show what kind of glory it is with which He will appear (δεῖξαι τίς ποτέ ἐστιν ἡ δόξα ἐκείνη, μεθ' ἧς μέλλει παραγίνεσθαι), so far as they were able to understand this (ὡς ἐνχωροῦν ἦν αὐτοῖς μαθεῖν), even in this present life He shows and reveals it to them.[15]

That which Christ had only spoken of, and which had not been revealed *until* the Transfiguration, was His coming again "in the glory of His Father" (ἐν τῇ δόξῃ τοῦ πατρός αὐτοῦ, cf. Matt 16:27). The glory of the transfigured Christ, then, is a foreshowing of the Paternal glory in which Christ is to appear at the Last Day.

In another passage, however, Chrysostom states with equal clarity that the righteous at the Last Day will see Christ, not merely as His disciples had seen Him on Tabor, but "in the very glory of the Father" (ἐν αὐτῇ τοῦ πατρός τῇ δόξῃ).

---

14. See the relevant section in my thesis, ibid., pp. 37–43.
15. Op. cit., 1 (549).

For not thus shall He come hereafter. For then, so as to spare His disciples, He disclosed only as much of His brightness as they were able to endure; whereas later He shall come *in the very glory of the Father*, not only with Moses and Elias, but also with the infinite angelic hosts, with archangels, with cherubim, with those infinite heavenly companies.[16]

Thus, "the very glory of the Father", which is here referred to as an even greater glory than that which was revealed at the Transfiguration, will be revealed only at the Last Day. What, then, is the difference between the glory of Christ at the Transfiguration and the glory of the Second Coming?

Now this apparent inconsistency[17] is resolved only when one looks more closely at the context in which our second passage appears. Firstly, it is important simply to note that both passages come from the same homily. What Chrysostom is actually saying here is that the revelation of Christ's glory at the Last Day will not be on the humble scale of Tabor – where we have an intimate disclosure of Christ's divine glory before two prophets and three disciples – but rather that it will be of such cosmic proportions that it will involve the infinite myriads of the heavenly Powers (μετὰ τῶν δήμων τῶν ἀπείρων ἐκείνων, cf. Luke 9:26). The underlying presupposition here, therefore, is that the greater the participation in Christ's glory, the greater the manifestation of that glory (cf. "all mine are thine, and thine are mine, *and I am glorified in them*", John 17:10: emphasis mine). Hence, Christ's glory at the Last Day will be greater than that of the Transfiguration, because it will also reveal the glory of the heavenly hosts, suffused with and bearing witness to the divine glory of Christ (cf. "The heavens declare the glory of God; and the firmament proclaims the work of his hands", Ps 18 [19]:1). It is, therefore, the manifestation of the full majesty of Christ's *heavenly status* that Chrysostom refers to here as "the very glory of the Father", that heavenly glory which is also proper to the pre-eternal and consubstantial Word of God. Thus, Chrysostom is not suggesting here that the glory shown at

---

16. Ibid., 4 (554).
17. See E. Briere, "Scripture in Hymnography" (Oxford D. Phil. thesis, 1983), p. 441, n. 89.

the Transfiguration is *qualitatively* inferior to that of the Last Day, but that it is by comparison a humble foreshowing of that very same glory which will be unleashed at the Second Coming. In this, Chrysostom's position greatly resembles that of Irenaeus, who, when speaking of the glory of the Millenium and the final glory of the Kingdom of Heaven, makes no qualitative distinction and speaks of the same Paternal glory.[18]

Hence, Chrysostom does regard the Transfiguration as a genuine eschatological revelation, even though in terms of scale he does not see it as a perfect or accurate manifestation of the glory of the future Kingdom (οὐκ ἐπίδειξις τοῦ πράγματος ἀκριβῆς).[19] Even the Light of Tabor, writes St John in the *Exhortation* to his friend Theodore, can only be but a dim image of the future things (ἀμυδράν τινα τῶν μελλόντων εἰκόνα).[20] For only at the Last Day shall we have a "face to face" vision of the Incarnate Word.[21] At His Second Coming, therefore, the righteous will see Christ,

... not as they then on the mountain, but in far greater brightness (ἀλλὰ πολλῷ λαμπρότερον). For not thus shall He come hereafter. For whereas then, to spare His disciples, He discovered so much only of His brightness as they were able to endure.[22]

Most significantly, Chrysostom also explains why this had to be the case:

The glory of incorruptible bodies does not emit a light similar to that of this corruptible body (οὐ τοσοῦτον ἀφίησιν τὸ φῶς, ὅσον τοῦτο τὸ σῶμα τὸ φθαρτόν), nor is it of a kind which is accessible to mortal eyes, but incorruptible and immortal eyes are required in order to see it. For then on the mountain He revealed only so much [of this light] to them as was possible for the beholders' eyes to see without being afflicted; yet even so they could not bear it and fell on their faces.[23]

---

18. Veniamin, "Transfiguration", loc. cit.
19. *Adhortationes ad Theodorum Lapsum* I.11 (SC 117:51–6).
20. Ibid. (87); see also *De futurae vitae deliciis* 6 (PG 51:352).
21. Ibid. (91–3).
22. *Homilia LVI in Matthaeum* 4 (554).
23. Op. cit. (57–64); see also: *Ad Viduam Iuniorum* 1.3 (SC 138:211–15).

So the glory that was revealed on Tabor, the glory of Christ's divinity, is the very same glory that the incorruptible bodies of the righteous will receive in the Celestial Kingdom. This glory is perceived as light. But this light, says Chrysostom, which will be revealed more fully at the Last Day, is not a natural or physical light, for it is not "accessible to mortal eyes".[24] The reason why, then, the three disciples were unable to bear *even* the glory revealed at the Transfiguration was because the supranatural and immaterial nature of this light is fully perceptible only to incorruptible and immortal eyes.[25]

It is important to note here, however, that this was according to Chrysostom a vision which the apostles actually experienced also with their physical, bodily eyes, even if only in an imperfect manner. Hence their physical reaction to it. But even though the three disciples actually saw Christ transfigured by His divine glory, they were nevertheless unable to contain the vision because, as St John explains, they were still subject to corruption and death.

This highlights another important aspect in Chrysostom's appreciation of the significance of the Transfiguration: that of the glorification of the human body. In his *De futurae vitae deliciis*, St John says the following:

Because the word concerning the Kingdom was until then unclear to those that heard it... He was transfigured before His disciples, thereby revealing to them the glory of the future things and, as in an enigmatic and dim way, showing what our bodies will be like. And whereas then He appeared with garments, it will not be so at the resurrection. For then our body will need neither garments, nor abode, nor shelter, nor any other such thing.[26]

Thus, the whole human person, body as well as soul, has been called to participate in the glory of which the Transfiguration is but a humble foreshowing.

---

24. Cf. for example St Basil of Caesarea, who says that this light is "contemplated only by the mind" (διανοίᾳ μόνῃ θεωρητόν), *Homiliae in Psalmos* 44:5 (400BD).
25. *Homilia LVI in Matthaeum* 3 (553).
26. *De futurae vitae deliciis* 6 (PG 51:352).

The Gnosiological Context

Let us now turn to the gnosiological context in which we should understand the revelation of God in Chrysostom. Firstly then, in his address to the eunuch Eutropius, St John insists that a clear distinction should be made between those things pertaining to God in Himself (τὰ τῆς θεότητος) and those things pertaining to God's action or operation in the world (τὰ τῆς οἰκονομίας).[27] In reference to this distinction Chrysostom first emphasizes the immutable and inaccessible nature of God:

> Most high was He, and lowly was [His economy]; Most high, not in locality, but in nature (οὐ τόπῳ, ἀλλὰ φύσει). He was uncompounded, His essence indestructible, His nature was incorruptible, invisible, incomprehensible, always being, the same being, beyond angels, superior to the heavenly powers, surpassing reason, transcending the intellect, being impossible to see, [He was] simply believed in.[28]

God in Himself, in His essence and nature, is invisible (ἀόρατος) and incomprehensible (ἀπερινόητος), and as such can neither be seen (ὀφθῆναι μὴ δυνάμενος) nor comprehended (νικῶν λογισμόν, ὑπερβαίνων διάνοιαν).

But if this is so, how does God reveal Himself to man? In the same passage, Chrysostom provides us with the following answer:

> When He wishes to show Himself, He does not appear as He is, nor is His bare essence revealed – for no one has seen God as He is. For at His condescension even the cherubim trembled: He condescended, and the mountains smoked; He condescended and the sea dried up; He condescended, and Heaven was shaken; for had He not condescended, who could have borne it? Therefore, He appears not as He is, but as that which the beholder is able to see. That is why He sometimes appears aged, and sometimes young, sometimes in fire, and sometimes in a breeze, sometimes in water, and sometimes in weapons, not changing His essence, but fashioning His appearance according to the different circumstances (σχηματίζων τὴν ὄψιν πρὸς τὴν ποικιλίαν τῶν ὑποκειμένων).[29]

---

27. *In Eutropium Eunuchum II* 9 (PG 52:403).
28. Ibid. (404); and cf. *Homiliae in Ioannem XV* 1 (PG 59:98).
29. Ibid.

The key word in Chrysostom's description of the divine economy is "condescension" (συγκατάβασις),[30] for it is by His condescension that God reveals Himself to man. He does this, says Chrysostom, not by suffering change in His essence, but by conforming, shaping or adapting Himself to the capacity of His creature.[31] Chrysostom is not here referring to created effects in God's revelation to man, for συγκατάβασις denotes the loving descent and participation of *God Himself* in the life of His creature.[32] So, it is precisely God's συγκατάβασις which reveals His love for mankind, his φιλανθρωπία, and which finds its ultimate expression in the Incarnation – the hypostatic condescension of the Son and Word of God, in the flesh.

Here we find a remarkable resemblance between Chrysostom's concept of condescension and the Cappadocian,[33] or rather the Basilian, distinction between the essence and energies of God.[34] As far as I am aware, this distinction, just as in St Basil, is made explicit in a single passage, in Chrysostom's *De incomprehensibili Dei Natura*, where in fact the word "economies" is used rather than "condescension". Here, Chrysostom in reference to St Paul's passage on the partial knowledge of God (1 Cor 13:9, ἐκ μέρους γινώσκομεν καὶ ἐκ μέρους προφητεύομεν), simply says of St Paul: "that he does not say this of the essence, but of the economies"

---

30. See also *Homiliae in Ioannem XV* 1 (PG 59:98); and cf. *Adhortationes ad Theodorum Lapsum* I.11 (SC 117:140,[61]–142,[64]): ὅσον δυνατὸν ἢ καὶ μὴ θλίψαι, which again is due to God's condescension and *philanthropia*.
31. Cf. *Homiliae in Ioannem XV* 1 (PG 59:98), where the nature of God is described as shapeless (ἀσχημάτηστος). What is seen, therefore, cannot be the essence of God.
32. Compare here Chrysostom's understanding of God's shaping or adapting Himself *out of love* for His creature to the *Acta Iohannis'* polymorphic depictions of Christ, employed in order to demonstrate the radical unknowability of an all powerful *Deus philosophorum*, see: E. Junod and J.-D. Kaestli, eds., *Acta Iohannis*, in *Corpus christianorum, series apocrypha*, vol. 2 (Brepols–Turnholt, 1983), pp. 692–94; and Veniamin, "Transfiguration", pp. 16–24.
33. Cf. St Gregory Nazianzus, *Oratio XL* 6 (PG 36:364BC); and cf. *Oratio XVI* 9 (PG 35:945C); and see: Veniamin, "Transfiguration", pp. 93–5.
34. St Basil of Caesarea, ibid., p. 86, n. 2.

(οὐ περὶ τῆς οὐσίας τοῦτο φησίν, ἀλλὰ περὶ τῶν οἰκονομιῶν).[35] Now bearing in mind also the created–uncreated distinction in Chrysostom,[36] the implications become clear: While in Basil we find the schema essence–energies,[37] in Chrysostom there is the schema essence–economies (or essence–condescension). And while their terms may differ, their meaning is in fact the same.[38] Neither of these two great Fathers develops the theme further; indeed in both instances their main concern was to refute the claim of the Anomoeans (the followers of Aëtius and Eunomius) that human reason and the human intellect are capable of penetrating into the divine mysteries to the point of apprehending even the essence of God. And as we know, it is only in the fourteenth century that the full significance of this distinction is made clear by the Hesychasts.

The Transfiguration, then, clearly falls within the realm of τὰ τῆς οἰκονομίας. As such it is yet another example of the συγκατάβασις of God. On Tabor the pre-eternal divine glory manifested in and

---

35. *De incomprehensibili Dei Natura* I (SC 28bis:124,[280–1]).
36. In particular, see: ibid. (126,[302]–128,[320]), where Chrysostom maintains that no created power can know the essence of God, and that even the angels cannot fully bear His condescension. Also, his *Homilia in Ioannem* XV 1 (PG 59:98), where, after stating that only the Son and the Spirit can see God the Father (Μόνος οὖν αὐτὸν ὁρᾷ ὁ Υἱὸς καὶ τὸ Πνεῦμα τὸ ἅγιον), he asks the following rhetorical question: Ἡ γὰρ κτιστὴ φύσις ἅπασα πῶς καὶ ἰδεῖν δυνήσεται τὸν ἄκτιστον; On the distinction of essence and energies or condescension of God in Chrysostom, see: Theodore N. Zissis, *Ἄνθρωπος καὶ κόσμος ἐν τῇ Οἰκονομίᾳ τοῦ Θεοῦ κατὰ τὸν ἱερὸν Χρυσόστομον*, Analecta Vlatadon 9 (Patriarchal Institute for Patristic Studies: Thessalonica, 1971), esp. pp. 65–9.
37. For a thorough analysis of the place and significance of the essence–energies distinction in Basil of Caesarea, see the fine study by G. D. Martzelos, *Οὐσία καὶ ἐνέργιαι τοῦ Θεοῦ κατὰ τὸν Μέγαν Βασίλειον* (University of Thessalonica Th. D. thesis, 1984).
38. See the chapter *Ὁ Ἰωάννης Χρυσόστομος καὶ οἱ Καππαδόκαι*, in P. K. Chrestou, *Θεολογικὰ Μελετήματα· Γραμματεία του Δ´ Αἰῶνος* (Patriarchal Institute for Patristic Studies: Thessalonica, 1975), esp. pp. 265–6.

through the theandric Christ appears to Peter, James and John as a brilliant light.

The Language of Holy Scripture

Now with the benefit of what we have learned about Chrysostom's gnosiological framework, let us also examine what he says about the language of Scripture in the description of the Light of Tabor. In his *In Eutropium eunuchum*, Chrysostom explains:

> When He wishes to say something about Himself, He uses human images. As for instance, He went up to the mountain, "and was transfigured before them, and His face shone as the light, and His garments became white as snow". He revealed, he says, a little of His divinity, He showed them the indwelling God… The Evangelist, then, wanted to show His brilliance, and so he says, "He shone". How did He shine? Tell me. "Exceedingly." And how do you say? "As the sun"… Why do you say so? Because I have no other star brighter. And He was white, "as snow"? Why "as snow"? Because I have no other matter whiter. That He did not shine in this way is indicated by the following: And the disciples fell to the ground. If He had shone as the sun, the disciples would not have fallen (for they saw the sun every day, and did not fall); but because He shone more than the sun and more than the snow, that is why, unable to bear the brilliance, they fell down.[39]

The revelation on Tabor demonstrates that the language which Scripture employs in order to describe the revelation of God to man should not be interpreted literally, but rather, as St John puts it, it should be understood θεοπρεπῶς, that is to say, "in a manner befitting God".[40] Thus, we should raise our minds to the meaning that the words of Scripture seek to convey.[41] According to Chrysostom, therefore, Scripture likens the Light of Tabor to the sun and snow because there

---

39. *In Eutropium Eunuchum II* 10 (PG 52:404–5); see also: ibid., 11 (405) and *Homilia LVI in Matthaeum*, 4 (PG 58:555). Cf. Chrysostom's interpretation of the phrases ὡσεὶ πυρός, ἐν εἴδει περιστερᾶς and ὡς φερομένης πνοῆς βιαίας, in *Homiliae de Pentecoste* 1.5 (PG 50:460). His explanation, ἵνα μηδὲν αἰσθητὸν ὑποπτεύσεις περὶ τοῦ Πνεύματος, could be applied equally to the description of Christ's resplendence at His Transfiguration.
40. Cf. *In Eutropium Eunuchum II* 7 (402–3).
41. Ibid., 9 (404).

is nothing brighter within the realm of human experience to which this particular light might be likened. St John is thus not interested here in metaphor or figurative language. Like Diodore of Tarsus, Chrysostom was not given to the allegorical interpretation of Scripture, which makes his interpretation here all the more striking.

The Bright Cloud

But what of the bright Cloud of Tabor? Firstly, like Origen before him,[42] Chrysostom regards the appearance of the Cloud as a direct reply to St Peter's proposal to build three tabernacles. The Cloud appears, therefore, as a divine tabernacle – a tabernacle, as Chrysostom puts it, which is not made by the hands of men (ἀχειροποίητος, cf. Acts 7:48, 17:24; Isa 16:12).[43] Secondly, the purpose of this Cloud, the brightness of which he contrasts with the thick darkness of the Cloud of Sinai (Exod 20:21; 19:16), was to instruct rather than to threaten or frighten.[44] Thirdly and most significantly, the bright Cloud also marks the beginning of a further stage in the revelation on Tabor. In fact, Chrysostom sees it as the prelude to the Voice of the Father. However, it is interesting that the Cloud itself is not identified exclusively with the Father,[45] nor for that matter with any Person of the Holy Trinity in particular. It is simply regarded as a manifestation of God: Οὕτως ἀεὶ φαίνεται ὁ Θεός.[46] Therefore, the

---

42. See: *Commentarius in Matthaeum* 12. 42 (*GCS* 40:165,9⁻15); and Veniamin, "Transfiguration", p. 60.
43. *Homilia LVI in Matthaeum* 3 (PG 58:553).
44. Ibid.
45. Ibid. Although a cursory reading of this passage might give the impression that Chrysostom simply refers to the Father as God, as indeed he does in, for example, εἰ γὰρ δυνατὸς ὁ Θεός; . . . εὔδηλον ὅτι καὶ ὁ Υἱὸς ὁμοίως, it will be observed upon closer examination that this is not in fact so in the case of the Transfiguration Cloud. Chrysostom's main concern here is to make clear that in emanating from the Cloud, the voice was immediately recognized as coming from God: Ἵν' οὖν πιστεύσωσιν, ὅτι παρὰ τοῦ Θεοῦ ἡ φωνὴ φέρεται, ἐκεῖθεν [*sc.* from the Cloud] ἔρχεται.
46. In further support of this, Chrysostom also gives the following Scriptural examples: νεφέλη γὰρ καὶ γνόφος κύκλῳ αὐτοῦ, Ps 96 [97]:2; κάθηται ἐπὶ νεφέλης κούφης Isa 19:1; ὁ τιθεὶς νέφη τὴν ἐπίβασιν αὐτοῦ,

Voice of the Father emanates from the Cloud in order to assure the disciples of its divine provenance. And so a subtle distinction can be discerned here between the *Cloud*, which denotes the presence of God, and the *Voice from the Cloud*, the purpose of which is to bear witness to and confirm the divine Sonship of the Saviour.

However, there is in Chrysostom no explicit statement regarding the nature of the Cloud beyond what has already been said, namely, that it is simply a manifestation of God. But there is a small passage in his homily on the Transfiguration, which offers, perhaps, a more positive indication as to what Chrysostom believes the bright Cloud to be. He says:

> There is probably nothing more blessed than the apostles, and especially the three, who even in the Cloud were made worthy to be under the same roof with the Master.[47]

Of course, the general point being made here is that there can be no greater blessing for us than to be with Christ. The context of this passage, however, is eschatological. Being with Christ, therefore, is the blessing that the apostles received, and it is also the one thing that all Christians should strive and hope for. But there is also a strong emphasis here on the three disciples, who received the extra special distinction of being with Christ even in the Cloud (καὶ ἐν τῇ νεφέλῃ).

What, then, is the significance of being in the Cloud? On one level, it is possible that Chrysostom is simply making a statement of fact: Peter, James and John were with Christ more often even than the other apostles – even, that is, in the Cloud. While this is undoubtedly true, it still does not offer a satisfactory explanation of this passage, because it does not take into consideration either the strong eschatological perspective of the passage in general, or the special emphasis which Chrysostom places on the Cloud in particular. A better explanation perhaps would be that the three

---

Ps 103 [104]:3; νεφέλη ὑπέλαβεν αὐτὸν ἀπὸ τῶν ὀφθαλμῶν αὐτῶν, Acts 1:9; and ὡς υἱὸς ἀνθρώπου ἐρχόμενος ἐπὶ τῶν νεφελῶν (= word order given by St John), Dan 7:13; and cf. Eusebius of Caesarea, Veniamin, "Transfiguration", p. 78, n. 4.
47. Op. cit., 4 (554).

disciples were indeed blessed to be in the Cloud with Christ, because this was a further and deeper revelation of the Celestial Kingdom. This harks back to the Cloud as the Tabernacle of God – a place where God is. In the Cloud, the three disciples experienced the heavenly bliss of the righteous – the blessed life of the future Kingdom.[48] This would imply, therefore, that the bright Cloud is not merely an indication of the presence of God, but that it is itself a description of the three disciples' *participation* in the Life of God.[49]

In conclusion, therefore, we can say that the significance of the Taborian Light in St John Chrysostom is predominantly eschatological, for it reveals the future blessed state of the righteous in the Kingdom – the glory of the Father. This bears a remarkable similarity to Irenaeus' strong eschatological perspective; especially when one pauses to consider the heavy emphasis that the Bishop of Lyons places on the *Paterna lux*. But the similarity between these two theologians does not end here, for St John, like St Irenaeus, makes no *qualitative* distinction between the Light of Tabor and that of the Kingdom. In taking up and reaffirming the Irenaean position, however, Chrysostom elaborates upon the Taborian theophany in such a way as to indicate also its anthropological implications, which in turn of course tell us more about his theological presuppositions.

Thus, by virtue of man's mortal and corruptible nature, such a light as was revealed on Tabor cannot be experienced fully in this life. Its nature is of a kind that is not only non-physical or immaterial,

---

48. For a similar interpretation, see the Basilian contribution, Veniamin, "Transfiguration", pp. 86–8.

49. Cf. Chrysostom's appreciation of the Taborian Cloud to that found in a contemporary work, by Archimandrite Sophrony, *Видет Бога Как Он Есть* [*We Shall See Him As He Is*] (Essex, 1985), p. 159 (*Апостолы Петр, Иаков и Иоанн на Фаворе были объяты нетварным Светом, и в этом осиянии восприняли невещественный голос Отца, свидетельствовавшего о Христе, как о возлюбленном Сыне Своем*), where the Transfiguration Cloud is not distinguished from the Transfiguration Light; and cf. also, p. 172. Thus, it was this same light which proceeded to envelope the three Apostles on Tabor, and it was out of this very same light that the Father's Voice was recognized as proceeding.

but also such as surpasses both discursive reason and transcends the intellect, and therefore the Taborian Light cannot be likened to or contrasted with any created light. Indeed, examined within the wider context of St John's gnosiology – that is, within the context of his distinction between God in His condescension towards us and in His essence or nature – it is not difficult to appreciate how these factors conspire to point not only to the supranatural, but also (I would add) to the uncreated character of the Taborian Light.

Equally striking, and this is the point on which I would like to close, is the agreement between Chrysostom and the Cappadocians, on the one hand, and between Chrysostom and the Hesychasts of the fourteenth century, on the other. Moreover, I would also maintain that St John's estimation of the relationship between the Light of Tabor and the divine economy is fundamentally the same as that of St Gregory Palamas: That though the Taborian Light is uncreated and denotes the manifestation of God Himself, nevertheless it is in no wise a revelation of His divine essence.[50]

---

50. *Homiliae xxxiv* and *xxxv* (PG 151:424–36 and 436–49).

THE RESURRECTION OF THE HUMAN BODY IN THE CHRISTOLOGY OF ST CYRIL POPE AND PATRIARCH OF ALEXANDRIA

"Without the Resurrection," said a *Staretz* of our own age, "there is nothing!"

Truly. Unless Christ be risen from the dead, unless the tomb of the Lord were found "empty", the Christian *kerygma* would indeed be useless. As St Paul puts it: "If Christ be not raised, your faith is vain" (1 Cor. 15:17).

But why do the saints speak about the Resurrection in such uncompromising terms? Quite simply, because if the Resurrection of Christ is merely a beautiful metaphor, "then they also which are fallen asleep in Christ are perished", and "we are of all men most miserable" (1 Cor. 15:18–19), for nothing but death and corruption – nothing but non-being – would await us.

Christians, however, *know* that Christ is risen; and they know that His Resurrection signifies our resurrection, and so together with St Paul they affirm that "now is Christ risen from the dead, and become the firstfruits of them that slept... For as in Adam all die, even so in Christ shall all be made alive" (1 Cor. 15:20–22). The Resurrection of Christ the New Adam, then, is a foreshowing of our own resurrection, of our intended place in the Kingdom of Heaven.

However, within the mystery of Christ's glorious Resurrection is also contained the mystery of the way in which we have been called to share in the very Life of God the Holy Trinity; and it is here that we arrive at the fundamental doctrine of the Church concerning the resurrection of the body.

Put simply, the whole of our humanity – body as well as soul – has been called to live eternally with God. This is the significance of the salvific work of Christ: that by His Incarnation, Crucifixion, Resurrection and Ascension, Christ has raised human nature to the right hand of God the Father, to the level of Divine Being.

Significantly, the only human person, the only human hypostasis thus far to have achieved this blessed state is, of course, the Most Holy Mother of God and Ever-Virgin Mary, through whom the Son and Word of God became flesh.

I say "significantly", because in our attempt to look a little more closely at the question of the resurrection of the body, I have chosen to turn briefly to St Cyril, Pope and Patriarch of Alexandria (d. 444), for it was he who first defended the Holy Virgin as Theotokos (*Birthgiver* or *Mother of God*) against the Nestorians – those who falsely taught that Christ was merely a man in whom the divine Logos dwelt. It is no coincidence, then, that references to the subject of our inquiry abound in St Cyril of Alexandria, for the theme of the resurrection of the human flesh of Christ is inextricably intertwined with our appreciation of the Holy Virgin as Theotokos.

Interestingly, St Cyril of Alexandria refers not to the Resurrection but to the Transfiguration as the clearest recorded manifestation that we have of that reward, the *misthon*, or glory (cf. Rom. 8:18) which the righteous – those who take up their Cross and follow Christ (Luke 9:23–24) – will receive at the General Resurrection.[1] Cyril describes this reward in terms of "participation (*methexis*) in eternal life and glory",[2] and "vision (*thea*) of glory";[3] interchangeable terms which describe the life of the Kingdom. For Cyril, the vision of Christ transfigured is perceived as a prefiguration of the participation of the saints in the glorious life of the Kingdom, which will be inaugurated at the Parousia.

By Kingdom we mean that vision of glory, in which He will appear at such time when He will shine upon those on earth.[4]

A little further on in the same work, Cyril suggests that Peter's words (Luke 9:33) might have been due to his mistaking the Transfiguration for the end of the world and the *kairos* of the promised participation of the righteous in the Life of God.[5] He goes on to explain, however, that this could not have taken place at that particular time, since Christ had not yet completed His redemptive work. Man was, therefore, still subject to the power of death and corruption and consequently incapable of enduring the revelation of Christ's divine glory.[6]

This point brings us directly to the significance of the resurrection of the body of Christ: In his *Commentary on John*, St Cyril refers explicitly to the reason for Christ's appearance to St Thomas and to all the apostles in His resurrected human body.

What need was there for the showing of His hands and side, if, in accordance with the depravity of some, He did not rise with His own flesh? If He wanted His disciples to believe differently concerning Him, why did He not rather appear in a different frame, and by putting the form of the flesh to shame, draw them towards a different understanding? But it was most important that He show Himself carefully at that time so that they should believe in the future resurrection of the flesh; so important that even when the time seemed right to change the fashion of His body into ineffable and supranatural glory, He providentially deigned to appear once again as He was before, so that He should not be thought of as having any other body than that in which He had even suffered death on the Cross. That the glory of the Holy Body could not have been borne by our eyes (if indeed Christ had wanted to reveal it before ascending to the Father), you will easily understand, when you consider the Transfiguration on the mount which was revealed to the holy disciples. For the blessed Evangelist Matthew writes that Jesus took "Peter and James and John, and went up to the mountain, and He was transfigured before them, and His face shone as lightning, and His garments became white as snow", while they, unable to bear the vision, fell on their faces. Most prudently, then, our Lord Jesus Christ, not yet having transformed His Temple into its due and proper glory, still appeared in His original shape, wishing that the belief in the Resurrection should not be transferred to a shape or body other than that which He took from the Holy Virgin, and in which He was crucified and died according to the Scriptures; for the power of death extended only over the flesh, from which it had been set free.[7]

The strong soteriological perspective in Cyril's Christology is more than apparent here. The underlying presupposition is clear enough: Christ could not truly be said to have redeemed mankind – human flesh, by which Cyril means human nature in its totality – unless He had also resurrected His own human body.

Christ, then, deigned to appear before His disciples still bearing the signs of corruptibility on His hands and side – marks which, properly speaking, should no longer have been present on His resurrected and therefore incorruptible body[8] – so as to make it absolutely clear that He had risen with the very same body that He had received from the Holy Virgin.

St Cyril adds that the Resurrection must have been of the body of Christ, since its very purpose was to release human flesh from the power of death and corruption.[9] Following here the *Logos-sarx* schema,[10] Cyril says that "the power of death extended only over the flesh", that is, over the humanity but not the divinity of Christ; for death and corruption could not be said to have any dominion over the Person of Christ, the divine Logos, who is by His very nature Life itself.[11] Cyril describes the mystery thus:

If His dead body had not risen, what kind of death was vanquished, and how was the power of corruption rendered powerless? Not by the death of one of the rational creatures, by a soul, or by an angel, nor even by that of the Word of God Himself. Since, therefore, the power of death extends only over that which is by nature corruptible, it is with respect to this [the body] that the power of the Resurrection should reasonably be understood...[12]

The resurrection of the human flesh of Christ – soul and body – is thus an absolute prerequisite for the Salvation of man. In Cyril physical death is understood as "the exodus of the human soul from the body",[13] and as a result of this exodus of the soul it is the body which suffers corruption. It is not the soul, therefore, but the body, which, being of its nature corruptible, is in need of being rendered incorruptible. Thus, by the Death and Resurrection of the body of Christ, the power of corruption was "rendered powerless".[14] Hence, the Holy Body, which the Apostle Thomas was allowed to touch, bears witness to the future resurrection of our own bodies in incorruption.

Furthermore, the glory of the body of Christ as revealed at the Transfiguration is regarded as a preview of His Resurrection glory,[15] not as it was revealed to St Thomas and the others immediately following the Resurrection, but as it was revealed to them from the Ascension onwards.

This does not mean, of course, that the body of Christ had not already been glorified at the time of the Resurrection. On the contrary, Cyril maintains that Christ, if He so desired, could have revealed His body in "its due and proper glory" immediately following His Resurrection; but that His disciples would not have been able to bear such a manifestation before Christ's Ascension to the Father – before, that is, the disciples had received the sanctification of the Holy Spirit. St Cyril illustrates this point by referring to the reaction of the three disciples on the mount, who were unable to endure the vision of the transfigured Christ.

Interestingly, St Cyril also maintains that Christ breathed the Holy Spirit on His disciples on the first day of His Resurrection (John 20:22). Now this at first sight appears to suggest that the disciples, well before the Ascension, were in fact ready for the vision of Christ in glory. But this, according to Cyril, is not the case. It is clear that in St Cyril the period between the Resurrection and the Ascension is seen as one of preparation for the disciples. (At this point the dynamic nature of the life in Christ in St Cyril becomes apparent.) St Cyril says that the Holy Spirit had been dwelling in and sanctifying the disciples since the first appearance of Christ in Jerusalem, so as to prepare them for the Ascension – the vision of Christ glorified – Pentecost, and all that was to follow.[16]

In St Cyril, then, it is the Transfiguration glory that is a foreshowing of that vision of Christ glorified which man has been capable of receiving since the Ascension. Consequently, the Ascension marks for Cyril a most important turning point in the history of man's receptiveness to the vision of God.

Let us pause here in order to consider the fascinating corollary to this assertion: that man is, subsequent to the Ascension, capable of both receiving and enduring the vision of Christ glorified. Explicit scriptural accounts of post-Ascension visions of Christ are relatively few. Most of these are either directly or indirectly connected with the Conversion of St Paul. They are: the Martyrdom of Stephen the Protodeacon (Acts 7:55–56); the Conversion of Saul (Acts 9:3–7, 27; 22:6–11, 15; 26:12–19; cf. Gal. 1:15–16); the Vision of Ananias (Acts 9:10); the Foundation of the Church in Corinth (Acts 18:9–10); St Paul's Vision in the Temple (Acts 22:17–21); and following St Paul's appearance before the Sanhedrin (Acts 23:11); to which an explicit reference to the vision of Christ in 2 Cor. 4:6 may be added. Also, the Vision of St John the Divine (Rev. 1:12–18). Compare 1 Cor. 15:5–8, where St Paul makes no distinction between the visions of Christ during the period between the Resurrection and the Ascension and his vision of Christ on the road to Damascus. However, it is also true that Paul at the time of this vision had not yet received the Holy Spirit (Acts 9:17–18). This would constitute an exception among these references to the vision of Christ in glory, since, in accordance with St Cyril's view of the scheme of things, Paul's own spiritual state at that time could have been no more advanced than that of the three disciples at the Transfiguration. Indeed, this would account for his inability to endure the revelation, and his resulting blindness – elements which are not present in other instances of post-Ascension visions of Christ. None the less, St Paul's vision was one of Christ glorified. Moreover, it would also follow that these post-Ascension visions of Christ are regarded as examples of what must have been the common experience of all the apostles.

The Resurrection of Christ, therefore, together with His Ascension signify, firstly, the glorification of the human nature of

Christ Himself – of His human body and soul. And secondly, they reveal the intended glorification of our whole human person, our whole hypostasis – soul *and body*.

In our brief inquiry, then, into the significance of the resurrection of the body of Christ, St Cyril grants us a glimpse of his panoramic theological vision. In his theology – that is, in his balanced vision of Christ as the *Theos Logos* – we see how one theme leads us to and is inextricably and organically bound up with another. Hence, in seeking to understand better the full significance of the Resurrection of Christ *for us*, we are once again brought before the mystery of the whole Divine Economy: the Birth, the Passion, the Death, the Resurrection, and the Ascension of the Son and Word of God truly made flesh.

"Without the Resurrection, there is nothing!" Truly, because without the Resurrection there is no Christ. But Christ is Risen! And to them that believe, He has given eternal Life.

ENDNOTES

1. *Homiliae Diversae IX in Transfigurationem* (*PG* 77:1009C–1012B); and cf. his *Commentarii in Iohannem* 20:22 (Pusey 3:1098d–e).

2. Ibid. (*PG* 77:1009C).

3. Ibid. (1012AB).

4. Ibid.

5. Ibid. (1013BC).

6. *Commentarii in Matthaeum* 200 (Reuss:218); and cf. Chrysostom, "The Transfiguration of Christ in Greek Patristic Literature: From Irenaeus of Lyons to Gregory Palamas" (Oxford D. Phil. thesis, 1991), pp. 99–100 (hereafter cited as Veniamin, "Transfiguration").

7. *Commentarii in Iohannem* 20:19, 20 (Pusey 3:1091e–1092c).

8. Ibid., 20:26, 27; 28 (1105d–1106b; 1108d–e). Note too that Christ retained the wounds on His resurrected body up to and including (but *not* after) the moment of His Ascension to the Father, in order to convince even the angelic powers of His bodily Resurrection, ibid.,

20:26, 27 (1106b–1107c). Interestingly, St Cyril is unmoved by Rev. 1:7 (and perhaps Zach. 12:10, though this is *not* supported by the *LXX* version), which, it must be conceded, actually refer to those who pierced Christ rather than the *Wounds* of Christ *per se*: "and every eye shall see him, *and they also which pierced him*". It is probable that St Cyril has 1 Cor. 15:42 in mind: "So also is the resurrection of the dead. It is sown in corruption; it is raised in incorruption".

9. Cf. also ibid., 20:20; 26, 27 (1092c; 1103b–d).

10. Cyril elaborates on the constitution of the human nature of Christ in his later antinestorian works, see for example, Veniamin, "Transfiguration", pp. 132–134.

11. Ibid., 20:24, 25 (1102d); cf. also 11:11 (Pusey 2:679c) and *Commentarii in Lucam* 22:19 (*PG* 72:908C–909A).

12. *Commentarii in Iohannem* 20:19, 20 (Pusey 3:1092c).

13. Ibid., 11:11 (Pusey 2:679b). See Plato's definition of death in his *Phaedo* (*OCT* 64 C and 67 D).

14. Cf. also the *Homiliae Diversae IX in Transfigurationem* (*PG* 77:1013C); *Commentarii in Lucam* 22:19 (*PG* 72:909A) and *Commentarii in Iohannem* 20:28 (Pusey 3:1108d–e).

15. Note that Pope Leo I, the Great (440–461) refers to the Transfiguration as a manifestation of the glory of the deified human nature of Christ, and not of the Godhead itself, *Homilia 51*. 2 (*PL* 54:310B).

16. Op. cit., 20:22, 23 (1099a–e). We should also note here that Pentecost in Cyril is the day on which the disciples received not the Holy Spirit, but the gift of languages and the power to preach the word of truth *from* the Holy Spirit. The vision of Christ *in glory*, however, came with the Ascension.

THE TRANSFIGURATION OF CHRIST AND THE DEIFICATION OF MAN IN ST MAXIMUS THE CONFESSOR

THE COMPLEX AND CONVOLUTED STRUCTURE of his thought and literary style, coupled with the highly allegorical character of his exegesis, all make reading St Maximus the Confessor (c. 580 – 662) an extremely difficult task. This is unquestionably a feature common to most, if not to all, of his theological *scholia*; but one, it should be noted, which does not apply to his letters and ascetical writings, suggesting that the difficult character of his theological works may be deliberate[1] – intellectually analogous, perhaps, to the ascetic effort required of the faithful in reading the intentionally difficult character scripts of names on icons.

A further complication in Maximus, of which the reader soon becomes aware, is that the headings of many *scholia* often appear to be misleading, as they seem to bear little or no direct resemblance to their content; often due to the fact that the

---

1. For example, cf. the clarity of expression in Maximus' *Epistulae xlv* (*Clavis Patrum Graecorum* 3:7699; PG 91:364–649), his *Liber asceticus* (CPG 3:7692; PG 90:912–956), and his *Capita de Caritate* (CPG 3:7693; PG 90:960–1080); see also St Photius, op. cit., 192 (B); 193 (83,$^{26\text{-}31}$; 84,$^{7\text{-}11}$).

relevant *scholion* is to be taken within the context of a much wider entity or unit.

Nevertheless, despite these initial difficulties and apparent obstacles, to the persevering student is revealed a depth of meaning and an originality of thought which is second to none in patristic literature.[2] The tight cohesion of Maximus' thought is matched only by his profound understanding of the spiritual life, which pervades his theology. Indeed, taken at any given point, the Confessor's thought immediately brings one into contact with the whole of an extremely complex and all-embracing vision of God, man and the cosmos.

The cyclical or repetitious character of his thought is equally evident in St. Maximus' treatment of the Transfiguration of Christ – reflected in the overlapping and intertwining of the numerous themes and motifs contained therein. Indeed ultimately, the uniqueness of his contribution to the question of the Transfiguration resides chiefly in the very application of his method to the subject, in the incorporation, that is, of the Taborian revelation into the vast landscape of his theology.

Maximus' treatment of the Transfiguration comes, not surprisingly, in the shape of *scholia*, which are to be found mainly in his *Quaestiones et dubia*, believed to have been composed during his Cyzicus stay, that is, by 626;[3] and in his *Ambigua*. The Transfiguration is encountered in the second part of the latter work – the part which Sherwood calls *Ambigua II* (*PG* 91:1061–1417) – written during Maximus' early African stay (628 – 630),[4]

---

2. Compare, for example, what St Photius writes in reference to Maximus' *Quaestiones ad Thalassium* in his *Bibliothèque* 192 (A) (Henry 3:80,25–81,9).

3. P. Sherwood, *An Annotated Date-List of the Works of Maximus the Confessor*, in Studia Anselmiana, no. 30 (Rome, 1952), 26 item 13.

4. Ibid. 31–32 item 26 and cf. item 43; and cf. also H. U. von Balthasar, *Die Gnostischen Centurien* (Freiburg im Breisgau, 1941), 152. Sherwood also calls this period (628–630) "the period of adjustment". It is during this period that the matter which was worked out while St Maximus was still at Cyzicus (upto 626) was actually composed. Furthermore, its purpose was to refute the arguments of the Origenists of the period,

and containing his most detailed treatment of the subject. Next, references are also to be found in his *Capita theologica et oeconomica*, written some time between 630 and 634, the period immediately preceding the outbreak of the Monothelete Controversy, which began in 634 with the publication of the Synodical epistle of Patriarch Sophronius of Jerusalem (c. 560 – 638).[5] And finally, we have two very brief references in his *Scholia in de divinis nominibus*,[6] as well as a single allusion in his *Scholia in de coelesti hierarchia*. All of these works, then, actually predate the Monothelete Controversy, and, as will become evident in this study, do not touch upon the question of the two wills of Christ.[7]

The influences evident in St. Maximus' treatment of the Transfiguration are many and varied, ranging from the early Apologists through the so-called Alexandrian school (particularly Origen and Cyril of Alexandria) to Gregory of Nyssa and Dionysius the Areopagite.

As in the case of Dionysius, the concept which dominates St. Maximus' vision of the Transfiguration of Christ, and indeed of his theological system as a whole, is that of the *deification* (θέωσις) of man. But Maximus is not content simply in describing

while at the same time retaining their positive elements, ibid.; and see idem, *The Earlier Ambigua of St Maximus the Confessor and His Refutation of Origenism*, in Studia Anselmiana, no. 36 (Rome, 1955).
5. Sherwood, *Annotated Date-List* 35 item 37; and cf. von Balthasar, *Gnostischen Centurien* 155.
6. No works from PG 4 are included in Sherwood's *Date-List*.
7. More recent writers on Maximus do not give consideration to the aspect of the Transfiguration in his works, being more concerned with the Monothelete Controversy, for example, see Alain Riou, *Le Monde et l'Église selon Maxime le Confesseur*, Théologie Historique 22 (Paris, 1973); Jean Miguel Garrigues, *Maxime le Confesseur*, Théologie Historique (Paris, 1976); Fancois-Marie Léthel, *Théologie de l'Agonie du Christ*, Théologie Historique 52 (Paris, 1979); Νίκου Ἀ. Ματσούκα, *Κόσμος, ἄνθρωπος, κοινωνία κατὰ τὸν Μάξιμο Ὁμολογητή* (Athens, 1980); Felix Heinzer, *Gottes Sohn als Mensch: Die Struktur des Menschens Christi bei Maximus Confessor*, Paradosis 26 (Freiburg, 1980); and also Pierre Pirret, *Le Christ et la Trinité selon Maxime le Confesseur*, Théologie Historique 69 (Paris, 1983).

the otherness of such a vision. His fundamental concern is above all ascetic and therefore refreshingly practical. Hence, most prominent among the theological themes touched upon by Maximus is that of the *process* by which the vision of Christ transfigured may be attained, addressing the question: What relevance does the deification of the assumed human nature of the divine Logos have for our own lives? It is no coincidence, therefore, that it is by focussing on Maximus' treatment of the Transfiguration that the clearest and most succinct answer to this fundamentally significant question is to be found.

St. Maximus' vision of Christ transfigured is comprised of two discernible elements: firstly, that of the *deified humanity* of Christ, and secondly, that of the *noetic* manifestation of his *divinity*. Both elements are evident in his *scholion* on the Dionysian phrase, "his visible theophany" (τῆς ὁρατῆς αὐτοῦ θεοφανείας),[8] where Maximus maintains that *visible* refers to the vision of "his divine body" (τὸ θεῖον αὐτοῦ σῶμα) or "the animated flesh" (ἡ ἐμψυχωμένη σάρξ) of Christ, which bears witness to the Incarnation as an event of permanent significance. St. Maximus proceeds to contrast Christ's visible theophany to what he calls his *noetic* theophany, which refers to the *intelligible* revelation of the *divinity* of Christ, received, that is, through the intellect (νοῦς), and which corresponds to St. Dionysius' noetic illumination (τῆς νοητῆς αὐτοῦ φωτοδοσίας).[9]

In this present life, however, the *noetic* theophany of Christ can only be experienced in part. For as St. Maximus adds, this vision "will be communicated to us then in a more perfect way through the intellect" (ἥτις κατὰ νοῦν ἔσται ἡμῖν μεθεκτὴ τότε τελειοτέρως). Hence, "a more perfect" noetic perception of the divinity of Christ is possible only in the Age to Come, that is, only when the saints will have reached the Christlike state of

8. *De divinis nominibus* 1.4 (PG 3: 592BC), which is analysed in my doctoral dissertation, "The Transfiguration of Christ in Greek Patristic Literature: From Irenaeus of Lyons to Gregory Palamas" (D. Phil. diss., Oxford University, 1991), 156–160 (hereafter cited as Veniamin, "Transfiguration").
9. Ibid.

incorruption and immortality.[10] Here, St. Maximus' holistic view of the human person is more than evident. In a more explicit way than his predecessors, Maximus shows that the human intellect is not unaffected by man's corrupt and mortal nature, for while it is certainly true, as St. Cyril of Alexandria had previously demonstrated,[11] that it is the body which actually suffers corruption and which is consequently in need of resurrection,[12] it is also equally true that man's corrupt and mortal state affects the operation of the *whole* human person, the *soul*, that is, as well as the body. Hence, the intellect, understood as the deepest and most responsive part of the soul, shares in and so also suffers from the present corruptibility of the human body.

St. Maximus' emphasis here on the future incorruptibility of the intellect may perhaps be traced back to a reference to

10. *Scholia in de div. nom.* (PG 4:197BC); cf. ibid. (1168AB); and cf. Veniamin, "Transfiguration", 156–157. On the question of the partial character of the Taborian revelation see, for example, St John Chrysostom, *Adhortationes ad Theodorum lapsum* I.11 (SC 117:140,$57-64$), also, *Ad viduam iuniorum* 1.3 (SC 138:211–215), and *Homilia 56 in Matthaeum* 3 (553); and cf. St Cyril of Alexandria, *Commentarii in Matthaeum* 200, in "Lukas-Kommentare aus der griechischen Kirche," edited by J. Reuss, *Texte und Untersuchungen* 130 (1984), 218, who give the same reason as does Maximus for this, namely, the limiting effects of death and corruption. For further discussion, see Veniamin, "Transfiguration" 120–121.

11. See, for example: *Commentarii in Iohannem* 20:19, 20 (Pusey 3:1091e–1092c), and Veniamin, "Transfiguration" 123–124.

12. For previous discussions concerning incorruptibility in relation to its effect primarily on the human body, and with specific reference to the vision of the Transfiguration, see St Irenaeus of Lyons, *Adversus haereses* 4.20.2 (SC 100**:630,$49-52$), and ibid., 5 (638,^{111}–640,^{117}); cf. Origen, *Fragmenta in Lucam* 140 and 225 (GCS 49:283,^{12}–284,^{17} and 335,$^{1-4}$); St Methodius of Olympus, *De resurrectione* 1.25 (GCS 27:252,^{21}–253,^{1}), and ibid., 3.16 (413,$^{8-9}$); St John Chrysostom, *Adhortationes ad Theodorum lapsum* I.11 (SC 117:140,$57-64$), also, *Ad viduam iuniorum* 1.3 (SC 138:211–215), and *Homilia 56 in Matthaeum* 3 (553); and St Anastasius I Antioch, *Sermo I in transfigurationem domini* 2 (PG 89: 1365A). For a more detailed discussion of these sources, see Veniamin, "Transfiguration" 39–40, 52, 53–54, 99–100, and 165–166.

the Transfiguration in St. Gregory of Nyssa, who expressed the view that the *soul*, when united with Christ, shines with the same incorruptibility as was revealed on Tabor.[13] Corruptibility, then, even if only implicitly, is ascribed by St. Gregory *also* to the human soul *before* its deification.

St. Maximus' reference to the *noetic* theophany of Christ, therefore, should be understood primarily as a comment on the *present* state of man, on his corrupt and mortal nature, which obstructs his intended noctic participation in the Divine Life. Nevertheless, it should also be noted here that God, even in the *eschaton*, will always remain *beyond* the capacity of the created human intellect: For "God surpasses every power and operation of the intellect", says St. Maximus, and man's participation in divine glory leaves "no impression whatever on the intellect of the one attempting to comprehend".[14] The reason for this is "because by nature it is neither possible for the uncreated to be contained by creation, nor for the infinite to be apprehended by the finite" (ἐπειδὴ μηδὲ χωρεῖσθαι κτίσει τὸ ἄκτιστον πέφυκε, μηδὲ περινοεῖσθαι τοῖς πεπερασμένοις τὸ ἄπειρον).[15] Here, St. Maximus provides us with a succinct summary of patristic gnosiology. The fundamental reason for the ultimate *unintelligibility* of God is the existential difference between creation (ἡ κτίσις) and God, the uncreated (τὸ ἄκτιστον); between the finite (οἱ πεπερασμένοι) and the infinite (τὸ ἄπειρον). Yet, despite God's ultimate unintelligibility, man, even in this life, is also called to participate *intelligibly* or *noetically*, that is to say, *with his whole being*, in God. And it is for this reason that both elements, the *visible* and the *noetic*, are present in St. Maximus' appreciation of Christ transfigured.

In *Ambiguum X*, where St. Maximus brilliantly develops the theme of *diabasis* or *transit* from the material to the intelligible

---

13. On the theme of incorruptibility in relation to the soul, see *Canticum Canticorum, homilia* 11 (Jaeger 6: 329,[6-14]); and cf. *De virginitate* 11.5 (SC 119:392,[1]–394,[9]).
14. *Ambiguum X* (PG 91:1160BC).
15. Ibid. (PG 91:1168AB).

and divine,[16] he goes into greater detail than do his predecessors concerning the process by which the three disciples experienced the vision of Christ transfigured; and in so doing, he provides us with an illuminating glimpse into his profound understanding of the Christian life. He explains that by the vision of all those elements which constituted the Taborian scene – the unapproachable light shining from the face of Christ, his bright garments, and the appearance of Moses and Elias – the three disciples "passed from the flesh to the spirit" (ἀπὸ τῆς σαρκὸς εἰς τὸ πνεῦμα μετέβησαν),[17] that is to say, they were transported from the plane of the physical and human to that of the spiritual and divine.[18]

Such a vision, however, presupposes a preparatory phase, one in which spiritual labour (ἄσκησις) is required. Maximus says that the disciples were made worthy of seeing the Transfiguration "because of their diligence in virtue" (δι' ἀρετῆς ἐπιμέλειαν), and that they underwent a cleansing or purification of the spiritual and *bodily senses* (τῇ ἐναλλαγῇ τῶν κατ' αἴσθησιν ἐνεργειῶν), through the *action* of the Holy Spirit (ἣν αὐτοὺς τὸ πνεῦμα ἐνήργησε). The action of the Holy Spirit, then, effected a *change* in the operation of their senses – not a natural but a supranatural change, in which "the veils of the passions were removed from their noetic power" (περιελὸν τῆς ἐν αὐτοῖς νοερᾶς δυνάμεως τῶν παθῶν τὰ καλύμματα). Moreover, by this fundamental change in their noetic power, the three disciples were "taught the spiritual λόγοι[19] of the mysteries revealed to them" (τῶν παραδειχθέντων

---

16. For the wider *schema* of this *diabasis*, see P. Sherwood, *The Earlier Ambigua* 33–40.
17. Op. cit. (1125D).
18. Cf. *Quaestiones et dubia* 191 (CChr series graeca 10:133,[17-24]).
19. Λόγοι in Maximus are the pre-existent principles of all things (τοὺς γὰρ λόγους τῶν γεγονότων ἔχων πρὸ τῶν αἰώνων ὑφεστώσας), *Ambiguum* 7 (PG 91:1080A); and cf. ibid. (1077C), which manifest the "good wills" (ἀγαθὰ θελήματα) of the Logos, *Quaestiones ad Thalassium* 13 (CChr series graeca 7:95,[8]); and cf. St Dionysius in *de divinis nominibus* (PG 3:824C), *vis-à-vis* man and the cosmos. They both define and differentiate one created thing from another, and at the same time lead all things to union

αὐτοῖς μυστηρίων τοὺς πνευματικοὺς ἐκπαιδεύονται λόγους) at the Transfiguration.[20]

Elements of all three stages in St. Maximus' so-called *threefold schema* of the Christian life may be observed here.[21] Firstly, his

with the divine Logos Himself, *Quaestiones ad Thalassium* 2 (CChr series graeca 7:51,7-30), which is the "divine purpose" (θεῖος σκοπός), ibid. (CChr series graeca 7:51,[13]). In fact, the many λόγοι *are* the one Logos: οἱ πολλοὶ λόγοι ὁ εἷς λόγος ἐστὶ, καὶ εἷς οἱ πολλοί, *Ambiguum* 7 (PG 91:1081BC). For a detailed discussion of the divine λόγοι in Maximus, see Lars Thunberg, *Microcosm and Mediator* (Lund, 1965) 67–69, and esp. 76–84; and more recently, J. van Rossum's 'The λόγοι of creation and the divine energies in Maximus the Confessor and Gregory Palamas' *Studia Patristica* 27 (1993), 213–217.

Von Balthasar has pointed out that the divine λόγοι in Maximus are identifiable neither with the divine essence nor with created things, see Hans Urs von Balthasar, *Kosmische Liturgie* (Einsiedeln, 1961) 113; and Thunberg, *Microcosm* 81. Vladimir Lossky, in his *Essai sur la théologie mystique de l'Église d'orient* (Paris, 1944) 91, identifies the λόγοι in Maximus with the divine energies; and cf. A. Riou, *Le Monde et l'Église selon Maxime le Confesseur* (Paris, 1973) 60; also Thunberg, *Man and the Cosmos* (New York, 1985) 137, which although more popular, nevertheless presents his further thoughts on the subject; and see also the work of Joseph P. Farrell, "Free Choice in St Maximus the Confessor" (D. Phil. diss., Oxford University, 1987). However, P. Sherwood, in his *The Earlier Ambigua* 179–180, holds strong reservations concerning Lossky's position, but, it must be said, these are presented only in a very cursory manner. Clearly, a fuller investigation into this question is required. Sherwood himself suggests in his "Survey of Recent Work on St Maximus the Confessor," *Traditio* 20 (1964) 435–436, that research into the question of *participation*, especially with regard to deification, would do much to clarify this whole area in Maximus. This key question is the subject of Eric D. Perl's doctoral dissertation, entitled "Methexis: Creation, Incarnation, Deification in Saint Maximus Confessor" (Ph.D. diss., Yale, 1991). Regrettably, Perl's treatment of the subject is philosophical.

20. *Ambiguum X* (PG 91:1125D–1128A).

21. The terms most commonly used by Maximus to describe the three stages are: "the practical" (πρακτική), "knowledge" (γνῶσις), and "theology" (θεολογία). For a systematic presentation of the *three-fold schema* in St Maximus, see V. Lossky, *Vision de Dieu* (Neuchâtel, 1962) 107–112; W. Völker, *Maximus Confessor als Meister des geistlichen Lebens* (Wiesbaden, 1965) 174–370;

emphasis on the disciples' "diligence in virtue" as a prerequisite for the vision of Christ transfigured corresponds to the practical stage (πρακτική), which is characterized by the cleansing of the passions and the cultivation of the virtues through the Holy Spirit. Secondly, the revelation of the spiritual λόγοι corresponds to knowledge (γνῶσις), that is, to the illumination of the intellect, which enables the νοῦς to receive the gift of spiritual contemplation (πνευματικὴ θεωρία).[22] The vision of Christ transfigured, broadly speaking, corresponds then to *spiritual contemplation*, which constitutes the first phase of the third and highest stage, that of theology (θεολογία), through which the Christian passes to the superior degree of mystical union with the Logos.[23]

Elsewhere, St. Maximus describes the progress towards perfection in terms of the eight days referred to in Luke 9:28. Man, he says, is called to strive so as to overcome the first of the eight days, which signifies man's impassioned, subnatural (παρὰ φύσιν) condition. Then he is required to surpass the six days, by which St. Maximus understands nature (τὴν φύσιν), which corresponds to man's natural state of being. Subsequently, man arrives at the supranatural state (καὶ γενέσθαι ἐν τῇ ὑπὲρ φύσιν), represented by the eighth day (ἥτις ἐστὶν ὀγδόη), which lies beyond the confines of time (ὑπερθετικὴ γὰρ τοῦ χρόνου αὕτη), and which also characterizes the future state (καὶ τὴν μέλλουσαν χαρακτηρίζει κατάστασιν).[24] Here we have yet another interconnected triad, which is employed by Maximus for paedogogical purposes, but which, though overlapping in certain respects with the previous one, does not correspond exactly with it. This too, however, is a description of the process by which the three disciples attained to the vision of the Transfiguration.

In his *Capita theologica et oeconomica*, St. Maximus refers to the two *forms* in which Christ is revealed to those who study the Holy

L. Thunberg, *Microcosm and Mediator* (Lund, 1965) 352–396; G. V. Florovsky, *Византийские Отцы* v–viii [The Byzantine Fathers of the Fifth to the Eighth Centuries] (Paris, 1972) 219ff.

22. Cf. op. cit. (1156AB).
23. Ibid. (1125D–1128A).
24. *Quaestiones et dubia* 191 (CChr series graeca 10:133,[17-24]).

Scriptures with great care. First, he speaks of Christ's common and more public form (κοινὴν καὶ δημωδεστέραν μορφὴν), by which he means the Incarnation. The Incarnation, however, to which St. Maximus applies Isa 53:2 – "and we saw him, but he had no form nor beauty" (καὶ εἴδομεν αὐτὸν, καὶ οὐκ εἶχεν εἶδος οὐδὲ κάλλος) – is a theophany which was not restricted to a particular group of people, but one which was openly seen by many (καὶ οὐκ ὀλίγοις θεατὴν). Nor is the experience of the Incarnation limited to a particular point in history; for in the thought of St. Maximus, this manifestation is appropriate "always and in everyone",[25] to those who are being initiated (τοῖς εἰσαγωμένοις ἁρμόδιος) into the divine mystery. St. Maximus also adds that it is on "the image of the first Parousia of the Lord that the word of the Gospel is established", and that this image or icon of the Incarnation actually purifies, through sufferings (διὰ παθημάτων), those whom St. Maximus terms the practical or active men (οἱ πρακτικοί). Here, practical or active men are those who have reached the first stage of perfection (πρακτική), and who are therefore engaged in the struggle for the acquisition and cultivation of virtue. Also significant is the term image (εἰκών), which is used in a similar way to the terms *symbol* and *type*, and which thus signifies much more than a mere *mental image* of the Incarnation. St. Maximus uses εἰκών in order to convey the attainability of the personal experience of Christ Incarnate.

In contrast to his more public manifestation, however, St. Maximus refers to a more secret form (κρυφιωτέρα μορφή) in which Christ is also revealed, such as was disclosed to the three disciples at the Transfiguration, and to which he applies the verse, "Thou art more beautiful than the sons of men" (ὡραῖος κάλλει παρὰ τοὺς υἱοὺς τῶν ἀνθρώπων, Ps 44:2). This, too, is a vision of Christ which is not exclusive to the three disciples on Tabor, but one which is granted to all those who, throughout the ages, have excelled in virtue.[26] Even so, relatively few in this life can attain

---

25. *Ambiguum* 7 (PG 91:1084CD).
26. *Quaestiones et dubia* 190 (*CCSG* 10:131,[6-12]).

to it (ὀλίγοις ἐφικτήν).[27] For this reason, the *form* of this second manifestation is seen primarily as a prefiguration (προδιατύπωσις) of the second and glorious Parousia. This vision is one "by which the Spirit is perceived by the intellect" (ἐφ' ἧς τὸ πνεῦμα νοεῖται), and which, through wisdom (διὰ σοφίας), transfigures towards deification (πρὸς θέωσιν) those whom St. Maximus calls gnostic men (γνωστικοί). It is important to note here that the place of knowledge (γνῶσις) and the gnostic men in Maximus contrasts significantly with that of *gnosis* and the gnostic man in the thought of Clement of Alexandria, where perfect *gnosis* is put forward as the highest state of perfection, and the state to which his true gnostic man must attain;[28] whereas in St. Maximus knowledge corresponds to the intermediate stage in his *schema* of man's progress towards deification.

Interestingly, Maximus also adds that the gnostic men experience the Transfiguration of the Word *within* themselves: "and with the Transfiguration of the Word within them (ἐν αὐτοῖς), they will see with an unveiled face the glory of the Lord mirrored within themselves" (ἀνακεκαλυμμένῳ προσώπῳ τὴν δόξαν κυρίου κατοπτριζομένους, cf. 2 Cor 3:18).[29] Here, the Transfiguration is referred to as an esoteric or inner vision of Christ in glory. Maximus makes no distinction, however, between the vision of the Transfiguration of Christ as experienced by the Apostles on Tabor and the Transfiguration as experienced by the gnostic men in the mirror of the soul.[30] Nevertheless, with the vision of the

---

27. *Capita theologica et oeconomica* II.13 (PG 90:1129C–1132A).
28. See, for example: *Stromateis* 4.22 (GCS 52:308), where Clement suggests that the true gnostic, given a hypothetical choice between knowledge of God and eternal Salvation, would prefer the knowledge of God.
29. *Capita theologica et oeconomica* I.97 (PG 90:1121C–1124A); and cf. ibid., II. 14 (1132A); and cf. also St Gregory of Nyssa, *De occursu domini* (PG 46:1156D).
30. The theme of the contemplation of the Image of God reflected in the mirror of the soul is one which had been developed by St Gregory of Nyssa. For examples of this in St Gregory, see *De virginitate* 11.5 (SC 119:392,[1]–394,[9]); *Canticum Canticorum, homilia IV* (Jaeger 6:103,[12]–104,[10]);

Transfiguration, the intellect is said to receive illumination, that is, it receives knowledge of God (γνῶσις Θεοῦ), and is thereby enabled to advance still further and attain to what St. Maximus calls spiritual contemplation (πνευματικὴ θεωρία).[31]

Even though very few in this life may attain to the vision of Christ transfigured, St. Maximus stresses that such a vision is by no means restricted to the three disciples. Since the word of God cannot be confined to one particular point in time, τινές in Matt 16:28 must also refer to all those who, down the ages, have excelled in virtue. Similarly, the words "will not taste of death" (οὐ μὴ γεύσονται θανάτου), once again referring in the first instance to the Apostles, who even before their natural death (φυσικὸς θάνατος) saw on Tabor the image (εἰκών) of the future brightness of the saints, also refer to that death, says Maximus, which all who are equal to the Apostles in virtue will experience, namely, that death which is experienced when one advances beyond the stage of natural contemplation. For by leaving behind all things caused (πάντα τὰ αἰτιατὰ καταλιπών), one arrives, through theological apophaticism (διὰ τῆς θεολογικῆς ἀποφάσεως), to the Cause (καὶ εἰς τὸν αἴτιον ἐλθών). Such as these, concludes St. Maximus, "will not taste of death", until the transfigured Lord has revealed himself to them, not cataphatically – no longer, that is, through his creation – but directly, in the unapproachable character of his hidden divinity, which is in accordance with apophatic theology.[32]

Furthermore, Maximus maintains that Christ's "coming in the glory of the Father with his angels" (ἔρχεσθαι ἐν τῇ δόξῃ τοῦ πατρὸς αὐτοῦ μετὰ τῶν ἀγγέλων αὐτοῦ, Matt 16:27) also means that God the Word appears transfigured to the worthy (τοῖς ἀξίοις) at each step of the way towards perfection. And to this he also adds that the worthy will perceive the glory contained in the *logoi* of the Law and prophets at a level of intensity proportionate to their stage of progress.[33]

---

ibid. *homilia XV* (440,7-10); and *De opificio hominis* (PG 44:161C–164A).
31. *Ambiguum X* (PG 91:1156AB).
32. *Quaestiones et dubia* 190 (CCSG 10:131,1–132,32).
33. *Capita theologica et oeconomica* II.15 (PG 90:1132AB).

Moreover, St. Maximus elaborates on the soteriological implications of the words: "the Son of man coming in his glory" (cf. Matt 16:28, which reads, ἐρχόμενον ἐν τῇ βασιλείᾳ αὐτοῦ), and "before they see that the Kingdom of God has come with power" (ἕως ἂν ἴδωσιν τὴν βασιλείαν τοῦ Θεοῦ ἐληλυθυῖαν ἐν δυνάμει, Mark 9:1). Firstly, he makes it clear that Christ, as the Son of God, "always possessed the glory" (ἀεὶ τὴν δόξαν κέκτηται) proper to his divine status. Therefore, "coming in his glory", as the verse clearly states, refers specifically to Christ as "the Son of man", and thus to the glorification of his assumed humanity (τὴν προσληφθεῖσαν ἀνθρωπότητα). Therefore, just as Christ glorified his assumed humanity on Tabor, being in the passible body (ἐν τῷ παθητῷ σώματι ὤν), so too will we in the Resurrection enjoy the transformation into incorruption of our body. And St. Maximus also adds that the phrase "come with power" is an allusion to the fact that "the incorruptible and eternal Kingdom hoped for by the saints is not yet realized". Even more important here, however, is St. Maximus' implicit identification of the Kingdom of God with his glory.[34]

In reference to the choice of the three disciples, St. Maximus also explains that not all men "stand before" the Lord in the same way. He draws a distinction between those who are being initiated (τοῖς μὲν εἰσαγωμένοις) and those who are capable of following him up to the high mount of the Transfiguration (τοῖς δὲ δυναμένοις ἀκολουθῆσαι αὐτῷ ἐπὶ τὸ ὑψηλὸν ἀναβαίνοντι τῆς αὐτοῦ μεταμορφώσεως ὄρος). The former experience Christ in the form of a servant (ἐν δούλου μορφῇ, cf. Phil 2:7); while the latter experience him in the form of God (ἐν μορφῇ Θεοῦ, cf. Phil 2:6). Maximus also states the following:

It is possible, then, that the Lord does not appear in the same way to all who are with him, but to some in one way, and to others in another, clearly varying the contemplation according to the measure of faith in each one (κατὰ τὸ μέτρον τῆς ἐν ἑκάστῳ πίστεως δηλονότι ποικίλλων τὴν θεωρίαν).[35]

---

34. *Quaestiones et dubia* 190 (*CCSG* 10:132,33-45).
35. *Capita theologica et oeconomica* II.13 (PG 90:1129C–1132A).

Notice that St. Maximus draws here on Origen. In Origen, however, the selection of the three Apostles is the result of their deeper perception of the Person of Christ as the divine Logos. Maximus' subtle shift of emphasis here from the criterion of *knowledge* to that of *faith* cleverly eliminates the possible intellectualistic connotations of Origen's interpretation, and is therefore essentially an attempt to correct Origen's view rather than an effort to endorse it.[36]

With regard to the divine Light shining from the face of Christ, it has already been noted that St. Maximus characterizes it as both unapproachable (ἀπρόσιτον)[37] and intelligible (νοητόν).[38] In further reference to the vision of the Transfiguration Light, St. Maximus says the following:

They learned mystically that the most blessed radiance (πανόλβιον αἴγλην) of his countenance brilliantly flashing forth (ἀκτινοφανῶς ἐκλάμπουσαν), and overcoming every operation of the eyes, is the symbol of his divinity which surpasses intellect and sense and essence and knowledge (τῆς ὑπὲρ νοῦν καὶ αἴσθησιν καὶ οὐσίαν καὶ γνῶσιν θεότητος αὐτοῦ σύμβολον εἶναι μυστικῶς ἐδιδάσκοντο)...[39]

Here, St. Maximus states that the disciples learned mystically (μυστικῶς ἐδιδάσκοντο) that the radiance emanating from the face of Christ is the symbol of his divinity (θεότητος αὐτοῦ σύμβολον εἶναι), which "surpasses intellect and sense and essence and knowledge" (ὑπὲρ νοῦν καὶ αἴσθησιν καὶ οὐσίαν καὶ γνῶσιν). This in St. Maximus is what is meant by the way of theological apophaticism (θεολογικῆς ἀποφάσεως) – theology *par excellence*.[40] Significant here is the use of the term *symbol*. In Maximus the term *symbol* denotes the manifestation of a hidden divine reality – hidden, because although revealed, it never ceases to remain a

---

36. Cf. *Commentarius in Matthaeum* 12.37 (GCS 40:152,[15]–154,9), *Contra Celsum* 6.77 (SC 147:372,[14-35]); and also 2.64 (SC 132:434,[1-14]); and see Veniamin, "Transfiguration" 48–49.
37. *Ambiguum X* (PG 91:1125D–1128A).
38. For example, see ibid. (PG 91:1156AB): θεὸς ὁ νοητὸς τῆς δικαιοσύνης ἥλιος ἀνατέλλων τῷ νῷ.
39. Ibid. (PG 91:1128AB).
40. See ibid. (1128B).

mystery.[41] The purpose of its revelation is always *soteriological*, and belongs therefore to the *divine economy*. The divinity of Christ, then, revealed on Tabor as *light* which "surpasses intellect and sense and essence and knowledge", will always remain beyond the comprehension of man, will always remain a mystery. Maximus also states:

> It was said earlier, then, that on the mountain the thrice blessed Apostles were mystically led by the radiant brightness of the Lord's face (in a way which is both ineffable and unknowable), towards the power and glory of God, which is completely incomprehensible to all beings (πᾶσι καθόλου τοῖς οὖσιν ἄληπτον); learning that the light of the invisible secret which appeared to the sense is a symbol (τῆς ἀφανοῦς κρυφιότητος τὸ φανὲν αὐτοῖς πρὸς τὴν αἴσθησιν φῶς σύμβολον εἶναι μανθάνοντες). For just as here the ray (ἀκτὶς) of the light which appeared overcame the power of the eyes, remaining uncontainable to them (ἀχώρητος αὐτοῖς διαμένουσα), so there also God surpasses every power and operation of the intellect (οὕτω κἀκεῖ Θεὸς πᾶσαν νοὸς δύναμιν ὑπερβαίνει καὶ ἐνέργειαν), leaving no impression whatsoever on the intellect attempting to comprehend (οὐδ᾽ ὅλως ἐν τῷ νοεῖσθαι τῷ νοεῖν πειρωμένῳ τὸν οἱονοῦν τύπον ἀφείς).[42]

The "light of the invisible secret" is of course a description of the divinity of Christ. Again, its manifestation is described by the term *symbol*. But even though Maximus affirms yet again the apophatic nature of its manifestation, he also asserts quite categorically that it "appeared to the sense". Hence, though ultimately surpassing "every power and operation of the intellect", the divine Light of Christ is nevertheless perceptible to man, even if only in an imperfect manner, and this is openly demonstrated in the case of the three Apostles, who actually experienced it on Tabor.

---

41. Of course, the mystery *par excellence* is the Incarnation itself. St Maximus maintains that Christ, in becoming man, in assuming fully the whole of our created nature, has become "the type and symbol for Himself", ibid. (1165D–1168A). Walther Völker, *Maximus Confessor als Meister des geistlichen Lebens* (Wiesbaden, 1965) 272–273 n. 5, also makes the pertinent point that "das σύμβολον, der τύπος ist immer durch die ποικιλία charakterisiert, die ἀλήθεια durch die ἁπλότης.

42. *Ambiguum X* (PG 91:1160BC).

In another passage, St. Maximus becomes more explicit on precisely why the divine Light of Christ is, and must always remain, a mystery. He writes:

> Thus the light of the face of the Lord which surpassed the human beatitude, appeared to the Apostles in accordance with apophatic mystical theology, according to which the blessed and holy Divinity is in essence above the ineffable and beyond the unknowable and infinitely transcendent of every infinity (ἡ μακαρία καὶ ἁγία θεότης κατ' οὐσίαν ἐστὶν ὑπεράρρητος καὶ ὑπεράγνωστος καὶ πάσης ἀπειρίας ἀπειράκις ἐξῃρημένη), having left them no trace of comprehension whatsoever – not even a faint one – after its manifestation, and not disclosing to any being the apprehension of by what manner or even quantity the same is both monad and triad; for by nature it is neither possible for the uncreated to be contained by creation, nor for the infinite to be apprehended by the finite (ἐπειδὴ μηδὲ χωρεῖσθαι κτίσει τὸ ἄκτιστον πέφυκε, μηδὲ περινοεῖσθαι τοῖς πεπερασμένοις τὸ ἄπειρον).[43]

The Light of the Transfiguration is identified here with the Divinity. And "in accordance with apophatic mystical theology", though the *uncreated* Light of Christ's divinity may be seen or perceived by the senses, in essence it will always remain incomprehensible to and beyond the capacity of the *created* human intellect. Its incomprehensibility, however, also resides in the mystery of the revelation of the blessed and holy Divinity (ἡ μακαρία καὶ ἁγία θεότης) as both *monad* and *triad* (ἡ αὐτὴ καὶ μονάς ἐστι καὶ τριάς). The Light of Christ, therefore, is the very same *Triune* Light of the Holy Trinity. And for this reason the Transfiguration Light itself is also a *Trinitarian* revelation.

This leads us on to the question of the significance of the bright garments of Christ. St. Maximus' treatment of the subject may be divided into two main themes. Firstly, the bright garments are seen as representing the spiritual *logoi* contained in Scripture and in creation; and secondly, they also reveal the two *ways* of theology, namely, the affirmative or *cataphatic* way and the negative or *apophatic* way.

---

43. Ibid. (1168AB).

Firstly, then, in the vision of Christ transfigured the Apostles were enabled to see that the bright garments of the Lord were a *symbol* of the words of Holy Scripture. Hence, their shining signifies the clearer, deeper meaning which the Old Dispensation acquired on Tabor: openly revealing the divine Logos as the one hidden behind and contained within the words of the Old Testament. Through the vision of the bright garments, therefore, the Apostles received the correct knowledge of God and, St. Maximus adds (indicating the close correlation between correct knowledge and the Christian life), they were thereby liberated from the inclination towards the world and the flesh.

In addition to this, however, the vision was also a *symbol* of the different kinds (διαφόρων εἰδῶν) of created things, all of which, when viewed spiritually and not simply according to the senses, draw us near to the Logos himself, who is their Creator.[44] This is what St. Maximus refers to as the natural contemplation of beings (φυσικὴ θεωρία τῶν ὄντων).[45] He maintains that both *symbols* are fitting to the revelation of the Logos, for in the words of Scripture, as also in the different forms of creation, the Logos is present, at one and the same time revealed and yet concealed: concealed, to those who are unworthy of coming into contact with such things as cannot be contained or comprehended; and revealed as Creator (κτίστης), Craftsman (δημιουργός) and Artificer (τεχνίτης) to those who have been cleansed of the passions.[46]

Moreover, Maximus identifies these two forms of revelation as laws, the natural (φυσικός) and the written (γραπτός), which, he says, are equal in value (ἰσότιμοι) to each other, implying thereby that the words of Scripture themselves would be totally incomprehensible outside the natural context of the created order. Significantly, however, both forms of revelation may be attained to *only through the Holy Spirit*.[47] The white garments reveal the *logoi* in Scripture and in created things, and the Logos is manifested analogously (ἀναλόγως ἐκφαίνεται) in the words of Holy Scripture, "by the power of the

44. Ibid. (1128BC).
45. Ibid. (1128CD).
46. Ibid. (1128BC).
47. Ibid. (1128CD).

Spirit"; and in created things, also "according to the Spirit", and, Maximus adds, through wisdom and knowledge.[48]

However, St. Maximus later points out that the Christian should strive to rise beyond even the natural contemplation of the bright garments of the Lord, that is to say, beyond the sensible, even beyond the divine and lofty concepts or meanings (νοήματα) contained in Scripture and the visible creation; and that we should actively strive to become rational or logical beings (λογικοί), moving through the Logos towards the Logos (διὰ λόγου πρὸς λόγον). At this point, Maximus alludes to the Egyptian woman, who, he says, in mistaking Joseph's speech as that of a lover, seized his garments (cf. Gen 39:11–18), in other words, she remained on the simple level of the sensible. This point is further emphasized by another Scriptural example, that of Mary Magdalene's vision of the resurrected Christ. St. Maximus explains that the reason why St. Mary was not allowed to touch the Lord at that time was because of her false perception of him, a perception which remained on the plane of the purely physical and human; wrongly apprehending the Creator, who had willingly subjected himself to birth and corruption, as being nothing beyond the senses (μηδὲν ὑπὲρ τὴν αἴσθησιν νομίζουσαν). He says that the way towards the deeper perception of the garments of the Logos, that is, the way by which the words of Scripture and the visible creation are illuminated in a manner befitting the Logos, is attained through superior contemplation (διὰ τῆς ὑψηλῆς θεωρίας), by that very same contemplation which the Apostles experienced on the mount of the Transfiguration. By this form of contemplation, says Maximus, and because of goodness (δι' ἀγαθότητα), one is enabled to recognize the *body* as representing *spiritual realities* and the *garments* as representing *sensible realities*.[49]

A similar contrast is made between the Transfiguration *Light* and the *garments* of Christ. St. Maximus says that they too are a joint indication (συνένδειξις), a manifestation of the true *logoi* of things spiritual or intelligible (τὰ νοητά) – also described here as

---
48. Ibid. (1160CD).
49. Ibid. (1132B–1133A).

things which surround him (τὴν περὶ αὐτὸν); and of things sensible (τὰ αἰσθητά) – also described as things which come after him (τὴν τῶν μετ' αὐτὸν).⁵⁰ Just as the eye without light cannot perceive sensible things, neither can the intellect without knowledge of God (γνώσεως Θεοῦ) receive spiritual contemplation.

Secondly, the Transfiguration teaches us mystically of the two ways of theology: the *apophatic* and the *cataphatic*. St. Maximus says that we are led to the apophatic and cataphatic knowledge both of God (περὶ Θεοῦ) and of things divine (περὶ τῶν θείων) through the *symbols* which are by nature akin to us (διὰ τῶν προσφυῶν ἡμῖν συμβόλων). It is, he adds, "through a respectful understanding of those things which exist" (δι' εὐσεβοῦς τῶν ὄντων κατανοήσεως) that the *logoi* of both theological ways are revealed. Any thing which pertains to the apophatic way is a *symbol* which *goes beyond the senses* (πᾶν τὸ ὑπὲρ αἴσθησιν σύμβολον εἶναι διδάσκουσα). All things which pertain to the second way, the cataphatic, may be grouped together as great deeds or things which God has done (μεγαλουργήματα), things that is, which are *sensible* (κατ' αἴσθησιν), and which are therefore perceptible to the human senses. St. Maximus then goes on to say that we can only believe in those things which go beyond sense, reason and intellect, and that even to attempt to understand them would be irreverent (ἀσεβές). As regards those things which are comprehensible, we may attempt to understand them, as far as it is possible for us to do so (ὡς ἡμῖν δυνατὸν), but only in a subtle way (ἰσχνῶς), through the apprehension of the images of the things of which we know him to be both Maker and Cause.⁵¹

Characteristically, St. Maximus' thought turns first to the Divine Person of Christ himself. Both ways of theology are to be found in the *theanthropos*, who as perfect God and perfect man contains within himself both the hidden mystery (κρυφιόμυστος) of his divinity and the theurgy (θεουργία), divine works or actions which are made manifest to men *par excellence* through his flesh.⁵²

---

50. Ibid. (1156AB).
51. Ibid. (1165BC).
52. Ibid. (1165D–1168A).

As already indicated, the way of apophatic theology is represented at the Transfiguration primarily by the Light of the face of Christ, which defeated the natural capacity of the Apostles. St. Maximus also refers to the apophatic way as mystical theology (μυστικὴ θεολογία), which discloses the positive character of the apophatic way, for in Maximus this is the way which concerns direct contact with the divinity itself. As a result of this coming into contact with the living God, one comes to know that "the blessed and holy divinity is in essence above the ineffable and beyond the unknowable and infinitely transcendent of every infinity".[53] Maximus' phraseology is clearly influenced here by the Areopagite.[54] The divinity of Christ, revealed on Tabor as light, is simply beyond the capacity not only of the human, but also of every infinity (καὶ πάσης ἀπειρίας), by which Maximus includes every created being. In continuing, Maximus' position becomes even clearer. Comprehension of the divinity is existentially impossible: "for by nature it is neither possible for the uncreated to be contained by creation, nor for the infinite to be apprehended by the finite" (ἐπειδὴ μηδὲ χωρεῖσθαι κτίσει τὸ ἄκτιστον πέφυκε, μηδὲ περινοεῖσθαι τοῖς πεπερασμένοις τὸ ἄπειρον).[55] The light shining from the face of Christ, therefore, represents the *apophatic* aspect of theology, because it is a revelation of the hidden mystery – the divinity of Christ.

The way of cataphatic theology, however, which refers to *theurgy*, is further divided by St. Maximus into three *ways* (τρόποι), namely, those of divine action (ἐνέργεια), providence (πρόνοια), and judgement (κρίσις). He states that on Tabor divine *action* is revealed in the shining bright garments of the Lord, for they represent the beauty and size of all created things which exist *around* the Creator (τὴν περὶ τοῦ δημιουργὸν εἶναι); thus, they are seen as an initiation into the mystery of the Logos as *Creator* of all things.[56] The appearance of Moses, on the other hand, signifies

53. Ibid. (1168AB).
54. Compare, for example, the kind of language used by St Dionysius in *De divinis nominibus* 1.4 (PG 3: 592BC).
55. Op. cit. (1168AB).
56. Ibid. (1168B).

the *providence* of God, evident in the Law by which the Israelites were guided from an erroneous understanding of things divine (identified by them with things material, corruptible and bodily – compare, for example, Exod 32:1–6 and 17–26), towards the positive affirmation of God as immaterial and incorporeal.[57] Also, the appearance of Elias represents the way of divine *judgement*, for it is through him that God in both word and deed punished those worthy of punishment, and dealt accordingly with the virtuous and the wicked (3 Kgs 16:29ff). Hence, through the appearance of Elias, the Logos is also revealed as Judge.[58] Here, then, St. Maximus presents us with yet another *threefold schema* (ἐνέργεια, πρόνοια, κρίσις), this time, however, in reference to the mystery of *theurgy*, or, more specifically, the mystery of the way in which God *operates* in the world – the cataphatic way.

Concerning the subject of conversation between Christ and Moses and Elias, St. Maximus suggests that it was not simply about Christ's *exodus* (cf. Luke 9:31). For the two prophets were instructed not only of the departure of Christ as foretold in the Law and the prophets, but also, perhaps, of the absolute incomprehensibility of the object (τὸ πέρας) of God's ineffable Counsel and also the divine economies which originate from it. Exceptions to the apophatic aspect in God's Counsel and economies, however, are those aspects of the divine economy – namely, his great Providence and Judgement – by which everything is driven in good order (εὐτάκτως) towards the end (τέλος) known only to God and his saints. St. Maximus adds that the saints truly know what will be, because by cleansing their soul through the virtues, and directing the inclination of their being towards things divine (τὰ θεῖα) – by which the entire visible creation comes together by nature – they have become responsive to the harmonious state of nature to such a degree that they are able, as it were, to *hear* the signs of the end of its present harmony (εὐκοσμία) as clearly as if they were being shouted out loud.[59]

---

57. Ibid. (1168C).
58. Ibid. (1168CD).
59. Ibid. (1169AB).

With regard to the significance of the words uttered by St. Peter (Matt 17:3–4; Mark 9:4–5; Luke 9:30 and 33), it is interesting that Maximus refrains from accusing him of confusing the Master with his servants or, even more seriously, of being under the influence of the devil.[60] On the contrary, St. Peter's words are perceived positively by St. Maximus as being full of allegorical significance. Hence, the three tabernacles represent the three states of Salvation (τὰς τρεῖς ἕξεις τῆς σωτηρίας). More specifically, the first tabernacle represents the practical state (πρακτική), which requires courage (ἀνδρεία) and prudence (σωφροσύνη), and of which Elias is the *type*; the second, represents that righteousness (δικαιοσύνη) which pertains to the state of natural contemplation (φυσικὴ θεωρία), and which was proclaimed through Moses; and the third tabernacle represents that pure perfection according to wisdom (τῆς κατὰ τὴν φρόνησιν ἀκραιφνοῦς τελειότητος), also referred to as theology (θεολογία), which of course may be seen in the Person of the Lord himself.[61] It should be added, however, that the gradation here applies more to the different states of Salvation than to a difference in the status of Christ and the two prophets.

Thus, for St. Maximus the focal point in the Transfiguration of Christ is the Person of the divine Logos; openly revealed on Tabor as the *alpha* and *omega* of the Old and New Dispensations, the origin and purpose of all creation. In his keen focus on the revelation of the Logos St. Maximus resembles the Apologists of the second and third centuries. Also important to note is that despite his intricate thought and convoluted style, Maximus' interest in the Transfiguration is far from being merely an intellectual exercise in speculative theology. This is especially evident in his broaching of the very concrete and practical question of the way in which the vision of Christ transfigured may be experienced by the faithful. Perhaps the most important doctrinal element in his treatment

60. Once again this interpretation is most probably in response to the negative conclusions to which Origen arrives concerning St Peter's words in his *Commentarius in Matthaeum* 12.40 (159–160); and in his *Fragmenta in Lucam* 146 (GCS 49:285).

61. *Capita theologica et oeconomica* II.16 (PG 90:1132BC); and cf. *Quaestiones et dubia* 192 (CCSG 10:134, ^{1}–135,^{16}).

of the Transfiguration, however, is St. Maximus' evaluation of the nature of the Taborian Light. Woven into his *scholia* on the Light of the Transfiguration is a recapitulation of all that has been said on the subject by his predecessors. He identifies the Light of Tabor explicitly with the divinity of Christ, and also points to the corollary to this assertion, namely, that as such it must also be both *uncreated* and beyond all comprehension. The revelatory paradox is that despite its uncreated nature and incomprehensibility, and despite also its transcending of every "intellect and sense and essence and knowledge", the Light of Tabor is nevertheless perceptible to the human senses. And finally, as a manifestation of divinity, the Light of Tabor is *in itself* a Trinitarian revelation.

THE SPIRITUAL FATHER AND CHILD RELATIONSHIP IN ST SYMEON THE NEW THEOLOGIAN

It would be difficult to overestimate the importance of the rôle of the Spiritual Father in the life of the Christian according to St Symeon the New Theologian (949 – 1022). The especial relationship which he formed at the tender age of fourteen with St Symeon the Studite, known also as Symeon 'the Devout' (ὁ εὐλαβής), undeniably ranks as one of the two most important events in the life of the New Theologian – the other being his vision of the Divine Light. These two events shaped his entire life and theological vision. Indeed, the centrality of an experienced guide in the Lord is clearly indicated in Symeon's own description of his very first experience of the Divine Light, in which he also saw his Spiritual Father.[1]

It is significant, therefore, that both of these elements – the Spiritual Father and the Divine Light – are found intertwined in the New Theologian's treatment of the Transfiguration of Christ,[2] where Symeon's chief concern is the practical question of how the Christian may ascend to the vision of Christ transfigured and contemplate the Light of His divine glory.[3]

Like SS Maximus the Confessor[4] and Andrew of Crete[5] before him, St Symeon also stresses the importance of the worthiness of the Christian as a prerequisite for the vision of the Transfiguration; but in so doing he also asks the following revealing rhetorical question:

How many have ascended and are even now ascending the Taborian mount, and have not at all seen the transfigured Lord, not because Jesus the Christ is not certainly present, for He is present, but because they are not worthy to be contemplators of His divinity?[6]

Thus, the vision of Christ transfigured is by no means granted to all Christians. Symeon adds elsewhere that this is often the case, even after great ascetic effort has been exerted on their part.[7] The reason for this, he says, is not because Christ does not exist ceaselessly transfigured in divine glory, but simply because not all are worthy to be contemplators of it. How, then, may we become 'worthy to be contemplators of His divinity'?

In order for the Christian to share in the very same vision of Christ that was granted to the three disciples on Tabor, it is first necessary to renounce the world (κόσμον ἅπαντα νόμισον καταλεῖψαι) and lay aside all cares for the things of the world;[8] and then to practice obedience, by placing one's self under the direction of a Spiritual Father, that is to say, under the guidance of one who is experienced in 'the things pertaining to the difficult work of virtue and the ascetic art' (τὰ τῆς ἀρετῆς καὶ τῆς ἀσκητικῆς τέχνης τὴν δυσκατόρθωτον ἐργασίαν),[9] thereby cutting off or sacrificing one's own will. Such a man, says Symeon, is found by persistently *beseeching* God to guide us to one capable of shepherding us well. And once found, he should be obeyed, just as though he were God Himself, even when his advice seems harmful to us and appears to go against our better judgment.[10] Indeed, adds Symeon, even when the disciple is inspired to remain with the Spiritual Father that he already has – envisaging, perhaps, a situation where one's Spiritual Father seems less experienced than others –, absolute and perfect obedience is again required of him. For, as he continues, it is 'better to be called a disciple of a disciple and not to live according to the fashion of one's own style of life, thereby gathering up the unprofitable fruits of one's own will' (κρεῖσσον γὰρ μαθητὴν μαθητοῦ ὀνομάζεσθαι καὶ μὴ ἰδιορρύθμως βιοῦν καὶ τρυγᾶν ἀνωφελεῖς καρποὺς τοῦ ἰδίου θελήματος). Thus, by sacrificing his own will, by not yielding to vainglory (κενοδοξία), sluggishness (ὀκνηρία) or apathy (ῥαθυμία), and by eagerly doing those things which he is advised, the disciple might, says Symeon, be saved.[11]

Especially worthy of note here is the fact that salvation for Symeon, though unequivocally the primary goal and purpose of the Christian life, is always viewed within the context of *the desire to seek after the vision of the light of God*. (There is, however, a subtle but vitally important distinction to be made between *desiring* to see Christ in glory and *expecting* to see Him thus. The former is regarded as a healthy spiritual state, while the latter lays one open to delusion of all kinds.) The *desire* for this vision, then, is a fundamental characteristic of the Christian's very mode of existence (τρόπος ὑπάρξεως); and consequently, the lack of such a desire is seen as unforgivable, since, according to St Symeon, it reveals one's spiritual condition as 'dead or blind or sick or paralysed and separated from the service of Christ'.[12]

In direct reference to obedience to one's Spiritual Father *vis-à-vis* the vision of the divine Light of Christ, St Symeon also adds the following:

If he leads you to the mountain, ascend eagerly, for you will there contemplate, I know well, Christ transfigured and shining brighter than the sun with the light of His divinity, and perhaps you will fall down unable to endure things which you have never seen (μὴ φέρων ὁρᾶν ἃ οὐδέποτε τεθέασαι), and you will hear from on high the Paternal voice, and see the overshadowing Cloud, and the Prophets standing in attendance and confirming Him to be the God and Lord of the living and the dead (cf. Matt. 22:32; Mark 12:27; and Luke 20:38).[13]

Of particular interest here is St Symeon's phrase, 'I know well' (εὖ οἶδα), which denotes that this is a vision of which he has had first hand experience. The New Theologian's appeal to personal experience is also reminiscent, *inter alios*, of the other two Theologians of the Church: John the Evangelist (as in for example, John 1:14: "and we beheld his glory, the glory as of the only begotten of the Father", 1 John 1:1–3, but also *passim* throughout his Gospel, Epistles and the Book of Revelation); and St Gregory of Nazianzus, in his *First Theological Oration*,[14] where we find that in addition to Scripture and Tradition, he appeals to his own direct personal experience as verification of the truth of both Scripture and Tradition, which are themselves based on *theoria* (θεωρία) – the vision of Christ in glory. Symeon thus appeals to Scripture and also to the Fathers, and although it is true to say that he only rarely identifies them by name, it is nevertheless clear that Symeon had both read the Fathers and was profoundly influenced by them.[15]

In his *Ethical Treatise*, St Symeon refers to the worthy disciple as the *hesychast* – one who practices silence[16] – and offers us a further insight into the effect of the mystical experience of the Transfiguration on him.

> Let the *hesychast* (ὁ ἡσυχάζων) become like those who went up to Tabor together with Christ and beheld the flashing radiance and the change of His garments and the light from His face, who seeing the bright Cloud and hearing the Paternal voice saying: 'This is my beloved Son', fell down on their face panic-stricken, so that he too may say as did Peter: 'Lord, it is good for us to be here'. Let us build three tabernacles, to you and your Father and your Holy Spirit, to the one rule (βασιλεῖα), for an eternal abode for soul and body and intellect, making them new by purification and edifying them to the summit by the variety of the virtues.[17]

Thus, in a mystical way, the hesychast becomes a participant in every aspect of the Transfiguration. There is no indication here that his vision is in any way inferior to that of the three disciples.[18] Indeed, we are told that the hesychast's reaction will be the same as that of St Peter. It is also worth noting that St Symeon interprets the words uttered by St Peter, firstly, in a Trinitarian sense, by ascribing three tabernacles to the Father, Son and Holy Spirit, and at the same time to their common rule or Kingdom – thereby signifying their co-equal status and unity; and secondly, in an eschatological and anthropological sense, where the three tabernacles of the Holy Trinity are presented as the place of eternal abode for soul (ψυχή), body (σῶμα) and intellect (νοῦς). Significantly, he also adds that soul, body and intellect – the human person in its totality[19] – are made new by purification, and that they are edified and thus raised up to the summit by the cultivation of the virtues. Note that *summit* or *mount* in Symeon signifies the attainment of divine knowledge and contemplation;[20] and also that divine knowledge is synonymous with contemplation,[21] which is often described as being accompanied by noetic *hearing*, as in the following short passage:

... then come and stand with us, O my brother, on the mount of divine knowledge and contemplation and together we shall hear the Paternal voice.[22]

Though not presented in a systematic way, there is in Symeon a discernible distinction between the different stages in the life of the Christian. He speaks of purification (κάθαρσις), the practice of the virtues (also referred to as the keeping of the commandments of Christ),[23] and the contemplation of the divine Light,[24] which is a characteristic element in man's progress towards deification (θέωσις).[25] Three stages, then, which broadly correspond to those found in such earlier writers as St Dionysius the Areopagite (κάθαρσις, φωτισμός, ἕνωσις or τελείωσις), and St Maximus the Confessor (who also employs the Evagrian schema, πρακτική, φυσική, and θεωρία).[26]

However, it is especially important to note in St Symeon the reciprocal relationship between purification (κάθαρσις) or purity (καθαρότης) and contemplation (θεωρία): 'when purity is acquired, it is followed by contemplation' (ὅτε ἡ καθαρότης προσγένηται, καὶ ἡ θεωρία συνέπεται).[27] Purification, then, leads to contemplation; but also, contemplation in its turn effects further purification.[28] Through the vision of God, the progressive nature of purification is revealed: 'little by little thou hast chased away the darkness, driven away the cloud, refined the materiality, cleansed the rheum from the noetic eyes, fortified and opened the eyes of the mind, taken away the veil of insensibility, and with these every passion and every fleshly pleasure has been put to sleep and completely cast out from me' (κατὰ μικρὸν μικρὸν τὸ σκότος ἐν ἐμοὶ ἀπεδίωξας, τὸ νέφος ἀπήλασας, τὸ πάχος ἐλέπτυνας, τὴν λήμην τῶν νοερῶν ὀφθαλμῶν ἀπεκάθηρας, τὰ ὦτα τῆς διανοίας ἀπέφραξας καὶ διήνοιξας, τῆς ἀναισθησίας περιῆρας τὸ κάλυμμα, σὺν τούτοις πᾶν πάθος καὶ πᾶσαν σαρκικὴν ἡδονὴν κατεκοίμησας καὶ τέλειον ἀπ' ἐμοῦ ἐξώρισας). Purification and contemplation are thus inextricably intertwined. Purification, moreover, involves physical and spiritual labours,[29] and here Symeon places possibly the heaviest emphasis on repentance and humility.[30] But even so, he insists that *only by the grace of the Holy Spirit* can one be made worthy to see God.[31]

As has already been shown, Symeon does not hesitate to invoke his own experience of the mystical vision of the Transfiguration. This may also be observed in an illuminating reference to the manner in which the divine Light of Christ is contemplated.

For we do not speak of that which we have not known, but we bear witness to that which we have known, that the Light shines even now; both by night and by day, both within and without: within, in our hearts, and without, in our intellect, never-setting, immutably, without change, without form, speaking, acting, living and giving life and turning into light those who are working. We testify that God is light... .[32]

Symeon's thought is clearly based on the Scriptural affirmation that God is light (1 John 1:5). Characteristically, he speaks of the experiential nature of the verification of this truth, appealing to his own experience of the divine Light – even if in this instance he uses the first person plural. The divine Light, he says, is visible by day or by night, and shines both *internally* and *externally*. When it shines from within, it is seen by the heart (καρδία);[33] when it shines from without, it is seen by the intellect (νοῦς).[34] The inner shining of the divine Light thus signifies deeper union with God.

St Symeon, however, does not include here the participation of the physical eyes of the body.[35] But while it is true that he often opposes the vision of the sensible light by the sensible eyes to that of the noetic light by the noetic eyes of the heart,[36] it is equally true to say that he does not deny the vision of the divine Light to the physical eyes of the body. In yet another reference to his own experience, he says: 'and then the first time, you dazzled my feeble eyes by the immaculate radiance of your countenance' (Καὶ τότε πρῶτον τῇ τοῦ προσώπου σου ἀχράντῳ αἴγλῃ τὰ ἀσθενῆ μου περιήστραψας ὄμματα).[37] Hence, the weak eyes of the body do see, even though they cannot contain or endure the vision of the blinding light of God. As immaterial, though, the divine Light is seen *immaterially* in material bodies by *the noetic eyes of the heart* (τὸ ἄϋλον ἐν ὑλικοῖς ἀΰλως καθορῶμεν φῶς, ὅπερ εἶπον, ὅτι ἦν Θεὸς ὑπερανάρχως, ἀόρατον τοῖς αἰσθητοῖς ὀφθαλμοῖς καὶ ἐνύλοις ἀπρόσιτον τοῖς νοεροῖς ὄμμασι τῆς καρδίας).[38] Note also, however, that as divine the Light is defined as *invisible* to the sensible eyes, and, though perceived, remains unapproachable (ἀπρόσιτον) *even* 'to the noetic eyes of the heart' (cf. 1 Tim. 6:16). It is essential, therefore, to appreciate that for Symeon the divine Light is nothing less than the manifestation of God Himself,[39] whether it be referred to as the light of the Holy Trinity,[40] or as the light of the *energies* or operation of Christ and the Holy Spirit,[41] or simply as the light of His divine glory.[42] It is, then, completely different to any other kind of light, for as divine it surpasses by nature every other light.[43] Consequently, it is described in the same terms that one would use in describing God. Hence, the divine Light shines, 'never-setting, immutably, without change, without form, speaking, acting, living and giving life' (ἀνεσπέρως, ἀτρέπτως, ἀναλλοιώτος, ἀσχηματίστως, λαλοῦν, ἐνεργοῦν, ζῶν καὶ ζωοποιοῦν),[44] and significantly, brings about transfiguration, 'turning into light those who are working' (φῶς τοὺς ἐργαζομένους ἀπεργαζόμενον), that is to say, those who are striving to fulfil the teaching of Christ.[45]

There can be little doubt that in St Symeon the New Theologian the Light, which is at one and the same time the Light of Christ and the Light of the Holy Trinity – the energies and operation of God *ad extra* – is understood as immaterial, noetic and divine. Moreover, the New Theologian's treatment of the Transfiguration Light is deeply connected with the ascetic character of his mystical theology. Significantly, in his description of the mystical ascent towards the vision of the transfigured Christ Symeon points to a fundamental paradox: that while the whole human person – intellect, soul and body – shares in this vision, nevertheless it is one which surpasses every aspect of our created being, since the Light of Christ remains unapproachable *even to the noetic eyes of the heart.*

But without doubt the single most important and unique contribution in St Symeon's ascetico-theological treatment of the Taborian Light stems from his own personal experience: namely, that the Divine Light may indeed be contemplated, just as it was by the three disciples on Tabor, by the person who has freely placed himself under the guidance of one who is truly experienced in the spiritual struggle for Christlike perfection. St John Damascene had rightly stressed the importance of silence and prayer in the ascetic struggle for the attainment of the vision of Christ transfigured in His Divine Light and glory; but it is St Symeon the New Theologian who completes the picture for us by underlining the important rôle of the Spiritual Father, of the inestimable value of an experienced and trustworthy guide in the Life in Christ.

Endnotes

1. *Catecheses* [*Cat.*] xxii (*SC* 104:372, ll. 100–108).

2. Consult Archbishop Basile Krivochéine's *Dans la Lumière du Christ* (Chevetogne, 1980), p. 229.

3. Allusions to the Transfiguration in Symeon are found *en passant*. For works ascribed to St Symeon, see J. Gouillard, 'Syméon le Jeune ou le Nouveau Théologien', *Dictionnaire de Théologie Catholique* 14/2 (1941), 2944–2947; and B. Krivochéine, 'The Writings of St. Symeon the New Theologian', *Orientalia Christiana Periodica* 20 (1954), 299–302; and A. Kambylis, ed., *Symeon Neos Theologos: Hymnen*, Supplementa Byzantina 3, *Texte und Untersuchungen*, series eds. H.-G. Beck, A. Kambylis, and R. Keydell (Berlin, 1976), pp. xix–xxi.

4. *Ambiguum X* (*PG* 91:1125D–1128A); and see my 'The Transfiguration of Christ in Greek Patristic Literature: From Irenaeus of Lyons to Gregory Palamas' (Oxford D. Phil. thesis, 1991), pp. 189, 195, and 208.

5. *Homilia in Transfigurationem Domini* (*PG* 97:936C); and Veniamin, op. cit., pp. 223 and 226.

6. *Ethical Treatise* [*Eth.*] ii (*SC* 129:452, ll. 121–126); and cf. ix (246, l. 380–248, l. 387), and Krivochéine, *Dans la Lumière du Christ*, p. 215, n. 18; and *Eth.*, iv (56, ll. 673–677), found in Krivochéine, ibid., p. 237, n. 19, where the divine light is said to be unapproachable to sinners: τὸ φῶς τὸ

ἀπρόσιτον... τοῖς ἁμαρτωλοῖς; and cf. also *Hymn* xxviii, Kambylis, op. cit., p. 246, ll. 73–83, and Krivochéine, ibid., p. 221, n. 33.

7. Cf. for example the words of advice that Symeon receives from his own Spiritual Father, in *Cat.* xvi (*SC* 104:242, ll. 54–57): 'Know this, my child, that neither fasting, nor vigil, nor physical toil, nor any other ascetic feat causes God to rejoice and appear to us, but only a humble, simple and good soul and heart' (Γίνωσκε, τέκνον, ὅτι οὔτε νηστεία, οὔτε ἀγρυπνία, οὔτε κόπῳ σωματικῷ, οὔτε τινὶ ἑτέρῳ τῶν δεξιῶν πράξεων χαίρει ὁ θεὸς καὶ ἐμφανίζεται, εἰ μὴ ταπεινῇ τε καὶ μόνῃ ἀπεριέργῳ καὶ ἀγαθῇ ψυχῇ καὶ καρδίᾳ).

8. *Hymn* xl, Kambylis, op. cit., p. 331, ll. 36–39, found in W. Völker, *Praxis und Theoria bei Symeon dem Neuen Theologen: Ein Beitrag zur Byzantinischen Mystik* (Wiesbaden, 1974), p. 98, n. 1; and see also Völker's section on ἀποταγή, pp. 97–111.

9. *Cat.*, xx (*SC* 104:330,ll. 3–6; 336, ll. 71–77); cf. *Eth.*, xv (*SC* 129:446, l. 41–448, l. 52); and in his *Epistula de Confessione*, in K. Holl, *Enthusiasmus und Bußgewalt: Eine Studie zu Symeon dem Neuen Theologen* (Leipzig, 1898), pp. 110–127. On the Spiritual Father in Symeon, see H. Graef, 'The Spiritual Director in the Thought of Symeon the New Theologian', in P. Granfield and J.A. Jungmann (eds.), *Kyriakon: Festshrift Johannes Quasten*, vol. 2 (Münster Westf., 1970), pp. 608–614; V. C. Christophoridis, *Ἡ πνευματικὴ πατρότης κατὰ Συμεὼν τὸν Νέον Θεολόγον* (Thessalonica, 1977); Krivochéine's chapter on 'Direction and Spiritual Fatherhood' in Symeon, *Dans la Lumière du Christ*, pp. 94–106; Völker, op. cit., pp. 111–129; and H. J. M. Turner, *St. Symeon the New Theologian and Spiritual Fatherhood* (Leiden, 1990); and see also more generally Irénée Hausherr, *La direction sprituelle en Orient autrefois*, in Orientalia Christiana Analecta 144 (Rome, 1955), Eng. trans. by Anthony R. Gythiel, *Spiritual Direction in the Early Christian East*, Cistercian Studies Series 116 (Kalamazoo, Michigan, 1990); K. T. Ware, 'The Spiritual Father in Orthodox Christianity', in K. G. Culligan, O. C. D., ed., *Spiritual Direction: Contemporary Readings* (Locust Valley, 1983), pp. 20–40; and Bishop Hilarion Alfeyev, *Saint Symeon, the New Theologian, and Orthodox Tradition*, Oxford Early Christian Studies (Oxford, 2000). Bishop Kallistos Ware, in 'The Spiritual Father in St. John Climacus and St. Symeon the New Theologian', *Studia Patristica* 18,2 (1989), 313–314, n. 20 [reprinted as the Foreword of Hausherr's *Spiritual Direction in the Early Christian East*, pp. vii–xxxiii; note 20 comes on p. xxix, and esp. 301–312 (pp. xi–xxvii)], is the first to bring out the important parallels between

Climacus' *To the Shepherd (Ad Pastorem)* and Symeon's letter *On Confession,* demonstrating thereby Symeon's indebtedness to Climacus.

10. Cf. St John Climacus' *Scala Paradisi,* Gradus IV 'On Blessed and Ever-memorable Obedience' (*PG* 88:717B); Eng. tr. by Archimandrite Lazarus (Moore) with an introduction by Muriel Heppell (Willits, CA: Eastern Orthodox Books, 1959), p. 91 [reprinted and revised by Holy Transfiguration Monastery, Boston, MA, 1979 and 1991], where he says: 'Let us trust with firm confidence those who have taken upon themselves the care of us in the Lord, even though they order something apparently contrary and opposed to our salvation. For it is then that our faith in them is tested as in a furnace of humiliation. For it is a sign of truest faith if we obey our superiors without any hesitation, even when we see the opposite of what we had hoped for happening'.

As an illustration of this, St John tells of a certain Acacius, under obedience to an elder 'who was extremely careless and undisciplined', and who 'tormented [Acacius] daily not only with insults and indignities, but even with blows'. However, Acacius' obedience, as St John is careful to point out, 'was not mere senseless endurance' but the result of a spiritual disposition born of discernment – cf. ibid. (680CD); pp. 67–68 – and this is confirmed by the fact that, five days after his repose, even from the grave Acacius replies to his disbelieving elder's question – 'Are you dead, Brother Acacius?' – with the following words: 'How is it possible, Father, for a man who is a doer of obedience to die?' Ibid. (720BD); pp. 92–93.

11. Op. cit., xx (*SC* 104:334, l. 44–336, l. 70); and cf. the following works which serve to illustrate the crucial rôle of the Spiritual Father in the life of the Christian: St Athanasius' *Vita Antonii* (*PG* 26:837–976); Palladius' *Historia Lausiaca* (C. Butler, *The Lausiac History of Palladius II*, Texts and Studies 6,2 (Cambridge, 1904), pp. 9–169); the *Apophthegmata*, alphabetical collection (*PG* 65:76–440); and the *Erotapokriseis* of SS Barsanuphius and John, ed. by Nicodemus of the Holy Mountain (reissued S. Schoinas, Volos, 1960); critical edition of Letters 1–124 by D. J. Chitty, *Patrologia Orientalia* 31,3, found in K. T. Ware, op. cit., 313, n. 12 (p. xxviii); the *Doctrinae Diversae* of Abba Dorotheus of Gaza, especially Oration V: 'That We Ought Not to Follow Our Own Understanding' (*SC* 92:250–266); and the *Scala Paradisi* of St John Climacus, especially Gradus IV: 'On Blessed and Ever-memorable Obedience' (*PG* 88:677–728). The list of such works is in fact endless. But perhaps the most significant patristic contribution to the subject since the time of Symeon is that of Staretz Sophrony of Essex, especially in his *О Молитве* [*On*

Prayer], in the section entitled 'The Rôle of the Father-Confessor', Eng. trans. Rosemary Edmonds (Monastery of Saint John the Baptist, 1996), pp. 87–118.

12. Cf. *Cat.*, xxix (*SC* 113:176, l. 137–178, l. 167), quoted in J. Meyendorff's *Christ in Eastern Christian Thought* (St. Vladimir's Seminary Press, 1975), pp. 194–195 and 239, n. 2. Meyendorff notes the similarity between this and a passage from Macarius' *Epistula Magna* (see W. W. Jaeger, ed., *Two Rediscovered Works of Ancient Christian Literature: Gregory of Nyssa and Macarius*, Leiden, 1954, p. 298): Τοὺς γὰρ ἀδύνατον ἡγουμένους τὴν κατόρθωσιν ταύτην διὰ τοῦ Πνεύματος ἐν ἀνθρώποις γίνεσθαι ἥτις ἐστιν ἡ ὄντως καινὴ κτίσις τῆς καθαρᾶς καρδίας. Also see *Eth.*, vii (*SC* 129:190, ll. 474–480); and D. L. Stathopoulos, 'The Divine Light in the Poetry of St. Symeon the New Theologian', *GOThR* 19,2 (1974), 101, n. 60.

13. *Cat.*, xx (*SC* 104:336, ll. 71–77).

14. *Oratio* XXVII [= *First Theological Oration*] 3 (*SC* 250:76, ll. 1–7): 'Not to all... does it belong to philosophize about God, not to all [τὸ περὶ Θεοῦ φιλοσοφεῖν, οὐ παντός]; the matter is not thus cheap and low. And I will add, neither always, neither with everyone, neither about everything [οὐδὲ πάντοτε, οἰδὲ πᾶσιν, οὐδὲ πάντα], but there is a when and a with whom, and an on what [ἀλλ' ἔστιν ὅτε, καὶ οἷς, καὶ ἐφ' ὅσον]. Not to all, because it belongs to those who have been examined and have advanced to *theoria,* and before these, have purified or are at the very least purifying the soul and the body' [ὅτι τῶν ἐξητασμένων καὶ διαβεβηκότων ἐν θεωρίᾳ, καὶ πρὸ τούτων καὶ ψυχὴν καὶ σῶμα κεκαθαρμένων, ἢ καθαιρομένων, τὸ μετριώτατον]. Found in J. S. Romanides, 'Critical Examination of the Applications of Theology', *Procès-Verbaux du Deuxième Congrès de Théologie Orthodoxe à Athènes (19–29 Août 1976)* (Athens, 1978), 424. And the same sentiments, though in a somewhat different context, may be found in St Gregory of Nyssa, *De Vita Moysis* 160–161 (*SC* 1ter:208, l. 1–210, l. 10): 'It is not for everyone to push themselves forward to try to comprehend the mysteries [τὸ μὴ πάντας ἑαυτοὺς εἰσωθεῖν πρὸς τὴν τῶν μυστηρίων κατάληψιν]. They [the faithful] should select one of their number who is able to grasp divine truth [ἀλλ' ἐπιλέξαντας ἐξ ἑαυτῶν τὸν χωρῆσαι τὰ θεῖα δυνάμενον]; then they should give careful attention to him [ἐκείνῳ τὴν ἀκοὴν εὐγνωμόνως ὑπέχειν] and accept as trustworthy whatever they learn from the man who has been initiated into divine truth [πιστὸν ἡγουμένους ἅπαν ὅτιπερ ἂν παρὰ τοῦ τὰ θεῖα μυηθέντος ἀκούσωσιν].' Translation taken from Maurice Wiles and Mark

Santer, *Documents in Early Christian Thought* (Cambridge University Prss, 1975; reprinted, 1993), p. 15. See also K. T. Ware, 'Tradition and Personal Experience in Later Byzantine Theology', *Eastern Churches Review* 3,2 (1970), 131–141.

15. Cf. Staretz Sophrony of Essex, whose style and theological method are remarkably similar to those of St Symeon.

16. Cf. St Andrew of Crete, *Homilia in Transfigurationem Domini* (PG 97:952AB); and St John Damascene, *Homilia in Transfigurationem Salvatoris Nostri Jesu Christi* 2, B. Kotter, ed., *Patristische Texte und Studien* 29 (Berlin, 1988), p. 437, ll. 5–15; and consult Veniamin, op. cit., pp. 227 and 236–237 respectively.

17. *Eth.*, xv (*SC* 129:446, l. 41–448, l. 52).

18. Cf. *Cat.*, xxxv, *Eucharistia i* (*SC* 113:310, ll. 66–69); and Krivochéine, op. cit., pp. 171–172.

19. Cf. B. Krivochéine, op. cit., p. 212, n. 6, for Symeon's division of the soul into the three faculties: the rational (λογιστικόν), the irascible (θυμικόν), and the appetitive (ἐπιθυμιτικόν). J. Darrouzès makes the point that the connection between the Holy Trinity and the *tripartite* division of the soul is one which is quite often encountered in Symeon – he refers mainly to instances where the division νοῦς, λόγος, ψυχή is employed. For further references, see *Eth.*, iv (*SC* 129:39, n. 3). In this particular instance, however, though unquestionably pointing to the triadological image in man, St Symeon is also emphasizing the eschatological place of the human *body* as well as that of the soul. Hence, 'soul and body and intellect'.

For a fuller investigation into the anthropology of the Fathers, with particular emphasis on the middle and later Byzantine periods, see the studies by Prof. Anestis Keselopoulos, Πάθη καὶ Ἀρετὲς στὴ Διδασκαλία τοῦ Ἁγίου Γρηγορίου τοῦ Παλαμᾶ [*Passions and Virtues in the Teaching of Saint Gregory Palamas*] (Athens, 1982); and John Chryssavgis, *Ascent to Heaven: The Theology of the Human Person According to Saint John of the Ladder* (Brookline, Mass., 1989).

20. Cf. Origen's understanding of the high mount as representing wisdom and knowledge; and Damascene's as representing love; and Veniamin, op. cit., pp. 48–49 and 235, respectively.

21. *Eth.*, iii (*SC* 122:408, ll. 247–253); quoted in Krivochéine, op. cit., pp. 210–211.

22. *Hymn* lii, Kambylis, op. cit., p. 416, ll. 79–81; and cf. Symeon's reference to the ears of the mind (τὰ ὦτα τῆς διανοίας), in *Cat.*, xxxv, *Euch. i* (SC 113:312, ll. 187–188).

23. Völker, *Praxis und Theoria*, pp. 233–288.

24. See Krivochéine, op. cit., pp. 229–255; and Völker, ibid., pp. 315–375.

25. See Krivochéine, ibid., pp. 411–419, especially, p. 414, n. 15. Note firstly, the difficulty in trying to define exactly what *theosis* is in Symeon; secondly, its dynamic character; and thirdly, the three stages of *theosis*: in this life, in the life beyond, and in the General Resurrection. Consult also Völker, *Praxis und Theoria*, pp. 432–455; and Stathopoulos, op. cit., 107, nn. 103–104.

For fuller details on the origin and meaning of *theosis* in Patristic tradition, see I. Popov, 'The Idea of Deification in the Early Eastern Church', *Voprosy philosophii i psikhologii* 97 (Moscow, 1909), pp. 162–213 (in Russian); J. Gross, *La divinisation du chrétien d'après les Pères grecs* (Paris, 1938); W. J. Burghardt, *The Image of God in Man According to Cyril of Alexandria* (Woodstock, 1957); G. Wingren, *Man and the Incarnation: A Study in the Biblical Theology of Irenaeus* (Philadelphia, 1959); Leon Contos, *The Concept of Theosis in Saint Gregory Palamas, With Critical Text of the "Contra Akindynum"*, 2 vols. (Los Angeles: University of California, 1963); J. E. Sullivan, *The Image of God: The Doctrine of St. Augustine and Its Influence* (Dubuque, Iowa, 1963); A. M. Allchin (ed.), *Sacrament and Image: Essays in the Christian Understanding of Man* (London, 1967); K. T. Ware, 'The Transfiguration of the Body', *Sobornost* 4,8 (1963), 420–434; reprinted (with revisions) in *Sacrament and Image*, ed. A. M. Allchin, published by the Fellowship of St Alban and St Sergius (London, 1967), pp. 17–32, 'The Mystery of God and Man in Symeon the New Theologian', *Sobornost* 6,4 (1971), 227–236, 'The Unity of the Human Person according to the Greek Fathers', in *Persons and Personality: A Contemporary Inquiry*, Arthur Peacocke and Grant Gillett (eds.), Ian Ramsey Centre Publications no. 1 (Oxford, 1987), pp. 197–206, 215–217; M. Lot-Borodine, *La déification de l'homme selon la doctrine des Pères grecs* (Paris, 1970); G. Mantzarides, *Deification of Man* (Crestwood, New York, 1984); J. A. Cullen, 'The Patristic Concept of the Deification of Man Examined in the Light of Contemporary Notions of the Transcendence of Man' (Oxford D. Phil. thesis, 1985); P. Nellas, *Deification in Christ* (Crestwood, New York, 1987); Norman Russel, 'The Concept of Deification in the Early Greek Fathers' (Oxford D. Phil. thesis, 1988).

26. Cf. Veniamin, op. cit., p. 158, n. 1; and pp. 188–191.

27. *Eth.*, v (*SC* 129:88, ll. 114–121); Krivochéine, op. cit., pp. 213–214. Also, contemplation presupposes ascetic struggle (ἄσκησις), *Cat.*, xxii (*SC* 104:388, ll. 312–320); Krivochéine, ibid., pp. 230–231. On the need for ascetic struggle, see *Eth.*, v (*SC* 129:116, ll. 511–519). Purification makes man worthy of contemplation, *Hymn* lv, Kambylis, op. cit., pp., 439, l. 82–440, l. 92; Krivochéine, ibid., p. 223, n. 38.

28. *Cat.*, xxxv, *Eucharistia i* (*SC* 113:320, ll. 185–190); Krivochéine, op. cit., p. 218, n. 27; and Stathopoulos, op. cit., 106, nn. 94–95.

29. See Völker, op. cit., pp. 87–288. Note also Krivochéine, op. cit., pp. 214–215, nn. 17–19, for references to the ascetic struggle, taking up one's Cross, and the keeping of the commandments of Christ, while at the same time underlining his unworthiness, and thereby underlining the free nature of the divine gift of contemplation. And again, Krivochéine, ibid., pp. 225 and 248, nn. 62–64, and p. 254.

30. *Eth.*, iii (*SC* 122:408, ll. 257–259); Krivochéine, op. cit., p. 211, n. 3; and Stathopoulos, op. cit., 101.

31. *Hymn* lii, Kambylis, op. cit., p. 348, ll. 120–125: καὶ τίς ἰσχύσει ἐξ ὑμῶν τοῦτον ποτὲ ἰδέσθαι ἐξ οἰκείας δυνάμεως ἢ ἐνεργείας ὅλως, εἰ μὴ αὐτὸς ἐκπέμψειε Πνεῦμα αὐτοῦ τὸ Θεῖον καὶ δι' αὐτοῦ τῷ ἀσθενεῖ τῆς φύσεως παράσχῃ ῥώμην, ἰσχὺν καὶ δύναμιν καὶ ἱκανὸν ποιήσῃ τὸν ἄνθρωπον τοῦ κατιδεῖν δόξαν αὐτοῦ τὴν θείαν, found in Krivochéine, op. cit., pp. 222–223, n. 37.

32. *Cat.*, xxviii (*SC* 113:136, ll. 102–109).

33. Symeon's heart was transfigured into light, see Krivochéine, op. cit., p. 236, n. 17; and cf. *Cat.*, ii (*SC* 96:264, ll. 286), where the shining of the light in our hearts brings knowledge or understanding of things divine: εἰ τὸ φῶς ἔλαμψεν ἐν ταῖς καρδίαις ὑμῶν (cf. 2 Pet. 1:19), εἰ φῶς ἐθεάσασθε τὸ μέγα (cf. Isa. 9:2;) τῆς ἐπιγνώσεως. Also, Krivochéine, op. cit., p. 244, n. 47: Light shines in the νοῦς and in the heart.

34. On the inner vision of the transfigured Christ, cf. St Maximus the Confessor, *Capita Theologica et Oeconomica* I. 97 (*PG* 90:1121C–1124A); and cf. ibid., II. 14 (1132A); Veniamin, 'The Transfiguration of Christ and the Deification of Man in Saint Maximus the Confessor', Κληρονομία 27, 1–2 (1995 issue; published 1996), 317–318; and idem, op. cit., pp. 193–194: that the gnostic men experience the Transfiguration of the Word *within*

themselves (ἐν αὐτοῖς).' With specific reference to the illumination of the human intellect (νοῦς), in his *Ambiguum X* (*PG* 91:1156AB), Maximus maintains that with the vision of the Transfiguration, the intellect receives knowledge of God (γνῶσις Θεοῦ), and is thereby enabled to advance *still further* and attain to what St Maximus calls spiritual contemplation (πνευματικὴ θεωρία), which constitutes the first phase of the third and highest stage of progress in the Christian life, that of theology (θεολογία), through which the Christian passes to the superior degree of mystical union with the Logos, ibid. (1125D–1128A); and Veniamin, ibid., 315; and idem, 'The Transfiguration of Christ in Greek Patristic Literature', p. 191.

Also, on the extraneous nature of the glory of Moses as compared to that of Christ, see St John Damascene, op. cit, 2, 437, ll. 5–15; and Veniamin, ibid., pp. 230–231. 'With 2 Cor. 3:7 in mind, St John adds that the glory of Moses was to be done away with (καταργουμένη), transitory, whereas that of Christ is perpetual and endures forever (δόξα διηνεκὴς καὶ διαιωνίζουσα), ibid., 17, p. 455, ll. 1–10.' However, 'there is no inherent difference between the glory revealed through Moses on Sinai and that of Christ on Tabor, for it is one and the same; but while Moses receives this glory from Yahweh, Christ possesses it *by nature*'. Note Krivochéine, op. cit., p. 237–238, n. 21: one must *become* light in order to see the Light – one must be *illumined*.

35. For Symeon this is an invisible vision of God's inexpressible beauty, Krivochéine, op. cit, p. 212: Ὁρῶσιν ἀοράτω", *Eth.*, iv (*SC* 129:68, ll. 856–857).

36. *Hymn* xxxiii, Kambylis, op. cit., p. 302, ll. 58–64: τὰ αἰσθητὰ τοὺς αἰσθητοὺς ὀφθαλμοὺς καὶ γὰρ μόνους φωτίζουσι καὶ λάμπουσι φῶτα, καὶ βλέπειν μόνον ἀπέχουσι τὰ αἰσθητά, τὰ νοητὰ οὐ μέντοι. πάντες οὖν ὅσοι βλέπουσι τὰ αἰσθητὰ καὶ μόνον, τυ[2]οί εἰσι τὰ νοερὰ ὄμματα τῆς καρδίας· τὰ νοερὰ οὖν ὄμματα τῆς νοερᾶς καρδίας καὶ νοερῷ φωτίζεσθαι ὀφείλουσι φωτί τε.

37. *Cat.*, xxxvi *Euch. ii* (*SC* 113:340, ll. 132–133); and cf. Krivochéine, op. cit., pp. 235–236 and 255.

38. *Hymn* xxxviii, Kambylis, op. cit., pp. 324, l. 81–325, l. 84.

39. Cf., e.g., *Hymn* xlv, Kambylis, ibid., p. 374, l. 6: τὸ γὰρ φῶς σου σὺ ὁ θεὸς μου τυγχάνεις, found in Stathopoulos, op. cit., p. 96.

40. Φῶς ὁ πατήρ, φῶς ὁ υἱός, φῶς τὸ ἅγιον πνεῦμα; ἓν γὰρ τὰ τρία φῶς εἰσιν, *Hymn* xxxiii, Kambylis, ibid., p. 300, ll. 1–3. Cf. the *Exapostilarion*

of Matins for the Feast of the Transfiguration: Φῶς ἀναλλοίωτον, Λόγε, φωτὸς Πατρὸς ἀγεννήτου, ἐν τῷ φανέντι φωτί σου σήμερον ἐν Θαβωρίῳ, φῶς εἴδομεν τὸν Πατέρα, φῶς καὶ τὸ Πνεῦμα, φωταγωγοῦν πᾶσαν κτίσιν.

41. *Hymn* li, Kambylis, ibid., p. 408, ll. 1–10; Krivochéine, op. cit., pp. 237–238; and his '"Essence créée" et "essence divine" dans la théologie spirituelle de S. Syméon le Nouveau Théologien', *Messager de l' Exarchat du patriache Russe en Europe Occidentale* 75–76 (1971), 151–170.

42. *Hymn* xlix, Kambylis, ibid., p. 392, ll. 22–24.

43. *Hymn* xxxviii, Kambylis, ibid., p. 324, ll. 70–71: ἐκεῖνος δὲ παντὸς φωτὸς ἐστὶ κεχωρισμένος, ὑπέρφωτος, ὑπέρλαμπρος, ἄστεκτος πάσῃ κτίσει.

44. The language used in this passage to describe the divine Light is echoed in the hymnography of the Feast of Pentecost in the Orthodox Church, which refers to the revelation of the Holy Spirit. Compare, for example, the phrases: ζωὴ καὶ ζωοποιοῦν and λαλοῦν, ἐνεργοῦν, διαιροῦν τὰ χαρίσματα, in the second and third *idiomela* of the Lauds for Matins.

45. Symeon says that in order to see the shapeless light, one must first become light: οἱ ἀπ' αἰῶνος ἅγιοι, οἱ πάλαι τε καὶ νῦν πνευματικῶς βλέποντες, οὐ σχῆμα ἢ εἶδος ἢ ἐκτύπωμα βλέπουσιν, ἀλλὰ φῶς ἀσχημάτιστον, ὡς καὶ αὐτοὶ φῶς ἐκ τοῦ φωτὸς Πνεύματος χρηματίζοντες, *Theological Treatise* 1,3 (*SC* 122:202, ll. 99–103); Krivochéine, op. cit., p. 237.

THE INTERPLAY BETWEEN MYSTICAL AND DOGMATIC THEOLOGY IN ST GREGORY THE SINAÏTE

S T. GREGORY THE SINAÏTE (c. 1265 – 1346), unlike his namesake, St. Gregory Palamas (1296 – 1359), did not play a directly active rôle in the *Hesychast Controversy* of the fourteenth century, even though his fame as a leading exponent of *hesychasm*[1] was rivalled perhaps only by Palamas himself (whose spiritual father, at least for a time, the Sinaïte almost certainly was).[2] But his unwillingness to become personally involved in

---

1. The contemplative mystical life centred on the practice of the Jesus Prayer. On the practice and significance of the Jesus Prayer in the Sinaïte, see Bishop Kallistos T. Ware's article, "The Jesus Prayer in St. Gregory of Sinai," *Eastern Churches Revue* 4, 1 (1972), 2–22.

2. Sources offer us no proof of direct contact between the two Gregories, and although Palamas is noted as having been, for a period of about eight years, under the spiritual direction of a certain Gregory the Great (Γρηγόριος ὁ πάνυ) as Father John Meyendorff puts it, "Ces détails biographiques ne correspondent pas avec ce que nous savons de Grégoire le Sinaïte, avec lequel on serait tenté d' identifier le maître de Palamas," *Introduction à l'étude de Grégoire Palamas* (Paris, 1959), p. 52. Bishop Kallistos Ware, however, considering both the chronological coincidence and geographical proximity, as well as the common circle of followers, friends and acquaintants, of the two Gregories from their

the theological disputations of his day ought not to diminish our appreciation of him as a theologian in the fullest and truest sense of the word, even if much of what he says, in doctrinal terms, is a synthesis of what had already been said before, because the originality of the Sinaïte's contribution in the Christian tradition lies specifically in the explicit intertwining of Orthodox doctrine with mystical theology.

This interplay, characteristic of St. Gregory's work as a whole, is nowhere more striking than in his *Discourse on the Transfiguration*,[3] which is nothing less than "an effusion of mystical and dogmatic theology."[4] Aimed at fellow ascetics, the *Discourse* concentrates mainly on those aspects of the Taborian theophany that pertain to the inner life of the *hesychast*. The theme of the divine Light of Tabor, identified by St. Gregory as the very same light that the *hesychasts* experience in prayer,[5] is most prominent, and indeed forms the pivot around which his entire sermon revolves. However,

---

time on Athos and later, arrives at the conclusion that "direct personal contact between the Gregories would seem intrinsically probable," cautiously adding, however, that this "cannot be proved," op. cit., 3, n. 2. David Balfour, on the other hand, goes one step further, and suggests, working on the principle of Occam's Razor (*entia non sunt multiplicanda praeter necessitatem*), that in view of the total absence of references supporting even the existence of a Gregory the Great, this must in all probability be none other than the Sinaïte himself, and attributes the silence of the sources to an embarrassing difference of opinion and parting of the ways of the two Gregories, which probably took place in Thessalonica, "St. Gregory of Sinai's Life Story and Spiritual Profile," Θεολογία 53, 1 (1983), 44–50. On the question of the Sinaïte's spiritual successors, see the work by Igumen Petr Pigol, *Prepodobnyi Grigorii Sinait i ego dukhovnye preemniki* (Moscow, 1999); and on his influence among the Slavs, see the fascinating observations made by Anthony-Emil N. Tachiaos, in his "Gregory Sinaites' Legacy to the Slavs: Preliminary Remarks", *Cyrillomethodianum* 7 (1983), 113–165.

3. See Balfour, "St. Gregory the Sinaïte: Discourse on the Transfiguration," Θεολογία 52,4 (1981), 644–680.

4. Ibid., 631.

5. See ibid., 631, nn. 1–4; cf. Hans-Georg Beck, *Kirche und Theologishe Literatur im Byzantinischen Reich* (Munich, 1977), p. 366; and esp. Eiji

his identification of the Light of Tabor with the triune God, in contrast to Palamas, is not presented in a systematic or expository fashion, and the essence–energies distinction, though implicit, is not at the epicentre of the discussion.[6] The Sinaïte's focus is simply but firmly fixed on the Christological and Trinitarian aspects of the Taborian revelation, and it is to these two areas in particular that we shall direct our attention in this study.

Following a line of thought which may be traced back to St. Gregory of Nazianzus in the fourth century,[7] the Sinaïte views the Christological and Trinitarian significance of the Taborian revelation as inextricably bound up with each other: the triune light of the Holy Trinity is manifested *in* and *through* the resplendent flesh of the Son and Word of God, of the Second divine Hypostasis.

And as the Son shone ineffably on Thabor in the light of His power, they clearly discerned the Father of lights (Jas. 1:17) through that voice from above and the Spirit through the resplendent cloud, and recognized the Trinity as an everlasting outpouring of light and brightness, truly flashing forth like lightning in the transfigured Christ.[8]

Hisamatsu, *Gregorios Sinaites als Lehrer des Gebetes*, published in the series Münsteraner theologische Abhandlungen 34 (Altenberge, 1994).

6. As is the case, for example, with Palamas' two sermons on the subject, namely, Hom. XXXIV, "On the Holy Transfiguration of Our Lord and God and Saviour Jesus Christ: In which it is proved that the Light of the Transfiguration is Uncreated," and Hom. XXXV, entitled "Another on the Transfiguration of the Lord: In which it is proved that although the Divine Light of the Transfiguration is Uncreated, it is not God's Essence." Eng. trans. in *Saint Gregory Palamas: The Homilies*, ed. and trans. by C. Veniamin (Dalton PA: Mount Thabor Publishing, 2013).

7. The Light of Christ on Tabor, says St. Gregory the Theologian, "is the divinity which was revealed to the three disciples on the Mount," in his *Oration on Holy Baptism* XL, 6 (*Patrologia Graeca* 36:364BC); this light, moreover, is nothing less than "that which can be contemplated in Father and Son and Holy Spirit (Φῶς δὲ λέγω, τὸ ἐν Πατρὶ καὶ Υἱῷ καὶ ἁγίῳ Πνεύματι θεωρούμενον); whose wealth is the oneness of nature and the unified outburst of brilliance."

8. *Discourse on the Transfiguration* 24. Translations taken from Balfour, loc. cit.

"In the transfigured Christ," then, is revealed "the Trinity as an everlasting outpouring of light and brightness, truly flashing forth like lightning" (τὴν Τριάδα ἐπέγνωσαν ὡς ἀληθῶς ἐν τῷ Χριστῷ ἀπαστράψασαν μεταμορφουμένῳ φωτοχυσίαν ἀέννοον καὶ λαμπρότητα). And echoing St. Irenaeus of Lyons (d. *c.* 202), the Sinaïte also refers to the Light of Christ as Paternal (τὸ πατρικὸν φῶς).[9] Christ is the begotten light (τὸ γεννητὸν φῶς); the Father, the unbegotten (τὸ ἀγέννητον).[10] Christ *is* the light, while the Father is the *source* of the light.[11]

St. Gregory also calls attention to the *Monarchia* of the Father, on the one hand, and to the mystery of the *perichoresis* or co-inherence of the divine Hypostases on the other. Commenting on Matt. 17:5, Gregory, speaking in the Father's name, says the following concerning the indwelling of the Father in His beloved Son:

"... in Him I shine and gleam and provide and purify and enlighten, and in Him I sanctify you. In the light of His glory you shall see Me, the unapproachable light. In Him you shall recognise Me and in Me you shall see Him; and that, firstly in order to put on [His] shape (μόρφωσις, cf. Phil. 2:6–7),[12] and secondly in order to be made perfect or that He may dwell within you here and deify you there."[13]

He also emphasizes the common *action* or *operation* of all three Hypostases of the Holy Trinity in the divine economy.

In Spirit you shall see the Son, in the Son you shall recognise the Father… He speaks in Me, and in Me and the Spirit He does nothing separately (αὐτὸς ἐν ἐμοὶ λαλεῖ καὶ ποιεῖ ἐν ἐμοὶ καὶ τῷ Πνεύματι δίχα οὐδέν); and I, speaking and dwelling through Him and in Him and with Him, perform the works in the Spirit; He Speaks in Me in the Spirit, and through Him I speak and do all things in the Spirit.[14]

---

9. Ibid., 27; reminiscent of the *paterna lux* of St. Irenaeus of Lyons, see Veniamin, "The Transfiguration of Christ in Greek Patristic Literature: From Irenaeus of Lyons to Gregory Palamas" (Oxford D.Phil. thesis, 1991), p. 32.
10. Ibid., 18.
11. Ibid.
12. Cf. ἐν μορφῇ Θεοῦ ὑπάρχων, μορφὴν δούλου λαβών.
13. Ibid., 18.
14. Ibid.

The grace of the Father is *one* and *common* to all three Hypostases, always communicated to the world *through* the Son and *in* the Spirit.[15] The common action of the divine Hypostases, which manifests a common will,[16] also discloses the oneness of the godhead – θεότης – and of God – Θεός. Indeed, outside the divine Hypostases there can be neither godhead nor God:

For the grace of the Father is one, fulfilled through the Son in the Holy Ghost (Μία γάρ ἐστιν ἡ τοῦ Πατρὸς χάρις δι᾽ Υἱοῦ ἐν Πνεύματι ἁγίῳ πληρουμένη); and there is one godhead and one God, worshipped in Father, Son and Holy Ghost.[17]

Furthermore, Christ was transfigured on Tabor "according to His humanity" (κατὰ τὸ ἀνθρώπινον),[18] and thus St. Gregory is keen to underline the *full* participation of His human nature in His divine glory. Participation in the divine glory of Christ, however, is synonymous with participation in the triune glory of the Holy Trinity, inasmuch as they are one and the same glory.

Elsewhere, the Sinaïte again refers to the *perichoresis* or mutual indwelling of the Father and the Son. The main emphasis this time, however, appears to be on the mode of union or participation of the *theandric* Christ in the communion of the Holy Trinity. Once again, rhetorically as the Father, St. Gregory says:

He is in Me unconfusedly, and I shine forth in Him immutably like lightning in divine majesty and Trinity. He is in Me singly, and I in Him triply; the first by reason of the assumption [of human nature], the second by reason of the existence of godhead.[19]

In this brief passage the Sinaïte describes the theandric Christ as resting in the Father "unconfusedly" (ἀσυγχύτως) and "singly" or "uniquely" (μοναδικῶς), by virtue of His "assumption"

---

15. See esp. Saint Gregory of Nyssa (*c.* 330 – *c.* 395), *To Ablabius: That There Are Not Three Gods* (*Patrologia Graeca* 45:125C); also Hom. XXIV, 1, and n. 364, in *Saint Gregory Palamas: The Homilies,* op. cit., pp. 191 and 578.
16. For the will of the Father in Christ, see for example: op. cit., 18: ἐν αὐτῷ ηὐδόκησα, καὶ ἐν αὐτῷ ἠθέλησα καὶ ἐξελεξάμην ὑμᾶς.
17. Ibid., 20.
18. Ibid., 18.
19. Ibid.

(πρόσληψις) of human nature. In other words, because of the uniqueness or exclusivity of the *prosopic union* of the divine and human in the single subject of the Hypostasis of the Son and Word of God, Christ may be said to be in the Father "singly" (μοναδικῶς). God the Father, on the other hand, as *cause* and *source* of the godhead – of the single majesty common to all three divine Hypostases – is said to reside in Christ "triply" or "triadically" (τριαδικῶς), "in divine majesty and Trinity" (θεοπρεπῶς καὶ τριαδικῶς), or, as St. Gregory also puts it, "by reason of the existence of godhead" (διὰ τὴν ὕπαρξιν τῆς θεότητος), which the Father "shines" in the theandric Christ "bodily" (ἐν αὐτῷ πᾶν τὸ πλήρωμα τῆς θεότητος *λάμπω σωματικῶς*).[20]

The same point is made in a later passage, couched in slightly different terms:

The Trinity is separated in Christ too without adding to itself, in the mode of existence on the one hand (τὸ μὲν γὰρ τῷ καθ᾽ ὕπαρξιν τρόπῳ) and in respect of essence on the other (τὸ δὲ τῷ κατ᾽ οὐσίαν λόγῳ), lest the Trinity become Quarternity, owing to the incarnation of the Son.[21]

Thus there are two modes by which the Trinity is seen to reside in Christ the God-man. Firstly, because of the *perichoresis*, co-inherence or interpenetration of all three Hypostases in one another; for which reason we can say that God the Son also possesses within Himself the Father and the Holy Spirit. This, moreover, must also apply to Christ's human nature: as a result of the *hypostatic* or *prosopic* union of the divine and human in the Son and Word of God, we are also obliged to confess that the *mode of existence* of Christ *in His humanity* is that of the Second Person of the Holy Trinity. The Trinity, therefore, resides in Christ *the God-man* in respect of His personal mode of existence.

Secondly, the Holy Trinity is also said to be in Christ according to a different mode of union, "in respect of essence." By this the Sinaïte refers to the single, common nature of the Holy Trinity, which each divine Hypostasis possesses in its entirety, but

---

20. Ibid.; and cf. Col. 2:9, ἐν αὐτῷ κατοικεῖ πᾶν τὸ πλήρωμα τῆς θεότητος σωματικῶς.
21. Ibid., 20.

which the human nature of Christ does not receive *essentially*. In the unique case of the Person of the Incarnate Logos, it is the *properties* or *energies* of the divine nature or essence, *but not the divine nature itself*, which are fully communicated to the human nature of Christ in the hypostatic union. In this way, significantly, the full integrity of the created assumed humanity of Christ is preserved. Implicit here, moreover, is the presupposition that if the human aspect of Christ also received its essence – its very being – from God the Father "in respect of essence," that is to say, essentially, then its nature would not in fact be human but divine, and we would be faced with an additional (divine and uncreated) element in the life of the Holy Trinity. For this reason, the two separate modes of union in the single Christ, the *hypostatic* and the *essential*, ensure the inviolate preservation of the Holy Trinity, and help us to appreciate that the Incarnation does not involve the introduction of another, "fourth element" into the Holy Trinity, which would result, as Gregory observes, in a "Quarternity, owing to the incarnation of the Son."[22] And so we see that the humanity of Christ is *hypostatically* united with, and thus inseparable from, God the Son, the Second Person of the Holy Trinity.

While St. Gregory identifies the Light of Tabor both as a revelation of the Hypostasis of God the Son and of all three Hypostases of the Holy Trinity, he distinguishes it from the divine essence *per se*. In contrasting the Sinaïtic theophany with that of Tabor, St. Gregory suggests, *inter alia*, that Sinai was a sign of "the unbearable and unapproachable character of the blessed essence" (τὸ ἄστεκτον καὶ ἀπρόσιτον τῆς μακαρίας οὐσίας αὐτοῦ)[23] – to which he later also adds the epithet "inconceivable"

---

22. St. Gregory also elaborates on the mystery of the threeness and oneness of the Trinity by means of the analogy of speech with mind and voice, ibid., 19.

23. Ibid., 4. Note that Gregory also ascribes the term "unbearable" (ἄστεκτον) to the divinity of Christ, attributing this to the imperfection of the three disciples, who had not been completely purified at the time of the Transfiguration (ἔτι γὰρ τὸ ἄστεκτον αὐτοῦ τῆς θεότητος οὐκ ἠδύναντο φέρειν διὰ τὸ ἀτελὲς τῆς καθάρσεως), implying, therefore, that the divinity is bearable for the perfect, that is, for those who have

(ἀκατάληπτος).²⁴ In reference to the manifestation of the omnipresent Son of God, St. Gregory becomes more explicit concerning the manner by which He communicates with man:

For He remains in His entirety in the bosom of the Father and the whole of Him is in us and is everywhere; and He proceeds ineffably and comes, and by what we mean His energy (ὅπερ ἐστὶν ἐνεργείας δηλωτικόν). But this too must be understood inexpressibly and as befits God.²⁵

Thus, Christ comes or reveals Himself not by His divine essence, but through His divine energy; by His revelatory action, which, being nothing less than the operation of God Himself, must also be understood in apophatic terms – ineffably and in a manner befitting God (ἀφράστως καὶ θεοπρεπῶς νοητέον). Indeed, Salvation is participation in the divine energies, for, as Gregory later adds, it is by the effulgence of the divine energies that the righteous are made to shine.²⁶

Elsewhere, in 113 of his *Chapters* (κεφάλαια or *Capita*), the Sinaïte, in reference to the gift of prayer, sums up all the above aspects of the divine economy in one sentence.

Prayer is God, who worketh all in all (1 Cor. 12:6), since there is one energy common to the Father, Son and Holy Ghost, working all things in Christ Jesus.²⁷

The main emphasis here is on the chief mode of man's communion with the triune God – prayer.²⁸ The identification of

---

been purified, ibid., and cf. 6. In the case of the divine essence, however, this term is noticeably left unqualified, thereby denoting unbearable in the absolute sense of the word.

24. Ibid., 25.
25. Ibid., 21.
26. Ibid., 27: ἐλλαμφθῶμεν τῇ τῶν ἐνεργειῶν σου ἐλλάμψει, ἀλλὰ μὴ βαρυνθῶμεν τῷ φωτὶ δι' ἀναξιότητα.
27. *Φιλοκαλία τῶν ἱερῶν νηπτικῶν*, Vol. 4 (Athens, 1976), p. 51: προσευχή ἐστιν ὁ Θεός, ὁ ἐνεργῶν τὰ πάντα ἐν πᾶσι, διὰ τὸ μίαν εἶναι Πατρὸς καὶ Υἱοῦ καὶ Ἁγίου Πνεύματος τὴν ἐνέργειαν, τοῦ ἐνεργοῦντος τὰ πάντα ἐν Χριστῷ Ἰησοῦ.
28. By prayer, of course, the Sinaïte as hesychast refers principally to the Jesus Prayer, which in concentrated form contains the essential

the gift of prayer with God Himself appears as the explicit corollary to the definition found in St. John Damascene (c. 655 – c. 750), namely, that "prayer is the manifestation of divine glory."[29] The Trinitarian formula simply serves to demonstrate that real and direct contact with God through prayer does not mean participation in the divine essence, but rather participation in the triune divine energy, which is nothing less than participation in God Himself. This, then, is "the energy and grace of that infinite light," as Gregory puts it in paragraph 8 of his *Vita*,[30] written by Kallistos I (Patriarch of Constantinople in 1350 – 1353, and again in 1355 – 1363),[31] which Adam lost after the fall.

The essence–energies distinction is not of course a new one; it had already been expressed in what was to become its most familiar form as early as St. Basil of Caesarea (c. 330 – 379),[32] and also in later writers, sometimes in the same language, as in Symeon the New Theologian (949 – 1022), though not consistently,[33] and sometimes in different

---

elements of both the Christological and Trinitarian doctrines of the Church: "Lord Jesus Christ, Son of God, have mercy upon me." St. Gregory also emphasizes the pneumatological dimension of the confession of Jesus as Lord, based on Scripture: "By our formula of prayer we give expression in the Spirit to the word that 'no man can say, Jesus is Lord, unless in the Holy Spirit'" (cf. 1 Cor. 12:3), ibid., 23; and Bishop Kallistos Ware, op. cit., 2–22..

29. *Homilia in transfigurationem salvatoris nostri Jesu Christi* 10: προσευχὴ δὲ θείας δόξης ἐμφάνεια.

30. Βίος καὶ πολιτεία τοῦ ἐν ἁγίοις πατρὸς ἡμῶν Γρηγορίου τοῦ Σιναΐτου συγγραφεὶς παρὰ τοῦ ἁγιωτάτου ἀρχιεπισκόπου Κωνσταντινουπόλεως Καλλίστου, edited by Ivan Pomjalovsky, in *Zapiski Istoriko-filologicheskogo fakulteta S. Peterburgskogo Universiteta* 35 (1896), 1–64.

31. Not to be confused with Kallistos II Xanthopoulos (Patriarch of Constantinople in 1397 for only three months), see Balfour, "St. Gregory of Sinai's Life Story and Spiritual Profile," op. cit., 32, n. 29.

32. *Epistula* 234, 1. This distinction, it should be noted, had also been expressed by writers before St. Basil, even if sometimes couched in rather different terms. For further details consult Veniamin, "Transfiguration", op. cit., *passim*.

33. See Veniamin, "Transfiguration", op. cit., p. 248, n. 5, and also as "The Spiritual Father and the Vision of Christ Transfigured in Symeon the New

language, as in John Chrysostom (c. 347 – 407),[34] but always, it should be noted, with the same gnosiological presuppositions in mind.

Reminiscent of the New Theologian in his at times unsystematic and non-technical employment of terms, the Sinaïte also speaks of Christ "as *essentially* partaken of because of His love for mankind."[35] The passage in question runs as follows:

> For it is He who gave the Law and spoke in the Law and was symbolically seen and truly visualized, and naturally invisible yet perceived in light and essentially partaken of for love of mankind (οὐσιωδῶς διὰ φιλανθρωπίαν μετεχόμενος) and admitted through purity, being the fount of kindness and abyss of light, at once light and cause of light, on the one hand because of His goodness, on the other because of His splendour, for He is, and is called, Light above cause and reason.[36]

Christ, by nature invisible (φύσει ἀόρατος), because of his love for mankind (διὰ φιλανθρωπίαν), makes Himself visible in light (ἐν φωτὶ καθορώμενος), and thereby allows us to share essentially (οὐσιωδῶς) in His divine life. The Sinaïte's somewhat ambiguous reference here to our essential partaking of Christ, prompted no doubt by 2 Pet. 1:4, is not discussed, but, given all that has been said about the manifestation of God through His divine energy, appears to be employed here in order to stress the reality of man's

---

Theologian," in Θεολογία καὶ Κόσμος σὲ Διάλογο [Theology and the World in Dialogue]: *Festschrift* for Prof. Georgios I. Mantzarides (Thessalonica, 2004), pp. 157–170; and cf. Basil of Seleucia, in "The Transfiguration of Christ in Greek Patristic Literature," op. cit., pp. 153–154.

34. Ibid., pp. 102–103, reworked as "Saint John Chrysostom and the Light of Tabor," the inaugural paper for the *Patristic and Byzantine Society* (Merton College, Oxford: Hilary Term, 1994), also published in *Alive in Christ*, Vol. X, no. 2 (Summer 1994), pp. 29–33; and cf. Maximus the Confessor, "The Transfiguration of Christ in Greek Patristic Literature," op. cit., p. 189, n. 3; and in "The Transfiguration of Christ and the Deification of Man," in Κληρονομία, Vol. 27, nos. 1–2 (1996), 313, 320–323.

35. Cf. Chrysostom's identification of God's love of mankind (φιλανθρωπία) with His condescension (συγκατάβασις), Veniamin, "Transfiguration", op. cit., p. 102.

36. *Discourse on the Transfiguration* 6.

communion with Christ, the fact that we have been called to share in *our* essence, that is, with our whole being, in Christ.[37]

Both the Christological and Trinitarian themes continue in the Sinaïte's references to the two prophets and the three disciples. Moses and Elijah, says Gregory, by their presence were declaring either the two natures of the Word, or, with Jesus, the three Hypostases of the Trinity.[38] The three disciples, on the other hand, whom the Sinaïte also regards as representing faith, hope and charity, the three powers of the soul, and the fulfilment of Matt. 18:16, are first and foremost representative of the Trinity.[39] Thus, the three disciples are symbolic witnesses of the Trinity and of the truth of the godhead; while the two prophets are primarily a type of the economy of Christ, Who is one and yet twofold in His nature. Together, then, the three and the two bear witness to the two principal dogmas of the faith.[40]

It is interesting, moreover, that Moses is regarded as being initiated into the mystery of God in three Persons: first on Horeb (= Sinai), where God the Holy Trinity, "He Who Is," was revealed to him; where, that is, he saw the Father legislating through the Son in the Spirit (ἐκεῖ μὲν Τὸν Ὄντα τριαδικὸν ἕνα Θεὸν ἐν γνόφῳ ἐθεάσατο πρότερον, τουτέστι τὸν Πατέρα δι' Υἱοῦ ἐν Πνεύματι νομοθετοῦντα); then on Tabor, where he comes face to face with Him "Who Is," one of the Holy Trinity, now made flesh (ἐνταῦθα δέ, Τὸν Ὄντα καὶ τῆς Τριάδος ἕνα σεσαρκωμένον ἐν Θαβὼρ), and recognizes in the transfigured Christ the fulfilment of all that had been previously revealed to him in symbols.

Now there (on Horeb) Moses had previously seen in the darkness that the one God "who is" was a triune God; that is, He saw the Father legislating through the Son in the Spirit, though most men – including the Jews themselves – foolishly thought there was only the Father; while

37. The Sinaïte is clearly less systematic in this regard than Palamas, see my own study, "*Divinae consortes naturae:* Notes on the Centrality of the Taborian Theophany in Saint Gregory Palamas," Κληρονομία, Vol. 28, nos. 1–2 (Thessalonica, 1996; published 1997), 85–103.
38. Op. cit., 10.
39. Ibid., 11.
40. Ibid., 15.

here, seeing Him "who is" and is one of the Trinity, incarnate on Thabor and shaped by the unapproachable light, and perceiving how His glory had shone forth, he rejoiced; he exulted as he recognised how all the symbolic figures of the Law had been fulfilled.[41]

The revelation to Moses on Sinai is thus firstly that of the *tri-hypostatic* nature of God, and secondly, on Tabor, that of the Incarnation of the Second Person of the Holy Trinity – the realization of all that had been prefigured on Sinai.[42]

In contrasting Sinai with Tabor,[43] the Sinaïte sees divine symbols revealed "both in the darkness of the old and later in the splendour of the Transfiguration." Of course, the term splendour suggests greater clarity of vision and understanding.[44] But the Transfiguration, according to St. Gregory, differs from Sinai chiefly in two respects: firstly, as the manifestation of the assumption and glorification of human nature by the Second Person of the Holy Trinity; and secondly, a fact which follows directly from the first, as the disclosure of "the earnest of the eternal beatitude," the glory in which the righteous will shine in the Age to Come.[45] As St. Gregory says, "His purpose was to show both the splendour of the glory to come and the pure beauty of the incarnation, by which God became truly man in a superhuman way."[46] These two new elements, then, unique to the Taborian theophany, constitute the true answer to the question posed by Christ at Philippi (Matt. 16:13–14; Mark 8:27–28; Luke 9:13–19).

Elijah too, says St. Gregory, recognizes Christ as the same Lord whom he knew in the fire and breeze.[47] Interestingly, he also speaks of the purifying and deifying effect of Elijah's vision of

---

41. Ibid., 8: πάντα τοῦ νόμου σύμβολα ὁρῶν ἐκβεβηκότα, ἠγαλλιᾶτο.
42. See also ibid., 5, where Moses is described as "a most initiated mystic seer of the symbols" (θεατὴς τῶν συμβόλων ἐκφαντορικῶς μυστικώτατος).
43. Ibid., 4, and 6.
44. Ibid., 16.
45. Ibid., 17, and 23.
46. Ibid., 7: ἵνα καὶ τῆς μελλούσης δόξης δείξῃ τὴν λαμπρότητα καὶ τῆς ἐνανθρωπήσεως αὐτοῦ τὴν εἰλικρινῆ ὡραιότητα, ἀληθῶς ἄνθρωπος γεγονὼς ὁ Θεὸς ὑπὲρ ἄνθρωπον.
47. Ibid., 9.

Yahweh on Horeb, curiously interpreting the light breeze, in which God was, as a manifestation not of a voice, but of light (αὔραν... λεπτὴν φωτός, cf. 3 Kgs. 19:12: φωνὴ αὔρας λεπτῆς). Indeed, the entire event is described in terms of vision, power and light.

And he saw a "great strong wind" such as crushes those initiated into hesychastic prayer, and an "earthquake" of the heart, and a "fire" of power which purifies; and finally a "light breath" of light [by which Elijah was deified],[48] in which God becomes superessentially intelligible to us in states of participation.[49]

St. Gregory also touches upon the question of the manner or state in which Moses and Elijah appeared by Christ's side at the Transfiguration. Christ, he says, summoned them in an instant to His side: Moses "from the grave" (ἐκ νεκάδων), Elijah "as from heaven" (ὡς ἐξ οὐρανοῦ).[50] The Sinaïte admits that while he is inclined to think that Moses probably appeared without his body, it must be conceded that "all things are possible to God, who vouchsafed that Elijah should superhumanly ride in the upper air with his body."[51] The three disciples, moreover, appeared imperfect compared to Moses and Elijah, although he holds that this does not mean that the two prophets were in any way superior to the three disciples, since, as the Sinaïte puts it, even in the two prophets at that time there was "the spirit of bondage" (πνεῦμα δουλείας ἦν ἐν αὐτοῖς).[52]

St. Gregory also follows the κάθαρσις–φωτισμός–θέωσις schema. The Transfiguration of the human nature of Christ hints

48. The words in brackets are my own addition to Balfour's translation. The line in question runs as follows: καὶ πνεῦμα μέγα κραταιὸν ὁρᾷ τῆς συντριβῆς τῶν περὶ ἡσυχίας εἰσαγωμένων καὶ συσσισμὸν καρδίας καὶ πῦρ καθαρτικὸν τῆς δυνάμεως καὶ αὔραν τὸ τελευταῖον λεπτὴν φωτὸς θεώμενος, ...
49. Ibid., 5.
50. Ibid.
51. Ibid. Note, however, that Elijah's bodily ascension is widely understood in a prophetic sense, see e.g. St. Gregory Palamas' Hom. XXI, 2, "On the Ascension of Our Lord and God and Saviour Jesus Christ," and esp. n. 312, in *Saint Gregory Palamas: The Homilies,* op. cit., pp. 171 and 572.
52. Ibid., 4.

mysteriously at our moral transformation (ἠθικῆς ἀλλοιώσεω).⁵³ In the very first paragraph of his sermon, St. Gregory refers to "all those who reflect as mirrors the vision of magnificent glory with unveiled countenance" (ἀνακεκαλυμμένῳ προσώπῳ κατοπτριζόμενοι, 2 Cor. 3:18)⁵⁴ – a Pauline reference, of course, especially significant in St. Gregory of Nyssa. While the contemplation of the divine light may also (to a certain degree)⁵⁵ be experienced by the senses,⁵⁶ as noetic or intelligible it is perceived primarily by the intellect or *nous*,⁵⁷ which thus receives illumination (φωτισμός).⁵⁸ Furthermore, at a certain point, the noetic light actually overpowers the senses (φωτὶ νικῶντι τὴν αἴσθησιν), and, as a result of a kind of ecstasy which removes what St. Gregory calls "the sensual perception of relationships,"⁵⁹ causes them to cease operating.⁶⁰ And it is at this point that one arrives at the stage of deification or perfection (θέωσις).

In summing up, then, we can say that in St. Gregory the Sinaïte's interplay of dogmatic and mystical theology the focus is

53. Ibid., 14.
54. Ibid., 1. Note also, that he refers here to the Maximian phrase, "from the flesh to the spirit" (ἀπὸ τῆς σαρκὸς εἰς τὸ πνεῦμα), meaning in this case, that having transfigured our intellect we may pass from the realm of the divine economy to that of theology proper, see esp. St. Maximus the Confessor, *Ambigua* X (*Patrologia Graeca* 91:1125D), and in his *Quaestiones et Dubia* 191; and also in Veniamin, in "The Transfiguration of Christ and the Deification of Man," op. cit., 313-314. It seems that St. Gregory is here already preparing his audience for the highly Trinitarian perspective of his sermon.
55. Ibid., 1: καὶ ὡς δυνατὸν ὀψόμεθα; and cf. ibid., 6, where the reason given for the three disciples' inability to endure the light of Christ's resplendent face is their imperfection (ἀτέλεια).
56. Ibid., 24: ὑπὲρ ἥλιον αἰσθητῶς τε καὶ νοητῶς τὸν ἑαυτῶν ὀρῶντες ἐν ὄρει δεσπότην ἐκλάμψαντα καὶ τὰ πάντα φωτίσαντα καὶ ἁγιάσαντα.
57. Ibid., 1, and 27.
58. Ibid., 7.
59. Ibid., 13, and cf. 12, where St. Peter's words are said to be the result of the ecstasy and inebriation of his intellect (μὴ εἰδὼς ἀπὸ τῆς ἐκστάσεως καὶ μέθης τὶ λέγει).
60. Ibid., 7, and 12: τῷ θείῳ φωτὶ κάτοχοι γεγονότες.

clearly on the Christological and Trinitarian "mode" by which the Light of Christ's divine glory is revealed. Indeed, the way in which St. Gregory describes its manifestation and the human person's participation in it is an explicit corollary of the doctrine of the hypostatic union of the two natures in Christ, and of the *Monarchia* of the Father, the *perichoresis* of the three divine Hypostases, and the single, common *energeia* or action *ad extra* in the mystery of the Holy Trinity. St. Gregory's view of the human person, moreover, is entirely positive, inasmuch as he maintains that the manifestation of God by His divine Light, although perceived primarily through the human intellect or *nous,* is also seen, to a certain degree even in this life, through the eyes of the physical body. And this in turn signifies our future hope: participation of the entire human person in Christ.

Partakers of Divine Nature
ST GREGORY PALAMAS
AND THE CENTRALITY OF THE
TRANSFIGURATION

THE VISION OF THE DIVINE LIGHT OF TABOR stands at the very epicentre of St. Gregory Palamas' theology, permeating and informing his every word. Many of the Church Fathers had written on the Transfiguration before Palamas,[1] and St. Gregory regarded himself as but a faithful exponent and continuator of their ascetico-theological tradition,[2] but none had integrated the Taborian theophany into the fabric of their theological vision in quite as comprehensive a manner as this particular Metropolitan of Thessalonica. It is, indeed, this all-encompassing Taborian perspective which constitutes Gregory's greatest contribution to the subject, and which justifies our appellation of him as Theologian *par excellence* of the divine Light of Tabor.

St. Gregory's fundamental concern, evident in all his works, is to affirm that even from this present life man is called to direct and unmediated communion with God Himself. Prayer is at one and the same time the chief means by which this communion is attained, and, in its truest form, the communion itself. Prayer as communion, prayer as theology, is nothing less than the face to Face encounter with the theandric Christ resplendent in His pre-eternal and divine glory – His Kingdom or Rule – just as He was revealed to His three disciples on Mount Tabor.

For St. Gregory Palamas (1347 – 1359) the divine Light of Tabor is unequivocally uncreated (ἄκτιστον). It is a light, therefore, but a light that is radically unlike any created light known to man. Though perceptible to both the senses and the intellect (the νοῦς), in the experience of deification (θέωσις) the Uncreated Light of Christ transcends every aspect of our createdness, including the human senses and the human intellect. Hence, it is both suprasensible and supra-intellectual. Moreover, St. Gregory accuses 'those who wage war against the Light' (τοῖς τοῦ φωτὸς πολεμίοις), that is, those who consider the Light to be both sensible and created, of basing their understanding not on Holy Scripture and Sacred Tradition but on 'the rational word of the Greeks', on the wisdom, that is, of this world.[3]

Palamas' ascetico-theological approach is further witnessed to by the *way* that he reads the Bible. His interpretation of Scripture is inextricably bound up with Tradition (to which he constantly appeals), which is rooted in the personal experience of the saints, the Fathers of the Church. As St. Gregory puts it in his *Homilia XXXIV*:

We have been taught by those who have been enlightened by Christ of those things which only they know with certainty (ὡς ἐδιδάχθημεν παρὰ τῶν ὑπὸ τοῦ Χριστοῦ φωτισθέντων, ἅτε μόνον ἀκριβῶς εἰδότων). For my mysteries are for me and for mine (Τὰ γὰρ μυστήριά μου ἐμοὶ καὶ τοῖς ἐμοῖς), says God by the prophet (cf. Dan. 2:27ff).[4]

In support of his own position on the uncreatedness of the divine Light of Tabor, Palamas focuses firstly on Christ, Who, he argues, had Himself identified the Light of Tabor with the Kingdom of God (Matt. 16:28ff, and parallels). Then he continues as follows:

The Kingdom of God is neither a servant nor created; for it alone is without master and unconquerable, and beyond all time and age (καὶ χρόνου παντῶς καὶ αἰῶνος ἐπέκεινα). It is neither possible for the

Kingdom of God to have a beginning nor to be subject to corruption. For it is, we believe, the inheritance of those who are being saved.[5]

The Transfiguration Light is, therefore, the very same Light in which Christ will shine at His Second Coming. Echoing Clement of Alexandria,[6] Palamas insists that the Light of Christ is His eternal glory and not a light which has been added to Him; one, that is, which He did not previously possess but which was assumed at the Transfiguration. It is wrong to conceive of the divine Light which shone around Christ as a phantasm (φάσμα) or a symbol (σύμβολον) that comes into being and then passes out of existence (γίνεσθαι καὶ ἀπογίνεσθαι).[7] Christ's Transfiguration was not a 'flash-in-the-pan' glorification. Such a view, argues Gregory, would imply that there are now three natures glorified in Christ: the divine, the human, and then that of the light. But although concealed beneath His flesh until His Transfiguration, Christ (the Light of Light) always possessed the light which was revealed on Tabor.[8] Thus, since this light is divine, being that of the Godhead, it must also be uncreated.[9] St. Gregory's fundamental gnosiological presupposition here is, of course, based on the sharp distinction between the created and the uncreated, in which there is no room for a third, metaphysical category.[10] Hence, if the Light of Tabor is divine, then it must also be uncreated, since by definition all things divine are also uncreated.[11]

In considering why Christ had taken the chiefs of the Apostles up to a high mount apart, Palamas concludes that it must have been in order to make a mystical disclosure. In refuting the idea that this disclosure was merely one of a created light, he asks the following long series of rhetorical questions:

What is so great and mystical about the vision of a created light, which both those who were chosen, before they were taken up, and those who were left behind had already had? What need was there for the power of the Spirit, by which they received the eyes or rather by which their eyes were changed in order to see that Light, if it were simply sensible and created? And how could a sensible light be the glory and Kingdom of the Father and the Spirit? And how could Christ come in such a (sensible) glory in the Age to Come, when there will be no need of air or light or space and suchlike, but there will be for us God beyond all? And if beyond all, then surely also beyond light (Εἰ δὲ ἀντὶ πάντων, καὶ ἀντὶ φωτὸς πάντως). Therefore, that light is again shown to be of the Godhead. For this reason, John, the most theological of the Evangelists, reveals by the Apocalypse concerning that future and eternal city, that "the city has no need of the sun or the moon to shine upon it, for the glory of God is its light, and its lamp is the lamb" (Rev. 21:23).[12] Does he not clearly show us here Jesus who is now on Tabor divinely transfigured; whose body is as a lamp, and whose light is the glory of the Godhead manifested on the mountain to those who went up with Him. And concerning those who shall dwell in that city, the same (Evangelist) says, "they need no light of lamp or sun, for the Lord God will be their light, and night shall be no more" (cf. Rev. 22:5). What is this light, then, in which there is no alteration or shadow of change (παρ᾽ ᾧ οὐκ ἔστι παραλλαγή, ἢ τροπῆς ἀποσκίασμα, Jas. 1:17)? What is this unchangeable and never-setting light? Is it not the Light of the Godhead? And Moses and Elias (and indeed Moses existing in His unembodied soul), how could they appear and be glorified by a sensible light? And these, appearing also in that same glory, spoke of His departure which he was to accomplish in Jerusalem. And how could the Apostles recognize those whom they had never seen, if not by the revelatory power of that light?[13]

Palamas rebukes 'those who are at present blaspheming' for reducing not only the Kingdom of God but also the power of the Holy Spirit to the level of a creature, and quoting 1 Cor. 2:9–10 (ἃ ὀφθαλμὸς οὐκ εἶδε, καὶ οὓς οὐκ ἤκουσε, καὶ ἐπὶ καρδίαν ἀνθρώπου οὐκ ἀνέβη, ἃ ἡτοίμασεν ὁ Θεὸς τοῖς ἀγαπῶσιν αὐτόν, ἡμῖν δὲ ἀπεκάλυψεν ὁ Θεὸς διὰ τοῦ Πνεύματος αὐτοῦ· τὸ γὰρ Πνεῦμα ἐρευνᾷ καὶ τὰ βάθη τοῦ Θεου), he holds that it is by this very power that things divine are revealed to the worthy.[14]

In connection with the nature and significance of the Bright Cloud, Palamas first regards it as the divine response in answer to Peter's words, manifesting the only tabernacle fitting for Christ.[15] He then goes on to ask *who* the Bright Cloud might be, and how or why it overshadowed them all at the Transfiguration. Interestingly, he concludes by saying that this again is the unapproachable light in which God dwells (1 Tim. 6:16, Μόνος ἔχων ἀθανασίαν, φῶς οἰκῶν ἀπρόσιτον), and with which He is clothed (cf. Ps. 103:23, ἀναβαλλόμενος φῶς ὡς ἱμάτιον... ὁ τιθεὶς νέφη τὴν ἐπίβασιν αὐτοῦ; and Ps. 17:12, Ἔθετο σκότος ἀποκρυφὴν αὐτοῦ, κύκλῳ αὐτοῦ ἡ σκηνὴ αὐτοῦ). Palamas maintains that this very same Light, because of its surpassing brilliance (δι' ὑπερέχουσαν φανότητα) which overshadows the beholder, is referred to sometimes as light and sometimes as darkness (ὥστε τὸ αὐτὸ καὶ φῶς ἐστιν ἐνταυθοῖ καὶ σκότος).[16] In support of the latter, St. Gregory appeals to St. Dionysius the Areopagite who refers to the divine Light as the dark cloud (γνόφος), in which those worthy of knowing and seeing God enter (γνόφον εἰπὼν εἶναι τὸ ἀπρόσιτον φῶς, ἐν ᾧ κατοικεῖν ὁ Θεὸς λέγεται, ἐν τούτῳ, φησί, γίνεται πᾶς ὁ Θεὸν γνῶναι καὶ ἰδεῖν ἀξιούμενος).[17] And he adds that it was this same light which later manifested itself as the Bright Cloud.

Therefore it was the same light which the Apostles saw shining first from the face of Christ which afterwards appeared as the overshadowing Cloud. But then it granted them sight by shining more obscurely (Ἀλλὰ τότε μὲν ἀμυδρότερον ἐπιλάμπον παρεῖχε τὸ ὁρᾶν); whereas later, shining more intensely, it became invisible by reason of its surpassing luminosity (ἐκφανὲν δὲ πολλῷ πλέον ὕστερον, ἀόρατον αὐτοῖς ὑπῆρχε δι' ὑπερέχουσαν φανότητα), and in this way, it overshadowed Jesus, the Sun of Righteousness (Mal. 4:2), who is the source of the divine and eternal light (καὶ οὕτω, τὴν τοῦ θείου καὶ ἀενάου φωτὸς πηγήν, τὸν ἥλιον τῆς δικαιοσύνης ἐπεσκίασε Χριστόν).[18]

Here, Palamas discerns two stages in the manifestation of the Transfiguration Light: the first, as light, when it is seen by the Apostles shining from the Face of Christ; and the second, in its appearance as the Bright Cloud, signifying an increasing intensity in its brightness, so much so that the Apostles could no longer look upon it. It surrounds Christ, adds Gregory, because He is the source of the divine and eternal light.

Interestingly, Palamas also identifies the Light of Tabor with the very first light which shone forth (Gen. 1:3–5), and proceeds to compare it to that of the sun. There was a time, he says, when the sun's light was not, and the light that was made to shine was clearly not, as we now see it, in the shape of a disc. The first is the progenitor or original light (πρωτόγονον), while the second, says

St. Gregory, is that physical light which was brought into existence on the fourth day of creation by Him who created all things. Hence, though there was a time when the divine Light was not in the assumed vessel of the human body of Christ, yet it always existed as pre-eternal and without beginning (προάναρχον).[19]

Palamas points out that St. Luke does not compare Christ's shining Face to any thing, nor indeed does he do so in the case of the bright garments (Luke 9:29); while St. Mark's comparison of Christ's garments to snow (Mark 9:3) simply serves to illustrate the inadequateness of the images employed; for snow, says St. Gregory, is indeed white, but it is not, by any stretch of the imagination, brilliant and dazzling (ἡ γὰρ χιὼν λευκὴ μέν ἐστιν, ἀλλ' οὐχὶ καὶ στίλβουσα).[20] Therefore, because the whiteness of snow, by itself, does not suffice to convey the delight (τερπνόν) of that vision, the quality of brilliance (τὸ στίλβειν) is also employed; for this light made Christ's garments brilliant, whereas material light, argues St. Gregory, does not make objects bright and white, but rather simply reveals their natural colour.[21] And by referring to both the Face and garments of the Lord, the Evangelist shows that His brightness is beyond anything that either nature (represented by His Face) or craftsmanship (represented by His garments) could achieve.[22] The peculiar terms used by the Evangelists in attempting to describe the divine Light are thus yet another indication of the supranatural quality of the Light of the Transfiguration (ὑπερφυὲς τὸ φῶς ἐκεῖνο).[23]

Palamas also refers to a grave contradiction in the contentions of his theological adversaries. At first, he claims, they maintained that the divine and supranatural and uncreated Light of Christ is both sensible and created; whereas now they insist not only on affirming the divinity of the Light of Christ but also on identifying it with the very essence of God.[24] Palamas concludes, therefore, that either the Barlaamites accept the divine Light as both created and as the essence of God, or they must be referring to two different essences and two different divinities or Godheads.[25]

In order to refute the Barlaamite position, and to show that the uncreated glory of God is not to be identified with the divine essence, Palamas points to the participation in that glory of both the angelic powers and the elect.

> And the Lord says in the Gospels that this (final) glory is not common to Himself and the Father alone, but also to the holy angels, as the divine Luke writes, "for whosoever shall be ashamed of me and of my words, of him shall the Son of man be ashamed, when he shall come in his own glory, and in his Father's, and of the holy angels" (Luke 9:26). Those therefore who endeavour to identify that glory with the (divine) essence, also say that the essence of God and the angels is one and the same, which is the ultimate impiety! And indeed not only angels, but also holy men participate in that same glory and Kingdom; but while the Father and the Son together with the divine Spirit possess this glory and Kingdom by nature, both the holy angels and men possess it by grace (χάριτι ταύτης εὐμοιροῦσιν). And both Moses and Elias, who appeared with Him in the same glory, demonstrate this to us.[26]

Note first that 'glory' and 'Kingdom' are used here synonymously. So too is the term λαμπρότης, 'brightness' or 'brilliance' (Κοινὴν μὲν οὖν ἡ δόξα καὶ ἡ βασιλεία καὶ ἡ λαμπρότης αὕτη τοῦ τε Θεοῦ καὶ τῶν αὐτοῦ ἁγίων), as is indicated by the Scriptural verse, 'the brightness of the Lord our God be upon us' (Ps. 89(90):17). Hence, according to Palamas, the divine and uncreated glory, Kingdom and brilliance is one and the same in God and in His saints. However, the same can not be said of the divine essence, for, as St. Gregory continues, no one – by which of course St. Gregory means none of the Prophets, Apostles or saints – has ever dared to say that the essence of God is one and the same in God and the saints (κοινὴν δὲ καὶ μίαν εἶναι τὴν οὐσίαν τοῦ Θεοῦ καὶ τῶν ἁγίων οὐδείς πω μέχρι καὶ νῦν ἐτόλμησεν εἰπεῖν).[27]

This distinction also holds true on the Christological plane, in the case of the two natures of Christ, where the divine brilliance is one and the same in the divinity of the Logos and (by virtue of the hypostatic union and the *communicatio idiomatum* which proceeds from it) in His flesh; whereas, as Palamas puts it, only Eutyches and Dioscorus would say that the essence is common to the Godhead and the flesh.[28] In fact Palamas, like St. Gregory the Sinaïte,[29] bases his Trinitarian theology on Christology, and this is particularly evident in his third letter to Akindynus, in which Palamas goes so far as to accuse Barlaam of atheism:

> For if (as we are told) God had no natural and essential energies, then he who says such a thing would be an atheist – for this again clearly means that there is no God; since the saints openly state that if there exists no natural and essential energy, then there would be neither God nor man in Christ who is venerated in those two energies and two natures – or, if we were to accept that there exist natural and essential energies of God, but that these were created, then we should also have to say that the divine essence from which they stem is created too. For if the natural and essential energies of the essence and nature were created, then the essence could not be uncreated. And then the divine providence and deifying power and the brightness of God, which was manifested on Tabor to Moses and Elias and to those who went up together with Christ, revealing His divinity and Kingdom, these too would also be created, if the (divine) nature alone were without beginning and everlasting and it alone were the uncreated light and the uncreated glory of God; therefore, the uncreated divinity is one, being of the one uncreated divine essence.[30]

Thus, the final glory is uncreated, and Palamas insists that all shall see the glory and brilliance of the Lord when He comes shining from the East to the West, in the same way as those who now ascend with Jesus. However, he reiterates, no one has found himself in the substance and essence of God, neither has any one seen or spoken of seeing the nature of God (οὐδεὶς δὲ ἔστη ἐν ὑποστήματι καὶ οὐσίᾳ Θεοῦ, καὶ Θεοῦ φύσιν εἶδεν ἢ ἐξηγόρευσε).[31]

In his interpretation of 'partakers of the divine nature' (2 Pet. 1:4), St. Gregory appeals to the authority of Maximus the Confessor:

> Listen now to the same Maximus who says, "He who is not participable according to His essence for beings, but willing to be participable in another way to those who are able, does not come out of His hiddenness according to essence". And again he says, "all of us in general become gods without becoming identical to His essence". And again, "the blessed Godhead is in essence above the ineffable and beyond the unknowable and infinitely transcendent of every

infinity, leaving no trace of comprehension whatsoever – not even a faint one – after its manifestation".[32]

Palamas continues in the same vein, appealing to, among others, SS. Athanasius, Basil, and Chrysostom. For Gregory, then, the nature of God is invisible and unparticipable, and this preserves the integrity of the Holy Trinity. His perspective is simply one of an ascetic seeking to describe, so far as is humanly possible, the mystery of the experience through prayer of man's union with his Creator. He refuses to accept a mode of union either according to essence (κατ' οὐσίαν) or according to hypostasis (καθ' ὑπόστασιν), because he sees the first as applying only to the unity of the Three Divine Hypostases, while he regards the second as unique to the prosopic or hypostatic union of the divine and human in Christ, the Second Person of the Holy Trinity.[33] The only other way of safeguarding the belief in a real and direct union with God, as Palamas sees it, is thus by that mode which is on the level of deifying Grace (κατὰ χάριν), which Palamas most frequently refers to as union or participation according to the divine energy (κατὰ τὴν θείαν θεοῦσθαι χάριν τε καὶ ἐνέργειαν).[34] Hence, while the divine essence is unparticipable (ἀμέθεκτος), indivisible and therefore simple, the divine energy is participable, divisible and therefore may be divided into many and different energies.[35] Palamas identifies the divine Light with all the energies of God, then, and in so doing appeals also to Basil the Great and Gregory of Nazianzus.[36]

Before moving on to the question of the way by which contemplation of the divine Light may be attained, it would be expedient to make certain brief observations concerning the divisibility and multiplicity of the divine energies in St. Gregory. In direct reference to the knowablility of the divine Light, it is important to note that St. Gregory affirms a fundamental mystery: that the divine Light is 'undividedly divided' (ἀμερίστως μεριζόμενον). In other words, with the manifestation of the divinity or Godhead to each person we are faced with the paradox that the whole divinity is present without suffering diminution in any way.[37] Furthermore, he argues that whereas we know it only in part in this life (cf. 1 Cor. 13:9), we shall know it in the life to come (Μετρεῖται μὲν οὖν οὕτω καὶ μερίζεται ἀμερίστως, καὶ τὸ μᾶλλον καὶ ἧττον ἐπιδέχεται τὸ φῶς ἐκεῖνο· καὶ τὸ μὲν αὐτοῦ νῦν, τὸ δ᾽ ὕστερον γνωρίζεται). As already indicated, however, this knowledge is not one of sensual perception or of noetic apprehension, because it is the result of the union or, rather, the communion of the created with the Uncreated, or better still, of the creature with the Creator. This, however, is not the case as far as the divine essence is concerned. The divine essence, unlike the divine Light, is perfectly indivisible and thus inapprehensible by the senses or intellect, and as such offers no prospect of an increasing or decreasing knowledge of it either in this life or in the life to come (Ἀμερὴς δέ ἐστι παντάπασι καὶ ἄληπτος ἡ τοῦ Θεοῦ οὐσία, καὶ τὸ μᾶλλον καὶ ἧττον οὐδεμία τῶν οὐσιῶν ἐπιδέχεται). And St. Gregory adds that it is the Messalians who falsely claim that those who are worthy actually see the essence of God (ἄλλως τε καὶ τῶν καταράτων Μεσσαλιανῶν ἐστιν ὁρᾶσθαι οἴεσθαι τὴν οὐσίαν τοῦ Θεοῦ τοῖς κατ᾽ αὐτοὺς ἀξίους).[38]

Now concerning the manner by which the contemplation of the divine Light of Christ may be attained, St. Gregory points first and foremost to prayer. Prayer, he says, is the ambassador or agent of the blessed vision, and this is why Christ Himself prayed immediately before His Transfiguration (ἵνα δείξῃ πρόξενον οὖσαν τὴν προσευχὴν τῆς μακαρίας ἐκείνης θέας),[39] even though (as consubstantial and undivided with the Father) He did not need to do so.[40] Faithful to the hesychast tradition, Palamas also stresses the importance of the cultivation of virtue: that it is through unceasing good works and earnest prayer toward God, and by the union according to the intellect that 'brightness' (ἡ λαμπρότης) is attained: ὅτι διὰ τῆς πρὸς Θεὸν κατ᾽ ἀρετὴν ἐγγύτητος, καὶ τῆς πρὸς αὐτὸν κατὰ νοῦν ἐνώσεως, ἡ λαμπρότης ἐγγίνεται καὶ ἀναφαίνεται ἐκείνη, πᾶσι διδομένη τε καὶ ὁρωμένη, τοῖς δι᾽ ἀγαθοεργίας ἀκριβοῦς, καὶ διὰ προσευχῆς εἰλικρινοῦς, ἀνατεινομένοις ἀδιαλείπτως πρὸς Θεόν.[41]

Like St. Basil of Caesarea before him, Palamas also speaks of the divine beauty (κάλλος) in relation to the Transfiguration.

This is not the divine nature itself, however, but rather that which *surrounds* the blessed nature; and it is this aspect of God which may be contemplated only by the intellect which has been purified (Κάλλος... μόνῳ τῷ τὸν νοῦν κεκαθαρμένῳ θεωρητὸν τὸ περὶ τὴν θείαν καὶ μακαρίαν φύσιν ἐστὶν).[42] He who looks upon the splendour and charisms of that light, says Gregory in a way which is reminiscent of Irenaeus of Lyons, participates in a *part* of it (μεταλαμβάνει τι ἀπ' αὐτοῦ).[43] And this is precisely why the face of Moses was glorified when he spoke with God.[44]

Palamas asserts that the divine Light, not being a sensible, physical light, cannot be seen merely by the physical eyes of the body. In order for our eyes to participate in this vision, it is first necessary for them to undergo a spiritual transformation, brought about of course *by the power of the divine Spirit*. This is how the three disciples were enabled to see the vision of the Light of Tabor: 'they were changed', says St. Gregory, 'and in this way they saw the change' (Ἐνηλλάγησαν οὖν, καὶ οὕτω τὴν ἐναλλαγὴν εἶδον).[45] The divine Light, then, is visible to the physical eyes of the body, and it was actually seen by the eyes of the Apostles at the Transfiguration[46] – even if only very briefly (καὶ ἑωρᾶτο τοῖς τῶν ἀποστόλων ὀφθαλμοῖς, καὶ ταῦτα οὐκ ἐκ πολλοῦ διαστήματος).[47] Explicitly identifying now the divine Light with the divine power, Palamas characteristically notes with caution that the divine power may be seen only by those who have the eyes of their heart purified (ἡ θεία δύναμις, διαυγάζουσα τοῖς ἔχουσι τοὺς ὀφθαλμοὺς τῆς καρδίας κεκαθαρμένους).[48]

Commenting on the significance of the words 'as the sun' in Matt. 17:2, St. Gregory echoes both SS. John Chrysostom and Maximus the Confessor,[49] who placed a strong emphasis on the noetic nature of the vision:

He [Matthew] said "as the sun", not in order to make one think of that light as sensible – Begone to the blindness of the intellect in those who are incapable of understanding any phenomenon which is superior to those within the realm of the senses! – but so that we should know, that what the sun is to those who live according to the senses, and see through the senses, Christ as God is to those who live according to the Spirit, and see in the Spirit, and there is no need for those who are godlike for another light in the vision of God: to those who are eternal He, and no other, is Light. For what need is there of a second light for those who possess the greatest?[50]

In response, it seems, to the view that the Transfiguration glory is not the highest form of theophany, but one which is inferior to the illumination of the νοῦς, St. Gregory argues that such a vision, far from being inferior to the intellect (οὐ τοῦ νοῦ χείρων),[51] is actually superior to it precisely because it is seen *in the divine Spirit*. The Light of the Transfiguration, therefore, cannot be a transitory glory, one which comes-to-be and then passes away, neither is it circumscribable, nor can it be subjected to the power of the senses (even if it is actually seen by the eyes of the body). Quoting Maximus again, St. Gregory adds that the vision of the Light of Tabor did not remain on the level of the Apostles' sensory perception, 'but passed from the flesh to the spirit' (ἀπὸ τῆς σαρκὸς εἰς τὸ πνεῦμα μετέβησαν), so that they underwent a change in the operation of their senses (τῇ ἐναλλαγῇ τῶν κατ' αἴσθησιν ἐνεργειῶν), through the *action* of the Holy Spirit (ἣν αὐτοὺς τὸ πνεῦμα ἐνήργησε), and in this way they saw that ineffable Light *when* and *as much as* the power of the divine Spirit granted or allowed them to see.[52]

As we have seen in the case of the Bright Cloud, Palamas discerns different levels of intensity in the shining of the divine Light, and also different levels of intensity in the measure according to which it is meted out to those who are worthy of receiving the vision (μέτρῳ δίδοται, καὶ τὸ μᾶλλον καὶ ἧττον ἐπιδέχεται, κατὰ τὴν ἀξίαν τῶν ὑποδεχομένων ἀμερίστως μεριζόμενον). Hence, the Face of the Lord shone as the sun, whereas His garments became white as snow; and while Moses and Elias appeared in this same glory, neither of them is said to have shone *as the sun*.[53] The three disciples, on the other hand, saw that light, but were unable to gaze upon it (τῷ δὲ ἀτενίζειν οὐκ ἠδυνήθησαν).[54] Beyond a certain level of intensity, moreover, the divine Light becomes *invisible* to both the transfigured eyes and the intellect, just as it proved to be in the case of the three Apostles, who for this reason are described as entering into a Bright Cloud (εἶτα τηλαυγέστερος λάμψας, ὡς ἠθέλησε, δι' ὑπερέχουσαν φανότητα τοῖς τῶν ἀποστόλων ὀφθαλμοῖς ἀόρατος ὑπῆρχεν, ὥσπερ εἰς φωτεινὴν νεφέλην εἰσελθών), which signifies the intensification of its brightness beyond human visual capacity.[55]

Most evident is the fact that for St. Gregory the basis of divine knowledge is not philosophical speculation but direct experience of God granted by the Holy Spirit Himself.[56] In a line of thought which may be traced back to Origen, he maintains that the bright garments of the divine Word represent the words of Scripture (τὰ ῥήματα τοῦ Εὐαγγελικοῦ κηρύγματος), the meaning of which, when contemplated in the Spirit, becomes bright and clear.[57] Only then is the Gospel understood in a divine way and as befits God (μᾶλλον δὲ θεοπρεπῶς καὶ ἔνθεον τοῖς ἐν Πνεύματι τὰ τοῦ Πνεύματος ὁρῶσι καὶ διασαφοῦσι τὰς ἐν τῷ γράμματι λέξεις θεοπρεπῶς).[58] Palamas also takes up Origen's interpretation of the term fuller (γναφεὺς) as referring to the wise of this present age (σοφὸς τοῦ αἰῶνος τούτου),[59] who are unable to explain or even to know things divine (οὐ δύναται διασαφῆσαι· καὶ τί λέγω διασαφῆσαι; Οὐδὲ γὰρ δύναται γνῶναι). And linking this to what St. Paul has to say about the unspiritual man (ψυχικὸς γὰρ ἄνθρωπος οὐ δέχεται τὰ τοῦ Πνεύματος, οὐδὲ δύναται γνῶναι, 1 Cor. 2:14), he concludes that he who is lacking in divine illumination, by attempting to penetrate things which he has never seen – his carnal mind being vainly puffed up with conceit (ἃ μὴ ἑώρακεν ἐμβατεύων, εἰκῇ φυσιούμενος ὑπὸ τοῦ νοὸς τῆς σαρκὸς αὐτοῦ) – mistakes divine and spiritual illuminations, which are beyond the intellect, for sensible phenomena (εἰς αἰσθητὰς παραγνωρίζει τὰς ὑπὲρ νοῦν καὶ θείας καὶ πνευματικὰς ἐλλάμψεις).[60]

St. Gregory also sees a difference between the shining Face of Christ and His garments, for whereas His Face shone as the sun, His garments became bright by virtue of their touching upon His body (τὸ μὲν γὰρ πρόσωπον αὐτοῦ ὡς ὁ ἥλιος ἔλαμψε, τὰ δὲ ἱμάτια ὡς ἐγγίζοντα τῷ σώματι ἐκείνου φωτεινὰ ἐγένετο). The significance of the splendour of the garments is that they represent the garments of glory with which those who are drawing near to God will be clothed; the cloak of sinlessness of which Adam because of his transgression was divested (καὶ διὰ τούτων ἔδειξε, τίνες αἱ στολαὶ τῆς δόξης, ἃς ἐνδύσονται κατὰ τὸν μέλλοντα αἰῶνα οἱ ἐγγίζοντες Θεῷ, καὶ τίνα τὰ ἐνδύματα τῆς ἀναμαρτησίας, ἃ διὰ τὴν παράβασιν ὁ Ἀδὰμ ἀπεκδυσάμενος, γυμνὸς ἑωρᾶτο καὶ κατῃσχήνετο).[61]

Palamas also refers to the significance of the number of days before the Transfiguration took place. In a way which is more reminiscent of Irenaeus than Origen, Palamas holds that the six days in Matthew and Mark refer unequivocally to the Light of the Paternal glory and Kingdom, which, of course, is more Irenaean than Origenist. And as regards the eight days in Luke, Palamas points out that eight persons were seen on the mount: Christ, Moses and Elias, the three disciples, together with the Father who spoke to them and the Spirit which appeared as a Cloud.[62]

Origen's influence is visible in Palamas' more mystical interpretation of the number of days, when he says that both numbers are correct, since six refers to things visible, and eight to things invisible.[63] The eighth day, moreover, represents the Age to Come: after the six days in which the world was created, and the seventh day, on which God rested, we have the eighth day, which symbolizes our passing from the sensible world to eternity. Palamas also brings in here the notion of the five senses – to which, he says, we can add speech – προφορικὸς λόγος, making a total of six –, by which we communicate with our environment. The Kingdom of God, therefore, is not only represented as being beyond sense, but also beyond word or speech (ὑπὲρ λόγον), and so in following what Gregory calls the good inoperation of these six senses (μετὰ τὴν καλὴν ἀνενεργησίαν τῶν ἑξαδικῶς τούτων ἐκτελουμένων), by which the seventh day is enriched, the eighth day is realized in us, though only, as he is quick to add, *by the greater power of the divine Spirit,* through whom the Kingdom of God is seen by those who are worthy (Καὶ ταύτην τὴν τοῦ θείου Πνεύματος δύναμιν, δι' ἧς ὁρᾶται τοῖς ἀξίοις ἡ τοῦ Θεοῦ Βασιλεία).[64]

Again like Origen, Palamas says that the words 'come with power' signify that the Kingdom of God, *which is always present, is made visible by the power of the Holy Spirit.* Furthermore, 'with power' here does not simply refer to those who happen to be present, but to those who actively stand with Christ, that is, to all those who are firmly established (ἐστηριγμένοις) in their faith in Him, and who, like Peter, James and John, are taken up to a high mount, whereby our natural ability (ταπεινότης) is surpassed, and we overcome the limitations of our createdness.⁶⁵ This indeed is why God reveals Himself on the mountain: to represent His *condescension* from His place on High, and, secondly, in order to reveal that the divine purpose in creating us is *to raise us up* from the lowly estate of our human existence to the level of divine Being, thereby making those who are of a created nature able to contain (in measure and as far as is safe) Him who cannot be contained (ὁ ἀχώρητος).⁶⁶

Concerning Peter's words, Palamas says that he did not wish to be separated from that Light: πρὸς ἔρωτα θεῖον καὶ πόθον ἐπαρθεὶς μείζονα, τοῦ φωτὸς ἐκείνου διαστῆναι μηκέτι θέλων. However the disciples were not yet perfect, since Peter did not understand that it was not yet time for the *apocatastasis*, οὔπω γὰρ ὁ καιρὸς ἐφειστήκει τῆς ἀποκαταστάσεως. Furthermore, Peter should not have placed Christ on an equal par with the two servants, Ἀλλ᾽ οὐδ᾽ ἐξισοῦν ἔδει τῷ Δεσπότῃ τοὺς δούλους διὰ τῆς τῶν σκηνῶν ὁμοιότητος.⁶⁷

And finally, just as a voice was heard emanating from the heavens at the Jordan (Matt. 3:17; Mark 1:11; Luke 3:21–22) and at St. Stephen's martyrdom (Acts 7:56), so too does the Transfiguration Cloud, from which the voice of the Father emanated, represent the supracelestial glory of God. Therefore, asks Palamas, in high rhetorical fashion, 'How then can the supracelestial (light) be a sensible light?' (Πῶς οὖν αἰσθητὸν φῶς τὸ ὑπερουράνιον;).⁶⁸

As stated at the beginning of this inquiry, what becomes increasingly apparent in reading St. Gregory is the centrality of the Taborian theophany. For Palamas, the Transfiguration stands as the icon of the divine purpose in the creation of man: to bestow upon humankind the gift of truly sharing in the divine Life of the Most Holy Trinity. Whether we are speaking of the divine Light, the glory, the Kingdom or rule, brightness, the divine darkness, the power, grace, divine energy or energies, or, indeed, of the nature of God in the sense employed by 2 Pet. 1:4, we are always speaking of that aspect of God's very Being to which we have been called to be united and participate in. Though full and perfect, this is not, and never will be, a union with or participation in the divine essence itself. Our communion with God is not a sharing in *what* God is, but rather participation in *how* God is. Man's union with God, therefore, is neither essential, which characterizes the unity of Three Divine Hypostases, nor hypostatic, which is found only in the mystery of the Incarnation of the Divine Logos; it is, rather, an energetic union, a union by grace, which is accomplished through the glorified human flesh of Christ by the power of the Holy Spirit. Thus, 'partakers of divine nature' signifies for Palamas the ultimate and sovereign gift of human existence on the level of divine Being, that of the Triune Godhead. As an energetic union with the Holy Trinity and not an essential one, the existential line of demarcation between the source of Life and those who share in this Life is never crossed. God the Holy Trinity alone is God, while man is called to be a partaker in the fullness of His Uncreated energy of Life. In other words, even in the Age to Come, the correct response to the Giver of Life and Maker of all things visible and invisible is prayer of thanksgiving, *eucharistic* worship, in which we 'commend ourselves and one another, and our whole life to Christ our God'.[69]

Endnotes

1. See Georges HABRA, *La Transfiguration selon les Pères Grecs* (Paris, 1973); J. A. McGUCKIN, *The Transfiguration of Christ in Scripture and Tradition*. Studies in the Bible and Early Christianity, vol. 9 (Lewiston and Queenston, 1986); and my own, 'The Transfiguration of Christ in Greek Patristic Literature: From Irenaeus of Lyons to Gregory Palamas' (Oxford D. Phil. thesis, 1991). The present study is a reworking of a section from the latter.

2. Strong objections have been expressed by a number of modern scholars *vis à vis* Palamas the traditionalist, for example, see E. von IVA´NKA, 'Palamismus und Vätertradition,' in *L'Église et les Églises. Études et travaux*

sur l'Unité chrétienne offerts à Dom Lambert Beaudouin, vol. 2 (Chevetogne, 1955), 29–46; idem, 'Zur hesychastischen Lichtvision,' *Kairos* 13 (1971), 81–95; and idem, *Plato Christianus: Übernahme und Umgestaltung des Platonismus durch die Väter* (Einsiedeln, 1964). Also see J.-P. HOUDRET's articles on Palamas and the Cappadocians, in *Istina* 3 (1974), 257–349; and R. D. WILLIAMS, 'The Philosophical Structures of Palamism,' *ECR* 9,1–2 (1977), pp. 27ff, especially note 8. However, compare A. DE HALLEUX, 'Palamisme et Scolastique. Exclusivisme dogmatique ou pluriformité théologique?,' in *Revue Théologique de Louvain* 4 (1973), 409–442; and idem, 'Palamisme et Tradition,' *Irénikon* 48 (1975), 479–493; and for a reply to de Halleux, see B. SCHULTZE, 'Grundfragen des theologischen Palamismus,' in *Ostkirchliche Studien* 24 (1975), 105–135. References found in K. T. WARE's article, 'The Debate about Palamism,' *ECR* 9,1–2 (1977), 46 and 61, note 41.

3. *Homilia XXXIV* (PG 151:432CD).

4. Ibid. (436BC).

5. Ibid. (432D).

6. See *Excerpta Theodoti* IV. 2 and V. 3 (GCS 17,2:106,$^{13-21}$ and 107,$^{6-7}$), *Stromateis* VI. 16. 140,3 (GCS 52:503,$^{12-13}$), and VENIAMIN, op. cit., pp. 41–43.

7. Ἁγιορειτικὸς Τόμος, P. CHRESTOU (ed.), Γρηγορίου τοῦ Παλαμᾶ· Συγγράματα, vol. 2 (Thessalonica, 1966), § 4, pp. 572,^{19}–573,^{19}.

8. CLEMENT OF ALEXANDRIA, op. cit.; and see also: JOHN DAMASCENE, *Expositio de Fide Orthodoxa*, B. KOTTER (ed.), in *Patristische Texte und Studien*, vol. 12 (Berlin, 1973), § 66, p. 165,$^{7-19}$; and VENIAMIN, op. cit., p. 232.

9. *Homilia XXXIV* (PG 151:433AB).

10. For a further discussion of Palamas' gnosiological framework, see B. KRIVOCHEINE, 'The Ascetic and Theological Teaching of Gregory Palamas,' *Eastern Churches Quarterly* 4 (1938, reprinted 1954), 1–16; G. I. MANTZARIDES, in his Παλαμικά (Thessalonica, 1973), Μέθεξις Θεοῦ' (Thessalonica, 1979), and 'Tradition and Renewal in the Theology of Saint Gregory Palamas,' *Eastern Churches Review* 9,1–2 (1977), 1–18; and K. T. WARE's articles, 'God Hidden and Revealed: The Apophatic Way and the Essence–Energies Distinction,' and 'The Debate about Palamism,' also in the *Eastern Churches Review* 7,2 (1975), 125–136 and 9,1–2 (1977), 45–63, respectively.

11. *In Defence of the Holy Hesychasts* (Ὑπὲρ τῶν ἱερῶς ἡσυχαζόντων) 1. 3. 26, in CHRESTOU, op. cit., vol. 1 (Thessalonica, 1988²), pp. 436,²¹–437,²².

12. Οὐ χρείαν ἔχει τοῦ ἡλίου οὐδὲ τῆς σελήνης, ἵνα φαίνωσιν αὐτῇ· ἡ γὰρ δόξα τοῦ Θεοῦ ἐφώτισεν αὐτήν, καὶ ὁ λύχνος αὐτῆς τὸ ἀρνίον.

13. *Homilia XXXIV* (PG 151:433C–436A).

14. Ibid. (429B).

15. *Homilia XXXV* (PG 151:441CD).

16. Ibid. (441D–444A).

17. Ibid. (444A); and also on light as both φῶς and γνόφος, see *In Defence of the Holy Hesychasts* 2. 3. 51, in CHRESTOU, op. cit., pp. 583,¹⁹–584,⁴, where Palamas again cites Dionysius.

18. Ibid. (PG 151:444AB); cf. JOHN CHRYSOSTOM, *Homilia LVI in Matthaeum* 4 (PG 58:554), and VENIAMIN, op. cit., pp. 106–107; and compare Chrysostom's appreciation of the Taborian Cloud to that found in Archimandrite SOPHRONY's Видеть Бога Как Он Есть (Essex, 1985), p. 159 (Апостолы Петр, Иаков и Иоанн на Фаворе были объяты нетварным Светом, и в этом осиянии восприняли невещественный голос Отца, свидетельствовавшего о Христе, как о возлюбленном Сыне Своем), where no distinction is made between the Transfiguration Cloud and the Transfiguration Light; and cf. also ibid., p. 172. Thus it was this same light which proceeded to envelope the three Apostles on Tabor, and it was out of this very same light that the Father's Voice was recognized as proceeding.

19. *Homilia XXXV* (PG 151:437D–440A); and cf. CLEMENT OF ALEXANDRIA, loc. cit., and in VENIAMIN, op. cit., p. 43ff.

20. Ibid. (440BC).

21. Ibid. (440C).

22. Ibid. (440C–441A).

23. Ibid. (440CD).

24. Ibid. (445BC). Cf. J. S. ROMANIDES, in his article, 'Notes on the Palamite Controversy and Related Topics,' *GOThR* 6 (1961/62), 198ff, who holds that this kind of statement is an example of 'cross–talk' between Palamas and Barlaam, because Barlaam was here following the post–Augustinian Latin tradition, which drew a distinction between

'the created *"lumen gloria"* of Latin theology "by which" or "in which" the elect will see the divine essence, and the uncreated glory which is this very same divine essence'. It does seem, as A. PARETSKY points out in his recent article, 'The Transfiguration of Christ: its Eschatological and Christological Dimensions,' *New Blackfriars* 72, no. 851 (July/ August, 1991), 323, n. 36, that AUGUSTINE himself surprisingly relegates the Transfiguration together with Abraham's vision of angels at Mamre and Moses' vision of the Burning Bush to the lowest form of vision, that according to the eyes of the body (*secundum oculos corporis*), while Isaiah's vision in the Temple is regarded as an example of a higher imaginative vision (*secundum quod imaginamur ea quae per corpus sentimus*). The third and highest form of vision, called spiritual, is that of a 'genuine apprehension of truth and wisdom *"secundum mentis intuitum"*', *Contra Adimantum* 28.2 (*PL* 42:171–72). Palamas states elsewhere, that the only illumination which the Baarlamites regard as suprasensible, beyond the senses, is that of knowledge, which they claim is superior to the divine light and the ultimate contemplation (Ὑπὲρ αἴσθησιν δὲ φωτισμὸν τὴν γνῶσιν μόνην λέγουσι, διὸ καὶ ταύτην κρείττω τοῦ φωτὸς καὶ τέλος πάσης ἀποφαίνονται θεωρίας), *In Defence of the Holy Hesychasts* 1. Question 3, in CHRESTOU, op. cit., p. 407,$^{16-18}$.

25. Ibid., 15 (177,$^{9-26}$).

26. *Homilia XXXV* (*PG* 151:445CD).

27. Ibid. (448A).

28. Ibid. (448A).

29. *Discourse on the Transfiguration,* D. BALFOUR (ed.), in 'St Gregory the Sinaïte: Discourse on the Transfiguration,' Θεολογία 52,4 (1981), 644–680; and see VENIAMIN, op. cit., pp. 254–270.

30. *Epistula iii ad Akindynum,* CHRESTOU, op. cit., vol. 1, § 4, pp. 298,^{11}– 299,^{8}; and see L. CONTOS, 'The Essence–Energies Structure of St. Gregory Palamas with Brief Examination of its Patristic Foundation,' *GOThR* 12,3 (1967), 283–294.

31. *Homilia XXXV* (*PG* 151:448AB). Cf. Saint Gregory is here quoting his namesake almost word for word, see Saint Gregory the Theologian, *Oration* XXVIII, 19 [*PG* 36:52B]: "But neither those whom we have just mentioned, nor any one else belonging to their ranks [of the prophets and saints] has either stood in the substance and essence of God, as the Scripture says (Jer. 23:18), or seen or described the nature of God"; and

Germanus of Constantinople, *Orationes* 2 (M.98.261A); found in Lampe. s.v. ὑπόστημα.

32. *Discussion of Theophanes with Theotimus,* in CHRESTOU, op. cit., vol. 2, § 13, pp. 236,[12]–238,[19]; cf. VENIAMIN, op. cit., pp. 199–200; and see V. KARAYIANNIS' *Maxime le Confesseur: Essence et Énergies de Dieu,* Théologie Historique 93 (Paris, 1993).

33. For a detailed discussion of Palamas' Trinitarian theology, see A. RADOVICH, *Τὸ Μυστήριον τῆς Ἁγίας Τριάδος κατὰ τὸν Ἅγιον Γρηγόριον Παλαμᾶν* (Thessalonica, 1973), pp. 102–143.

34. See, for example, *Epistula ad Gabram* (Πρὸς Γαβρᾶν), in CHRESTOU, op. cit., §§ 28–29, pp. 356,[13]–358,[20]; and for a fuller discussion on the nature and significance of the divine energies in St. Gregory, consult the excellent article by S. YANGAZOGLOU, 'Προλεγόμενα στή σπουδή τῆς Θεολογίας τοῦ Ἁγ. Γρηγορίου Παλαμᾶ περί τῶν ἀκτίστων ἐνεργειῶν,' *Γρηγόριος ὁ Παλαμᾶς* 739 (September–October 1991), 754–789, esp. 766–770 and 777–787.

35. *That Barlaam and Akindynus are the Ones who Divide the One Godhead into Two,* in CHRESTOU, ibid., § 12, pp. 270,[30]–273,[14]. On the question of participation in God according to Palamas, see G. I. MANTZARIDES, *Παλαμικά,*, pp. 179–268; and especially his *Μέθεξις Θεοῦ,* pp. 99–129.

36. *Discussion of Theophanes with Theotimus,* in CHRESTOU, ibid., § 9, pp. 231,[1]–233,[30].

37. *Homilia XXXV* (448B).

38. Ibid. (448BC).

39. Cf. also: St. JOHN DAMASCENE, *Homilia in Transfigurationem Salvatoris Nostri Jesu Christi,* in KOTTER, op. cit., vol. 29 (1988), § 10, p. 448,[9–22]: 'prayer is the manifestation of divine glory' (προσευχὴ δὲ θείας δόξης ἐμφάνεια), and that prayer becomes the ambassador or agent of the divine glory (τῆς θείας δόξης ἡ προσευχὴ καθίσταται πρόξενος). Note that in this second phrase Palamas uses the same term as Damascene, provxeno" 'ambassador' or 'agent'; and see VENIAMIN, op. cit., p. 236–237.

40. In contrast to the glorification of Moses, who suffered the transfiguration but did not effect it (Ἀλλ' ἔπαθε τὴν μεταμόρφωσιν, οὐκ ἐνήργησε), Palamas states that Christ possessed His glory as His own, and so did not need to pray (οἴκοθεν εἶχε τὴν λαμπρότητα ἐκείνην, διὸ οὐδὲ

προσευχῆς αὐτὸς ἐδεῖτο), *Homilia XXXIV* (*PG* 151:432BC). On this point, cf. St. JOHN DAMASCENE, loc. cit.; and VENIAMIN, op. cit., p. 237, n. 1.

41. *Homilia XXXIV* (*PG* 151:432A).

42. Ibid. (432AB); and cf. St. BASIL's phrase, διανοίᾳ μόνῃ θεωρητόν, *Homiliae in Psalmos* 44:5 (*PG* 29:400BD); and VENIAMIN, op. cit., pp. 84–86.

43. Cf. St. IRENAEUS OF LYONS, *Adversus Haereses* IV. xx. 5 (*SC* 640,$^{117-}$ 642,^{130}); and see E. LANNE, 'La vision de Dieu dans l'oeuvre de saint Irénée,' *Irénikon* 33 (1960), 311–320; and VENIAMIN, op. cit., p. 39f.

44. *Homilia XXXIV* (*PG* 151:432B); and on this point compare an interesting allusion which Palamas makes to St. MACARIUS, who says that the light which shone from the face of Moses, *Homiliae Spirituales* V. 10 (*PG* 34:516A); *De Patientia et Discretione* IV (868CD), now shines in the soul of the saints (τὴν δόξασν τοῦ προσώπου Μωσϋσέως νῦν ἐν τῇ ψυχῇ, κατὰ τὸν ἅγιον Μακάριον, δέχονται οἱ ἅγιοι), *In Defence of the Holy Hesychasts* 1. 3. 7, in CHRESTOU, op. cit., p. 416,$^{12-14}$.

45. *Homilia XXXIV* (433B).

46. Ibid. (411D).

47. Ibid. (444B).

48. Ibid. (433B).

49. Cf. VENIAMIN, op. cit., pp. 99f; and 186ff, respectively.

50. *Homilia XXXIV* (*PG* 151:429D–432A).

51. J. S. ROMANIDES, in his article, 'Notes on the Palamite Controversy and Related Topics,' *GOThR* 6 (1961/62), 198ff, where he makes the salient point that 'for Barlaam the knowledge derived from seeing the Old and New Testament glory is inferior to intellection'. Palamas certainly seems to be responding here to a view of the Transfiguration glory as inferior to another kind of illumination of the mind.

52. *Homilia XXXIV* (*PG* 151:429AB); and cf. MAXIMUS THE CONFESSOR, *Ambigua* X (*PG* 91:1125D) and *Quaestiones et Dubia* 191 (*CCSG* 10:133,$^{17-24}$); discussed in VENIAMIN, op. cit., pp. 188–189.

53. Cf. *Apocalypsis Petri* 17, in *New Testament Apocrypha*, E. HENNECKE, W. SCHNEEMELCHER and R., M. WILSON, eds., *New Testament Apocrypha*, vol. 2 (London, 1965), p. 680, where the light, emanating from 'the two men' with Christ, is described as shining 'more than the sun'; and see also:

J. D. KARAVIDOPOULOS, Ἡ Μεταμόρφωση τῶν Δικαίων στὴν Ἀπόκρυφη Ἀποκάλυψη Πέτρου,' *Κληρονομία* 24 (1992; actually published, 1994), 35–46.

54. *Homilia XXXV* (*PG* 151:448B).

55. Ibid. (444C).

56. See *In Defence of the Holy Hesychasts* 1. Question 3, in CHRESTOU, op. cit., p. 407,[2–3]; and cf. *Homilia XXXIV* (424AD). Note also the recent study by S. YANGAZOGLOU, 'Philosophy and Theology: The Demonstrative Method in the Theology of St. Gregory Palamas,' *GOThR* 41,1 (1996), 1–18; and cf. the appraisal of the tension between philosophy and theology in the later Patristic period in such modern scholars as G. PODSKALSKY, *Theologie und Philosophie in Byzanz: Der Streit und die theologische Methodik in der spätbyzantinischen Geistesgeschicte (14./15.Jh.), seine systematischen Grundlagen und seine historische Entwicklung*. Byzantinisches Archiv, Heft 15 (Munich, 1977); and H.-G. BECK, *Das Byzantinische Jahrtausand* (Munich, 1978).

57. VENIAMIN, op. cit., p. 65.

58. Cf. JOHN CHRYSOSTOM, *In Eutropium Eunuchum* II. 7 and 9 (*PG* 52:402–403 and 404), and VENIAMIN, op. cit., pp. 104–105

59. VENIAMIN, loc. cit.

60. *Homilia XXXV* (*PG* 151:441AB); and see *In Defence of the Holy Hesychasts* 1. Question 3, in CHRESTOU, op. cit., p. 407,[5–18]. It should have been the case, adds St. Gregory in another passage, that rather than talk about the manifestation of the light of Christ based on our human ideas and imperfect thoughts, we should obey the 'voices' of the Fathers and wait patiently with a pure heart to receive the correct knowledge by experience (Ἐχρῆν οὖν καὶ περὶ ἐν Θαβὼρ ἀπορρήτου Ἰησοῦ φωτοφανείας, μὴ λογισμοῖς δειλοῖς, ἀνθρωπίνοις δηλονότι, καὶ ἐπισφαλέσιν ἐπινοίαις ἀποφαίνεσθαι, ἀλλὰ πειθαρχεῖν ταῖς πατερικαῖς φωναῖς καὶ τὴν ἐν καθαρότητι καρδίας ἀκριβῆ διὰ τῆς πείρας ἀναμένειν εἴδησιν), ibid., 1. 3. 28 (439,[12–16]).

61. *Homilia XXXV* (*PG* 151:440AB).

62. The explicit identification of the Bright Cloud *exclusively* with the Holy Spirit may be traced back to St. AMBROSE OF MILAN (*c.* 339 – 397), *Expositio Evangelii secundum Lucam* VII.19 (*CCSL* 14:215,[216]). This exclusive identification appears later in the East, however, and, to the best of my

knowledge, is found no earlier than St. GERMANUS OF CONSTANTINOPLE (c. 634 – c. 733), see F. E. BRIGHTMAN, 'The *Historia Mystagogica* and other Greek Commentaries on the Byzantine Liturgy,' in *JTS* 9 (1907–8), 388, l. 22; St. ANDREW OF CRETE (c. 660 – 740), in his *Homilia in Transfigurationem Domini* (*PG* 97:952D–953A and cf. 936C); and St. JOHN DAMASCENE, *Homilia in Transfigurationem Salvatoris Nostri Jesu Christi,* in KOTTER, op. cit., § 4, p. 441,$^{25-26}$; and see also, VENIAMIN, op. cit., pp. 220–223 and 228.

63. Op. cit. (425B–428A).

64. Ibid. (425A–428C); and cf. ORIGEN, *Contra Celsum* VI. 77 (*SC* 147:372,$^{14-35}$), II. 64 (*SC* 132:434,$^{1-14}$), and ibid. (153,^{8}–154,^{9}); and see VENIAMIN, op. cit., pp. 48–49.

65. Ibid. (428CD).

66. Ibid. (428D–429A).

67. Ibid. (441BC).

68. Ibid. (444C).

69. From the Litany of Fervent Intercession, *Let us complete our supplication unto the Lord.* Translation taken from *The Orthodox Liturgy* of The Stavropegic Monastery of St. John the Baptist, Essex (Oxford University Press, 1982), pp. 67–68, 117, and *passim.*

BY WAY OF CONCLUSION

On Becoming Theologians

"HESYCHIA" AS A PREREQUISITE FOR THE
ENCOUNTER WITH GOD[1]

As Fr Sophrony of Essex writes, the Gospel teaches us that for a whole week before His glorious Transfiguration, our Lord, God and Saviour Jesus Christ performed no miracle, and spoke no word.[2] In short, in all three Synoptic narratives there is a significant period of silence before the Taborian theophany takes place (Matt. 17:1; Mark 9:2; Luke 9:28). Indeed, the Gospel of Luke specifies that it was while the Lord was praying that His wondrous change occurred (Luke 9:29). Prayer, silence and stillness – what the Fathers refer to as *hesychia* – preceded this great Biblical event: the manifestation of Christ's pre-eternal divinity in and through His assumed human flesh, and therefore also the revelation of God's purpose in His creation of man, as Christ, the divine hypostasis of the Logos, is beheld by

---

[1]. This article is dedicated to Archimandrite Zacharias, of the Monastery of St John the Baptist in Essex, England, who gave me the topic, made several key suggestions, and on whose writings it is largely based. Regrettably, however, it represents but a shadow of his vision, if that. It was first delivered, as a public lecture, at Holy Cross Greek Orthodox School of Theology in Brookline, Massachussetts, on October 18, 2013.
[2]. Archimandrite Sophrony, *Asceticism and Contemplation*, p. 177 [in Greek].

the three chosen disciples resplendent, even in the flesh, in the light of His divine glory.

As true and perfect God and true and perfect man the uniquely incarnate Person of the Son and Word of God is for us the measure of all things both divine and human. He is the Way – "No man cometh to the Father but by me" (John 14:6), and again as the Lord Himself says, "I have given you an example" (cf. John 13:15). And the example that we see here, in the Transfiguration of the Saviour on Mount Tabor, is that prayer and stillness – *hesychia* – precede the clear vision of God.[3]

Now this simple fact is of course attested to not only by the Transfiguration, but throughout Holy Scripture. Beginning with Genesis, we read of the Holy Spirit hovering in silence upon the waters before Creation bursts forth (Gen. 1:2–3); following the six days of Creation, God rests on the Sabbath, on the Seventh Day (Gen. 2:2–3),[4] which is also a foreshowing of the Lord's three-day burial; we notice the silence in Jacob's spiritual struggle, as he wrestled with God all night long, before meeting with his brother Esau, who wanted to kill him, after which he exclaims, "I have seen God face to face, and my life is preserved" [lit. "and my soul is saved"] (Gen. 32:24–30). In Exodus we find Moses and the people of Israel keeping silence, before Moses entered the cloud to be with God (Exod. 24:1–18). Similarly, Joshua and the Israelites kept silence for seven days after they camped outside Jericho, before the trumpets sounded and the walls came tumbling down, which was a clear sign that the Lord was working with them (Joshua 6:10–16); and Job's seven-day silence, before opening his mouth

---

3. Archimandrite Zacharias, "Fattening of the Soul through Hesychia" (unpublished article), p. 2.

4. Gen. 2:2–3: "And on the seventh day God ended his work which he had made; and he rested on the seventh day from all his work which he had made. And God blessed the seventh day, and sanctified it: because that in it he had rested from all his work which God created and made." As Fr Zacharias says, "God entered into His eternal Sabbath, that is to say, into His rest, which means that He sealed His creation with the seal of the perfection of His Holy Spirit", "Fattening of the Soul through Hesychia" (unpublished article), p. 3ff.

to speak with power (Job 2:13ff), that is to say, to speak inspired by God. And let us not forget Elijah's silence on Horeb and the fact that God was afterwards revealed to him in "the still small voice" (1 Kgs. 19:9–14). And of course, the greatest *hesychast* of all, the Mother of God and Ever-Virgin, who practiced silence in the Temple,[5] and through the period before she received the glad tidings of the Annunciation from Gabriel (Luke 1:26ff). And we find the Lord manifesting His power after stillness and silence on the Mount of Olives[6] and in the desert (e.g. Luke 5:16–17 and following). And the Resurrection itself takes place after "all flesh" had been stilled for three days, as we are taught by the beautiful hymn, "Let all mortal flesh be still", sung in place of the Cherubic Hymn on Holy Saturday. And the Holy Spirit came down upon the disciples at Pentecost while they too kept silence "with one accord in prayer" (Acts 1:14).[7] And to all these wonderful events we may add what the great Godbearer Ignatius of Antioch tells us about the Word of God Himself being born pre-eternally "of the silence of the Father" (Magn. 8:2).[8]

What the Transfiguration and all these other great events in the history of our salvation show us is that if we truly desire to meet God, and have a face to face vision of Him, we need first to prepare ourselves for that encounter through prayer and stillness – through

---

5. St. Gregory Palamas, Homs. LII and LIII, *On the Entry into the Holy of Holies of Our Exceedingly Pure Lady, Mother of God, and Ever-Virgin Mary*, in *Saint Gregory Palamas: The Homilies*, ed. and trans. by C. Veniamin (Dalton PA: Mount Thabor Publishing, 2013), pp. 407–444.
6. Matt. 24:3ff; Mark 13:3ff, where Christ prophesizes concerning the end of the world; Matt. 26:30ff; Mark 14:26; Luke 22:39ff, after which we have the agony in Gethsemane and the Passion; Mark 11:1ff; Luke 19:29ff, followed by Palm Sunday; Luke 21:37ff, the Last Supper. And John 8:1ff, after which the Lord teaches in the Temple.
7. "These all continued with one accord in prayer and supplication, with the women, and Mary the mother of Jesus, and with his brethren."
8. Gk. ὅς ἐστιν αὐτοῦ λόγος ἀπὸ σιγῆς προελθών, St Ignatius of Antioch, *Epistle to the Magnesians* 8:2: "... there is one God who manifested Himself through Jesus Christ His Son, who is His Word that proceeded from silence, who in all things was well-pleasing unto Him that sent Him".

hesychia. As the Psalmist says, "Be still and know that I am God" (Psalm 46:10). For, unless we know the Lord, we cannot be true theologians. And, more importantly, we cannot give a word of comfort to those to whom we have been called to minister – unless we ourselves have been comforted, by the Comforter.

So, prayer and silence must precede our encounter with God. Theology is the description of our encounter with God. And this encounter is also the prerequisite for our ministry to others as His servants.

Most significantly, the liturgical cycle of the Orthodox Church gives us ample opportunity to "be still" and focus on the "one thing needful" (Luke 10:42). Sunday, the weekly celebration of the Lord's Resurrection, and all the major feasts of the ecclesiastical year, prescribe *argia* for us, that is to say, resting from all of our usual work, not simply in order to cease working physically and mentally, but rather to help us to learn to focus on things eternal instead of things temporal. It is an important reminder, especially for us in our workaholic and stressed-out society, that all the things that the world considers important – money, power and fame – will in fact one day come to an end, and that inevitably each and every one of us will be faced with the question of eternity.

But having said all this, how do we attain to the kind of prayer and stillness that we find in the example given us by the Lord and His saints? Where is this kind of prayer and standing before God to be found? The answer to this question is that it is to be found in the heart – the spiritual centre of man's being, which coincides with, but is not limited to, our physical heart – and the way it is to be found is by following the example of Christ, which is the mystery of His descent from on high, and His Cross which reaches down into the nethermost parts of Hades.

Turning once again therefore to the example that the Lord gives in His Person, we find Him in the Garden of Gethsemane sweating "great drops of blood" (Luke 22:44), engaged in a prayer–dialogue with God the Father, as He is about to go forth to endure the Passion of the Cross for our sakes.

Now firstly, as the Son and Word of God, consubstantial with the Father, and equal in every respect with Him in His divine status, Christ's human will, as Saint John Damascene tells us, "always willed what the divine will willed it to will" (*Exact Exposition of the Orthodox Faith*, Book III). Therefore, there was never any possibility of Christ not following the will of the Father or diverging from it (*non posse peccare*);[9] for the divine will of the Father is also His very own divine will – for it is one and the same.[10] And Christ's human will was, from the very moment of His conception in His mother's womb, in perfect harmony with His divine will. And what is true of Christ, by virtue of the hypostatic union and of the *communicatio idiomatum* that follows it, also becomes a reality in us – by grace. Therefore, those who strive to follow His example and His way receive the privilege of existing on the plane of His divine will and life. Christ is our example of obedience and His way is the pattern of our life.

Secondly, Christ did not need to pray. As the divine Logos He was and is always in full and perfect communion with God the Father, once again by virtue of the *homoousion*. But He does pray, in His human nature, in order to give us the example that we human persons ought to follow, and this is emphasized by His agony in which He sheds drops of blood as He faces the prospect of death (Luke 22:44). Therefore, we too, following the example of Christ and His saints, whenever we find ourselves threatened by pain, suffering or death, learn to take the opportunity to enter into a prayer-dialogue with God, for thereby we transform anything that may befall us into a spiritual state.

Thirdly, death for Christ was by no means inevitable. On the contrary, as the very Source and Author of Life, death was totally foreign and unnatural to Him. Therefore, He did not need to die.[11]

---

9. *Non posse peccare*, as opposed, of course, to *Posse non peccare*.
10. Note the significantly telling title of one of St Cyril of Alexandria's most famous treatises on the Person of Christ, *That Christ is One*; and also what he says in his *Second Letter to Nestorius*, where he writes, "Scripture does not say that the Logos united a Prosopon to Himself, but that He became flesh."
11. Hom. XVI, *Saint Gregory Palamas: The Homilies*, ed. and trans. by

What we observe here is the reality of the hypostatic union of our nature in the single and unique person-hypostasis of the Son and Word of God – and all the things that follow naturally from it: the mystery of His two natural energies and two natural wills; we find Him in Gethsemane actually "fearing" death, or more correctly, "shrinking" from death. For, as Saint John of the Ladder explains, this is the mystery of the Lord, "fearing death but not being terrified by it" (Δειλιᾷ Χριστὸς θάνατον, οὐ τρέμει).[12] In other words, as the Author of Life it was unnatural for the Divine Logos incarnate to suffer death. For His human nature is the flesh of none other than the Son and Word of God, Who was in the beginning, and by Whom all things were made.

Christ's death, then, was innocent and totally voluntary. But He accepts the shame of death on the Cross, in order to reveal His boundless self-sacrificial love and the humble way of divine life (John 15:13, "Greater love hath no man...") that He describes so vividly in His Sermon on the Mount (Matt. Chapters 5–7), which we too must strive to follow if we wish to be with Him. For, unless we become like Him, we cannot be with Him (cf. 1 John 3:2).[13] But, by the Lord's death on the Cross, the power of death was completely vanquished, and joy came into the world – the joy of the Resurrection by Christ's triumph over death. And this is precisely what those who are willing to follow the way of Christ experience in their own self-denial, as they take up their cross and follow His Way (Matt. 16:24: "If any man will come after me, let him deny himself, and take up his cross, and follow me"; Mark 8:34; Luke 9:23 – of course, Luke adds "daily" or "every day", which gives even stronger emphasis) – joy, lasting joy that cannot be taken away from

---

C. Veniamin (Dalton PA: Mount Thabor Publishing, 2013), p. 115, the subtitle of which reads: "Also Teaching that God was Able to Redeem Man from the Devil's Tyranny in Many Different Ways but Rightly Preferred This Dispensation."
12. Step. 6, "On Remembrance of Death", in *The Ladder of Divine Ascent*.
13. As the Theologian says, "Beloved, now are we the sons of God, and it doth not yet appear what we shall be: but we know that, when he shall appear, we shall be like him; for we shall see him as he is."

us. Here we have the paradox that the Lord speaks of when He says, "He that loseth his life for my sake shall find it" (Matt. 10:39).

Gethsemane, therefore, understood theologically and not psychologically, is a remarkable confirmation of the reality of the Lord's Incarnation, of God's truly becoming man for our sakes, and, of giving us the authentic pattern of the Christian way of life.

Now this example is of vital importance to us, because it teaches us that whatever difficulty, suffering or misfortune may befall us, we too aught to use the pain that is experienced owing to the threat of death to open up a prayer-dialogue with God and enter into communion with the Physician of our souls and bodies; for by so doing, we are accepting the pain as from the Hand of God and thereby remarkably discovering our heart, and from the depths of our heart we are then able to truly speak to God. Thereby transforming whatever may befall us – psychological, emotional or even physical - into a spiritual state.

In his encomium for the Martyr Gordius, St Basil the Great exhorts us to "make voluntary that which is involuntary and not to spare life, whose privation is unavoidable."[14] St John Chrysostom teaches that it is not death, but "death in sin" that is evil.[15] And St Gregory Palamas, writing about a thousand years later, urges his people to resist sin "even unto death" if need be, and makes what seems to be a bold statement, when he says:

> Except for sin nothing in this life, even death itself, is really evil, even if it causes suffering. The company of the saints brought bodily sufferings upon themselves. The martyrs made the violent death which others inflicted on them into something magnificent, a source of life, glory and the eternal heavenly kingdom, because they exploited it in a good way that pleased God.[16]

---

14. Homily XVIII *On the Martyr Gordius*.
15. *On Statues* (Εἰς ἀνδριάντας) V, 2 (PG 49:71–72); found in G. Mantzarides, *Christian Ethics,* p. 653 [in Greek].
16. Hom. XVI, 33: *On the Dispensation of our Lord in the Flesh* ; trans. taken from, *Saint Gregory Palamas: The Homilies*, ed. and trans. by C. Veniamin (Dalton PA: Mount Thabor Publishing, 2013), p. 130.

As the saints show, following the example of Christ Himself, it is our spiritual disposition that really matters, the desire to learn the humble way of Christ. And so the mystery is that the more we embrace and follow His Way, the more we enter into the stream of His own life, and the more we receive His grace to live His commandments and become increasingly like Him, which, as the Transfiguration shows us, is the very purpose of our existence – to become by grace all that He is by nature.

Now in case this sounds rather theoretical, let us attempt to summarize this last point in simpler language. Archimandrite Sophrony used to say that we must learn to live by inspiration. In practical terms this simply means that, aided by the life in the Church, we must acquire the habit of turning to God at all times and in all things (cf. Eph. 5:20; Rom. 12:12).[17] So that before we act, before we speak, before we even think anything, we turn our hearts and minds to Christ our true God; and in that way, as the great Paul says (1 Tim. 4:5), all things may "be sanctified by the Word of God and by prayer", which is in fact the shape of the Divine Liturgy.

For in the Anaphora of the Divine Liturgy we are taught to refer "our whole life and one another unto Christ our God", acknowledging Him as the Giver of all good things, in thanksgiving, following His example, and thereby reversing the sin of our forefather, Adam.

And so, if we truly wish to become theologians in the tradition of our Fathers, then we must learn the ethos and spirit of the Divine Liturgy, which contains everything. To quote St Ireneaus of Lyons, a spiritual grandchild of the Apostles, "Our way of thinking is in harmony with the Eucharist, and the Eucharist confirms our thinking".[18]

---

17. Eph. 5:20, "Giving thanks always for all things unto God and the Father in the name of our Lord Jesus Christ." And Rom. 12:12, "Rejoicing in hope; patient in tribulation; continuing instant in prayer."
18. *Against the Heresies* IV, 18, 5.

Publications by Mount Thabor Publishing

Mary the Mother of God: Sermons by Saint Gregory Palamas.
Edited by Christopher Veniamin. 2005. Paperback: 92 pages.

Ecclesial Being: Contributions to Theological Dialogue by Constantine B. Scouteris.
Edited by Christopher Veniamin. Repr. ed., 2006. Paperback: 188 pages.

The Hidden Man of the Heart (1 Peter 3:4): The Cultivation of the Heart in Orthodox Christian Anthropology by Archimandrite Zacharias.
Edited by Christopher Veniamin. 2008. Paperback: 203 pages.

The Saving Work of Christ: Sermons by Saint Gregory Palamas.
Edited by Christopher Veniamin. 2008. Paperback: 150 pages.

On the Saints: Sermons by Saint Gregory Palamas.
Edited by Christopher Veniamin. 2008. Paperback: 80 pages.

Remember Thy First Love (Revelation 2:4-5): The Three Stages of the Spiritual Life in the Theology of Elder Sophrony by Archimandrite Zacharias.
Foreword by the Right Reverend Basil Essey, Bishop of Wichita. 2010. Paperback: 464 pages.

Born to Hate, Reborn to Love: A Spiritual Odyssey from Head to Heart by Klaus Kenneth.
Foreword by Christopher Veniamin. 2012. Paperback: 287 pages.

The Enlargement of the Heart: "Be ye also enlarged" (2 Corinthians 6:13) in the Theology of Saint Silouan the Athonite and Elder Sophrony of Essex by Archimandrite Zacharias.

Edited by Christopher Veniamin. Second American ed., with Indexes, 2012. Paperback: 277 pages.

Saint Gregory Palamas: The Homilies.
Edited and translated from the original Greek, with an introduction and notes by Christopher Veniamin. Second ed., 2014. Hardbound: 800 pages.

The Parables of Jesus: Sermons by Saint Gregory Palamas.
Edited by Christopher Veniamin. 2013. Paperback: 80 pages.

Miracles of the Lord: Sermons by Saint Gregory Palamas.
Edited by Christopher Veniamin. 2013. Paperback: 70 pages.

Mount Thabor Publishing
106 Hilltop Road
Dalton, PA 18414
Telephone (570) 319-1347
Fax (570) 319-1348
Email info@mountthabor.com
Website www.mountthabor.com